The Myths That Stole
CHRISTMAS

Seven Misconceptions That Hijacked the Holiday
(and How We Can Take It Back)

BY DAVID KYLE JOHNSON

For Johney
May you always cherish Christmas as much as I

Copyright © 2015 by David Kyle Johnson

HUMANIST PRESS

1777 T Street NW
Washington, DC, 20009

www.humanistpress.com

Printed book ISBN: 978-0-931779-67-1
Ebook ISBN: 978-0-931779-68-8

Editor: Luis Granados
Cover Design: Lisa Zangerl
Cover Illustration: © Courtesy, The Winterthur Library:
The John and Carolyn Grossman Collection.

CONTENTS

ACKNOWLEDGMENTS

This book has been years in the making. I'd like to thank all the Philosophy Department student aides and interns who helped with researching and proofing over the years (Ryan Klubeck, Elle Bulter, Samantha Feilsel, Elysia Balavage, Ashley Panko, and Gabriel Gross); my colleagues William Irwin, Greg Bassham, Regan Reitsma, and Tom Mackaman for their helpful feedback; my extremely efficient copy-editor Louise Spencely; Luis Granados, Jan Melchior and the great folks at Humanist Press; King Stimie for his made to order Krampus artwork; Brom, Monte Beauchamp and the Grossman Collection for the use of their artwork; and my wife Lori for supporting me though the process.

INTRODUCTION

[I]f there isn't a hell, as I suspect, I'd like to take a crack at saving Christmas myself—because I think it does need saving. You know why? 'Cause when the subject of Christmas comes up now, I notice so many people roll their eyes and say some variation of "Uh, I hate Christmas." Well, I'm not ready to throw Christmas under the bus... I have too many good memories wrapped up in the word "Christmas." To me it's about family and memories—and the looks on the carolers' faces when I set the dogs on them....So, how did we fuck it up? When did it become such a chore? Look at all these books and movies with titles like: How to Survive Christmas, Christmas Sucks, Skipping Christmas, Surviving Christmas. *And what do people say when it's over? "Hey, did you make it through the holidays?" Christmas shouldn't be something you make it through, like basic training or a colonoscopy...You shouldn't be looking at the open oven and thinking "Hmm, should I take the sugar cookies out or stick my head in?"*— Bill Maher *(Real Time with Bill Maher, November 21, 2014)*

What's Wrong with Christmas?

The fact that you are willing to consider that question at all reveals something because the question is loaded—it assumes that there is, in fact, something wrong with Christmas. So, if you formulated an answer instead of objecting to the assumption, you are willing to break one of the harshest social taboos and admit that Christmas isn't perfect. Christmas is not a holiday during which everyone is always happy and nothing is ever wrong. Like most people, you probably love Christmas but harbor a secret frustration with at least one aspect of it and wish that aspect would change. Or maybe you don't harbor your frustrations but instead

3

voice them loudly to all who will listen—like apparently Bill Maher's friends do. Either way, if you are frustrated with Christmas on any level, this book is for you. It will articulate your frustration, challenge your conception of Christmas, and perhaps even motivate you to change the way you celebrate.

Now, don't get me wrong. I don't hate Christmas—I love it. That's why I celebrate it. I buy gifts. I put up a tree. I deck my house in lights. My love of Christmas is what drove me to study it. But in no way do I think that Christmas is perfect. The list of complaints I have come across regarding Christmas is lengthy. Think about the last time you celebrated Christmas.

- Did you feel obligated to buy gifts for people who didn't really need or want them?
- Did you enjoy the trip to the mall or store to buy them?
- Could you really afford all the gifts you bought?
- Was it money well spent? Did you find the right gifts?
- Did you put them on credit? How quickly did you pay them off? Did Christmas sales save you more than the interest cost?
- How long did it take you to get tired of being bombarded with Christmas ads?
- Was the 15-minute gift orgy your children experienced on Christmas morning worth its price tag?
- Were your kids grateful? Or did the experience make you fear that you were helping to make them selfish and greedy?
- If they were grateful, did they thank you...or Santa?
- Did you feel a twinge of guilt for lying to your kids about Santa Claus?
- Did you feel obligated to put on a Christmas party? Did the preparations or the party itself add to your holiday enjoyment?
- Did you, or your partner, do most of the work to prepare for Christmas? Were they grateful? Were you?
- Did you *get* to visit family, or did you *have* to?
- Did you really need to hear about "The War on Christmas" again? Did you believe a word of what you heard?
- Did someone criticize the way that you celebrate? Were you made to feel like you didn't have enough religion in your holiday? Did someone try to make you feel guilty for celebrating because you aren't a Christian?[1]

No holiday brings more unwanted chores and more outrageous, unnecessary expenditures than Christmas; no holiday leads to more anxiety about money and no holiday raises more publicly contested controversial religious issues. And yet no holiday makes you feel guiltier for complaining about it.

Although it's still taboo, pointing out that Christmas is not perfect is nothing new. As early as 1850, when the modern consumer Christmas was in its infancy, Harriet Beecher Stowe said of Christmas that "There are worlds of money wasted, at this time of year, in getting things that nobody wants, and nobody cares for after they are got."[2] The twentieth-century author and Christian apologist C. S. Lewis observed, "you have only to stay over Christmas with a family who seriously [tries] to keep it...in order to see that the thing is a nightmare.... They look far more as if there has been a long illness in the house."[3] So we've known for a long time that most of the money we spend at Christmas is wasted. We've known for a long time that Christmas is often not a vacation but a chore.

Yet we can't give it up. If you announced that you were giving up on Christmas, you might as well just have announced that you were joining Al-Qaeda or ISIS. As the comedy movie *Christmas with the Kranks* (2004) (and the John Grisham novel, *Skipping Christmas*, on which it was based) pointed out quite nicely, nothing will get you shunned by your social group more effectively than not celebrating Christmas. Christmas enthusiasm enjoys a level of "protection" that religious doctrines had in the Middle Ages. Your friends won't ostracize you for not believing in the virgin birth. But say you are not celebrating Christmas—well then "you sir, are worse than Hitler."[4]

But the truth is, we've all secretly thought about skipping Christmas—at least to some degree. Again, if we can be honest with ourselves, we will admit that we loathe at least one aspect of the Christmas season; most of us loathe many. We don't really want to quit Christmas, however; we want Christmas to change. But if we are going to do anything about it, we have to fight against that social taboo, admit that it is okay to criticize Christmas, and then identify what is wrong with it.

But we can't stop there. We also have to be willing to change it, and that's not always easy. Once something has the veneer of an old-fashioned tradition, it seems impossible to change—even when that tradition is, literally, burning our houses down.

When the Christmas tree tradition began in Germany, it was common for people to put lit candles on the tree's branches.

As you can imagine, this wasn't exactly safe. Lighting small fires in dead trees tends to start bigger fires. This wasn't a huge problem in Germany where most houses were made of stone. If your Christmas tree did catch fire, your house would not burn down. You'd just throw the tree out and your house would smell like smoke for a while—but you likely cooked with fire inside your house anyway, so what else is new? Things didn't work out so well, however, for Americans who carried on this German tradition in houses made of wood. Hundreds of houses burned to the ground in Christmas tree-related fires. But did we let that stop us? Of course not. Although it made no sense to do this in an environment in which houses were made of the same combustible material as Christmas trees, because it was "tradition," we just kept right on doing it. Eventually laws were passed making it illegal to light candles in Christmas trees.[5] But in reality, it wasn't until the invention of a brand new old-fashioned tradition—the electric Christmas light—that people stopped. Nevertheless, the USFA still warns against lit candles in trees on their Holiday Fire Safety page.[6]

How silly we were to continue such an obviously harmful tradition, right? Yep, and we do exactly the same type of thing today. When holiday overeating was established as a tradition it made perfect sense and even served a purpose. As we will see when we discuss Myth #1, it originated in ancient agricultural societies as a way to take advantage of the only time in which food was plentiful and to fatten up for the winter—a season in which food would be scarce and through which many would not survive. But that kind of overeating makes no sense today. For most Americans, food is readily available all year round, winter poses no danger, and there is no need to fatten up for anything. Take that feast and plop it down in front of a first-world, western, industrial, motorized, televised, over-fed, "sit-down-to-work" society, and you get exactly what we have— a populace where 70 percent of adults are overweight, and 36 percent are obese.[7] Christmas of course is not the only culprit, but the average American puts on one pound every Christmas that they never take off.[8] Christmas feasting is literally helping to kill us—just like lighting candles in Christmas trees— and yet we just keep doing it.

And every year our collective house burns down just a little bit more. Not only are we a little bit fatter, but we're a little bit poorer, a little more in debt, a little more "at war," and a little more entrenched in the (not so innocuous) Santa Claus lie. But I want to motivate you to take charge of the way you celebrate Christmas. To be clear, I don't want you to celebrate just like I do or even to make every change I recommend. I'm not interested in endorsing one particular way of celebrating Christmas. I'm simply suggesting that you don't have to be satisfied with being frustrated with Christmas—that you can change what you want about the way you celebrate and make Christmas what you need it to be.

Wishing you a purr-fectly Happy Christmas!

To do this I am going to identify and debunk seven myths about Christmas—seven myths that I think are most responsible for our current Christmas conundrum—seven myths that have, as I have termed it, "hijacked the holiday." These myths have not only taken Christmas over but have made it harmful and even seem impossible to change. Christmas used to serve a useful social purpose but, thanks to these myths, now Christmas causes problems. It not only hurts our waistline, but it divides us socially and religiously, takes our money and puts us in debt, and threatens to make us all greedy and stupid. So debunking these myths is necessary if we are ever going to take Christmas back.

The first myth I will take on is the myth that Jesus is the reason for the season. It's not that there is anything wrong with religious Christmas celebrations, but Christmas originated as a pagan holiday and has always been celebrated in primarily secular ways. Yet this myth is used to control how Christmas is celebrated and to exclude others from doing so. Christmas should be for everyone, and everyone should feel free to celebrate as they wish.

The second myth is that there is a war on Christmas. There is not. And not only does this myth divide society on religious and political grounds, but it is used to marginalize people and even demonize them, turning good-natured inclusive efforts into acts of blasphemy that deserve a good punch. Christmas should unite us, not divide us. Yet if left unchecked, this myth could even threaten the very foundations of our democracy.

The third myth is that our modern Christmas traditions are old-fashioned, rooted in antiquity. In fact, they are almost all modern inventions, forced upon us by people with either a monetary, social, or political agenda. But since people are so hesitant to change ancient traditions, this myth hijacks the holiday by making it seem unchangeable—making it seem like there is nothing that we can do about its less-than-perfect aspects.

The fourth myth is that Christmas spending is good for the economy. This myth creates in us a sense of duty to spend at Christmas time. Even if we can't afford it, we feel like we are at least doing our duty as good capitalistic Americans by pumping money into the economy—even if we have to take on debt to do so. In reality, we are just shooting ourselves in the economic foot. Christmas spending is at best neutral, and at worst is simply wasting our money and setting us up for economic disaster. There are ways to spend our money at Christmas that would help the economy and create economic value—ways that actually trace back to the most ancient of holiday traditions—but they are usually not included in our modern Christmas shopping habits.

POSTCARD CIRCA 1900. © PD

The fifth and sixth myths go hand in hand. The fifth myth is that Santa Claus is St. Nicholas. He's not—and you won't believe where he really comes from. (It's not the devil, but it's damn close!) Of the seven myths, this one may be the most entrenched and it will be the most fun to take down. But it is also likely the least harmful myth—except for the fact that it helps feed the sixth myth: that the Santa Claus lie is a harmless rite of passage for children. Debunking the fifth myth will teach us that the Santa Claus lie has not been around for long, but debunking the sixth myth will reveal that we'd be much better off without it. Not only is it an immoral lie, and not only does it threaten our parental trustworthiness, but it's just bad parenting. It threatens to warp our children's sense of morality, make them greedy and retard their rational development.

Finally, the seventh myth is that there is nothing we can do—that Christmas can't change. Wrong. It has been changing and always will be. The only question is: will it change for the worse, or will we do something to make it change for the better? Can we make Christmas work for us, instead of against us, again? I'll close the book by summarizing a few changes we can enact to make this happen.

Right now, Christmas owns us. We do what it expects, when it expects it. We buy what we are told and when we are told; we spend where we are told and how much we are told. We even lie to our children and justify it in the name of Christmas joy. But instead, we should own Christmas. And debunking the myths that have hijacked the holiday is a necessity if we are going to take it back.

Jesus Is the Reason for the Season

WE NEED TO BEGIN BY ADDRESSING ONE OF THE most difficult myths. And while the title of this chapter may cause some people discomfort, I want to assure the reader that I don't mean to be disrespectful. The birth of Jesus may be the focus of your Christmas celebrations. In that way, Jesus may be the reason for *your* seasonal celebrations. If that's true of course that is perfectly fine. I'm not arguing against that at all. However, the phrase "Jesus is the reason for the season" is usually used to express a historical view, a kind of causal explanation for why humanity collectively celebrates in later December. That view goes something like this:

It all started with the birth of Jesus 2000 years ago, in year zero, with "The First Noel"—that is, the first Christmas—and we have been celebrating his birth with church services and charity ever since. Inspired by the Wise Men giving gifts to gentle infant baby

Jesus, we now give gifts to our children, and although the holiday has recently been commercialized, these tra ditions continue on pretty much as they always have.

In other words, according to this view, the historical cause of Christmas celebrations is the birth of Christ. That's where it started and that's why we celebrate as we do. If that had not happened, humanity wouldn't celebrate in late December at all. The birth of Jesus is the historical, causal root of Christmas.

This view is historically inaccurate. It is an empirical claim about who was celebrating, when they were celebrating, how and why they were celebrating that can be researched and verified. And, as we shall see, such research reveals that it is false. That's not to say that your motivation for celebrating at Christmas can't be whatever you want it to be. Of course it can! But, historically speaking, not one single sentence of the bold text above is true.

To see why, let us begin by turning our attention to the ancient world, thousands of years before Christ was born. There we will find the historical origin of holiday celebrations. We will then look at how Jesus's birthday was "tacked onto" those celebrations and follow how those celebrations changed (and didn't change) as a result. We will follow this path through to around the 1600s, right before Christmas was nearly stamped out by, perhaps ironically, fundamentalist Christian fervor.

Ancient Holiday Celebrations and Traditions

Secularists often quip that it is, in fact, *the tilt of the earth on its axis* that is the reason for the season. In the most precise way, of course this is true. The season of winter occurs because the earth's tilt draws the northern hemisphere away from direct sunlight. But this is also true, in a way, regarding Christmas. The causal explanation of why we celebrate during the holiday season ultimately does trace back to the tilt of the earth. Because it explains winter, it explains Christmas, because Christmas began as a way to deal with the onset of winter and the fear that spring would never return.

Think what it would have been like four thousand years ago as winter set in. First of all, people had no modern conveniences: no indoor plumbing, no central heating, no cars with heaters, and no refrigerators. They couldn't transport fruit and grains from a different hemisphere that was currently enjoying a growing season. There were no planes or cargo ships. Winter was a hard time. It was dark and cold—a time of want and despair. The young and old often didn't survive it. Today, it means we have to put on a coat and gloves before we go out. Back then, it meant you had to fear for your life.

Worse yet, the ancients didn't know about the tilt of the earth. They didn't know what caused the seasons. All they knew was that the sun kept getting lower in the sky and the days kept getting shorter. What if it never stopped? What if the sun kept getting lower until it disappeared? What if the daylight dwindled into nothing? What if winter lasted forever? It was a terrifying prospect indeed, and the ancients had no way of knowing this wouldn't happen.

At some point in time, people were so worried about this that they started performing rituals that they thought would ensure the return of spring. Since spring did subsequently return, they fallaciously concluded (as humans are apt to do) that their rituals worked.[1] They became convinced that if they didn't perform them, spring wouldn't return, so they started performing them on a regular basis, usually every year.

More than two thousand years before Jesus was born, the Mesopotamians observed Zagmuk. They believed that their god Marduk had created the world and life by claiming it from the monsters of chaos and imposing order on the world. However, every year, as plant life began to die and the world grew colder, Marduk had to battle them again—and he was always on the verge of defeat. The people believed that their earthly ruler needed to descend into the underworld to help Marduk fight the monsters of chaos that threatened an eternal winter. Only their defeat could ensure the return of spring. But how does one descend into the underworld? You have to die. Thus it was the tradition, every year, to kill the king to assist in the return of spring. Kings didn't much like being killed, however, so they adopted the practice of appointing a criminal or peasant as "king for a day." He would be crowned, get his every whim for food and woman granted, and then be sacrificed. When it was clear that the battle had been won and the days were getting longer again, the people celebrated. They would burn images of the defeated monsters in bonfires, exchange gifts, and have parties.

The Persians and Babylonians had a similar celebration called Sacaea. Like the Mesopotamians, the king's household would appoint a criminal as a "mock king," indulging his every whim, only to kill him later. They would also let a second criminal go free. However, in Sacaea, similar traditions were also practiced in individual households. There was no ritualistic sacrifice but there was social inversion. Masters and servants (owners and slaves) would trade places. The upper class would indulge the whims of the lower class, making them "mock kings of the household." It's unclear how far the indulgence went, but it most certainly involved the master serving the "mock king" the household's best food and drink.[2]

Some of these traditions survived nearly unaltered beyond the Middle Ages. (We'll see this later in wassailing rituals when we discuss Myth #3.) Some are still alive today. In Europe, many communities still play at appointing a "boy bishop" or a "mock king" for a day. In Great Britain, on what is known there as "Boxing Day" (the day after Christmas), officers and enlisted men in the military trade places. This includes the officers serving the enlisted men their meals.

These ancient traditions also traveled across the ancient world. In the north, among the Norse, they became Yule celebrations. Complete with a Yule log, which was probably an echo of those Zagmuk bonfires, the Norse Yule included heavy drinking and feasting. It also included evergreen plants. In the extreme north, where it is extremely cold, evergreens were considered a sign of life. While everything else was dying, evergreens stayed green. Bringing their branches inside was thought to help preserve life inside the house throughout the winter. Similar observations were made about holly and mistletoe, which not only stayed green but bore fruit throughout the winter—clearly they are ultra fertile. To be under mistletoe supposedly is to be under the influence of its fertility, and you simply must kiss (or make love to) whoever is nearest. It was also thought that evil spirits were not so fond of prickly evergreen needles. So surrounding your door with evergreens was thought to ward off evil spirits. And finally, candles were also lit in windows and around the house to fight back the darkness.

Most importantly, the ancient traditions traveled to Rome and by 500 BCE became Saturnalia. Saturn was a god of the harvest and of peace and equality. Saturnalia, as a celebration of this god, reflected those attributes. It was a harvest festival of abundance (food, drink) and of peace and equality. According to Lucian of Samosota, Saturn had ordered:

Let every man be treated equal, slave and freeman, poor and rich...no one may be ill-tempered or cross or threaten anybody.... Each man shall take the couch where he happens to be. Rank, family, or wealth shall have little influence on privilege [that is, on a man's place at the table]. All shall drink the same wine, and neither stomach trouble nor headache shall give the rich man an excuse for being the only one to drink the better quality. All shall have their meat on equal terms. The waiters shall not show favor to anyone.... Neither are large portions to be placed before one and tiny ones before another, nor a ham for one and a pig's jaw for another—all must be treated equally.... When a rich man gives a banquet to his servants, his friends shall aide him in waiting on them.[3]

Fueled by alcohol, Saturnalia was obviously a time of debauchery and sex as well. It also included small gift giving, visitation, and bonfires. And it didn't just last a day, but many—usually starting around December 17 and lasting until the twenty-third (about the time most Christmas parties happen today). Practices of gift giving around the New Year (Kalends) arose as well.

December celebrations made perfect sense in an agricultural community such as Rome. The harvest was in, so it was about the only time that there was plenty of food and drink. Also, it wouldn't be time to plant again until the spring, so there was no work to be done. Additionally, they had to thin the herds before winter, so December was the only time of year the Romans had access to fresh meat. It was the perfect time to party and fatten up for the harsh times of winter.

Combined with the Roman Kalends celebration, December was a fun time to be Roman. However, without these celebrations, it would have been the darkest time of year—and not just in the literal sense. The Romans had reason to fear winter just as much as the Mesopotamians, but they turned the darkest, most frightening of days into the most wonderful time of the year by simply believing that they were. Isn't that the magic of the holidays? They fool us—we fool ourselves—into believing that the darkest, gloomiest, most miserable days of the year are actually "the hap-happiest season of all."

Saturnalia and Kalends, however, were not the only things going on in Rome during December. Many deities celebrated their birth on or around December 25. Among them were sun gods like the Roman Sol Invictus and the Persian Mithra. The reason sun gods were believed to be born on this day is because the ancients believed it to be the date of the winter solstice. Although I'm not sure why they thought it was this day instead of when it actually falls (on December 21 or 22), I think this has a fairly simple explanation: on December 25, the days start getting noticeably longer. It is the day it becomes clear that the sun will make its comeback—that it will be reborn. "And if that is when it is reborn," they reasoned, "that must be when it was born in the first place." Obviously, this most likely influenced the date on which Jesus's birth was eventually celebrated—but the story of this influence is not simple. So let's start from the beginning with the story of Jesus's birth.

The Biblical Nativity

It's important to realize that celebrating Jesus's birth on December 25 has nothing to do with information that is provided about Jesus's birth by the Bible.

The Apostle Paul was perhaps the first to write of Jesus, around 50 CE, and the author of the Gospel of Mark, around 70 CE, was the next. However, neither mentions anything about when Jesus was born. In fact, they don't mention anything about Jesus's birth at all. We don't get an account of Jesus's birth until the Gospels of Matthew and Luke, which were written almost a century after Jesus was born—perhaps later. Unfortunately, neither gives us knowledge about Jesus's birth because—and even Christian biblical scholars agree on this—the veracity of both accounts is highly questionable. They are likely just myths.

Let me be clear. I'm not suggesting, as some secular scholars do, that Jesus never was born (and thus never existed).[4] I am simply reporting what the majority of biblical scholars agree upon—that the stories found in Matthew and Luke that describe events surrounding Jesus's birth are very likely not historically accurate and instead were stories invented by the authors of those gospels for theological purposes. In reality, we know almost nothing about the historical event of Jesus's birth.

Why do biblical scholars think this? Good question.

First, we know that the gospels of Matthew and Luke were not actually written by apostles named Matthew and Luke or any other apostles for that matter. (These gospels were attributed to Matthew and Luke long after they were written). There are many clues that this is the case.[5] Most telling is the fact that the gospels were originally written in Greek, yet the apostles of Jesus would have spoken Aramaic. And even if they had (unlike others in their time) lived into their nineties—long enough to have been alive when these gospels were written—it's unlikely that they would have learned to speak Greek, much less have learned read and then write Greek.[6]

In fact, no eyewitness to the events of Jesus's life (and certainly not his birth) would have spoken Greek, much less been literate in it. So, the gospels could not have been written by eyewitnesses. At best, they are records of oral traditions that circulated generations after the events they are supposed to describe—traditions that, over time, crossed a linguistic barrier to eventually reach the Greek-speaking world. However, any oral tradition that was passed on through so many people (and languages) would not have been reliable. Anyone who has played the game "telephone," where a message is passed down from person to person, knows how stories get changed as they are repeated.[7]

Worse is the fact that each of the two nativity stories works against the veracity of the other. They are completely different and even contradictory. (If you don't believe me, please read them for yourself and check what I am telling you here. They can be found in the first two chapters of Matthew and Luke.)

Let's start with their differences. In Matthew, we get Herod, the Wise Men, the slaughter of innocents, the star, and an angel appearing to Joseph. That's it. No angel appearing to Mary, no census, no shepherds, no host of angels in the sky, no inn and manger, and no temple presentation. Those things are all in Luke, which is lacking the aforementioned elements that are in Matthew. Also, the genealogies the two gospels present for Jesus are different and contradictory.[8]

Every Christmas, nativity plays and crèches push these stories together, but they have to ignore elements of each to do so because the two stories also contradict each other. First, the basics of each story are different. Notice that Matthew's story begins in Bethlehem. The Holy Family lives there and baby Jesus is born there without incident. After this, the Wise Men show up in Jerusalem to meet Herod, not in Bethlehem to meet Jesus. At first it seems this meeting takes place the day Jesus was born—so maybe they have time to make it to Bethlehem that night. However, we then learn that Herod has every baby two years old and younger killed, based on what the Wise Men told him about how long they had been following the star. Presumably, the star appeared the night Jesus was born, and the Wise Men had been following it for two years! By the time the Wise Men got to Jesus, he would have been at least two years old—and

LUKE'S STORY: **(A)** Holy Family lives in Nazareth. **(B)** Trip to Bethlehem for census (7 CE). **(C)** Birth of Jesus (in Bethlehem). **(D)** Visit Jerusalem on the way back for presentation of infant Jesus. **(E)** Travel back to Nazareth (so Jesus is from there).

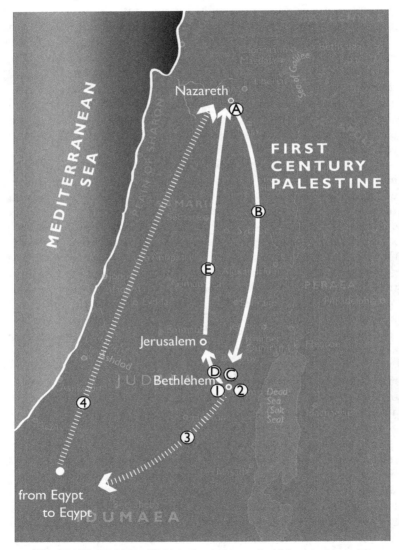

MATTHEW'S STORY: **(1)** Holy Family lives in Bethlehem and Jesus is born there. **(2)** Two years later, Magi visit Holy Family in Bethlehem. **(3)** Holy Family flees to Egypt to avoid Herod's slaughter of innocents. **(4)** After Herod dies (4 BCE), Holy Family moves to Nazareth (so Jesus is from there.)

still living in Bethlehem. Indeed, when they arrive at the Holy Family's house in Bethlehem (notice, a house, not a manger behind an inn) Jesus is a young child, not a baby. The Wise Men warn the Holy Family of Herod's plans, and the family flees to Egypt. Once Herod is dead, they move to Nazareth, a town they have never even been to before.

Luke, on the other hand, starts with the Holy Family living in Nazareth, not Bethlehem. Mary becomes pregnant, but they have to travel to Bethlehem because of a census issued by Caesar Augustus, while Quirinius is governor of Syria. There Jesus is born in the manger outside the inn. The shepherds visit and, eight days later, Jesus is circumcised. Shortly after, they visit the temple in Jerusalem to "present" him to the Lord and then head straight back home to Nazareth. That's it. No flight to Egypt, no Magi, nothing else. If you were to trace the journeys traveled in both stories, you would see that there is no overlap.[9] (See Figure 1)

Additionally, the time frames of both stories are different. Matthew places the birth of Jesus during the reign of Herod the Great, and we know that Herod the Great died in 4 BCE Since there had to be time for the Wise Men to arrive, for Herod to order the slaughter of the innocents, and for the Holy Family to leave Egypt and wait there for Herod's death, the latest that Jesus could have been born, according to Matthew, is around 7 BCE Luke, on the other hand, specifically places the birth of Jesus during Quirinius's reign as governor in Syria. Although he held office in Syria prior, Quirinius was not governor of Syria until 6 CE, a full nine years after Herod died.[10] He remained governor until 12 CE, but he did issue a census around 7 CE So, 7 CE is a fair approximation for estimating when Luke thought the birth of Jesus took place. But although the dates look similar, 7 BCE and 7 CE are a full 13 years apart.[11]

Clearly, Matthew and Luke are telling different stories. The only thing they have in common is Jesus's parents' names (Mary and Joseph), the city in which Jesus was born (Bethlehem), the city in which Jesus grew up (Nazareth), and a virginal conception. Is this evidence that there was a true story of Jesus's birth that was floating around, that contained these elements, of which both Matthew and Luke were aware? Were they just elaborating on an already existing story?

Not necessarily.

Most of these elements are found in other places available to both Matthew and Luke, for example the Gospel of Mark.[12]

Mark mentions Jesus's mother by name[13] and that Jesus was from Nazareth.[14] They both might have known of a Jewish tradition that the Messiah would be born in Bethlehem, the City of David,[15] and Matthew actually tells us why he thought Mary was a virgin. He quotes Isaiah 7:14: "Behold, the virgin shall be with child, and shall bring forth a son, and they shall call his name Immanuel." It's likely that Luke had the same passage in mind.[16] The only thing that can't be explained without coincidence is the agreement between Matthew and Luke on the name "Joseph" for Jesus's father. That was not in Mark or apparently any other written source. So perhaps it was established oral tradition that Jesus's father was named Joseph.

What is clear is that both Matthew and Luke had a common goal: to tell a story of Jesus's birth depicting him as special from the beginning and that was consistent with what they thought was supposed to be true of Jesus (that he was born to a man named Joseph and the virgin Mary, in Bethlehem, but grew up in Nazareth). They just made up different stories that accomplished this. For Luke, Jesus grew up in Nazareth because his family lived there, and he was only born in Bethlehem because of the census journey. For Matthew, Jesus was born in Bethlehem because his family lived there, and he only grew up in Nazareth because his family moved there after they fled to Egypt to avoid Herod's wrath. Luke heralds Jesus's specialness with angels while Matthew does this with Magi.

Some claim that they may not have invented these stories but borrowed them. Secular scholars claim that both Perseus and Attis were born of virgins and that Mithras was born in a cave and was visited by both shepherds and wise men. They claim that Krishna was born without a sexual conception, was foretold by an angel, was born during a "tax journey," was heralded by a star, and had wise men visit with gifts. Kings also tried to kill Krishna by slaughtering innocents, and he had to flee to a foreign country to hide.[17] My research, however, suggests these claims are largely exaggerated.[18] You can, for example, only see such grandiose similarities between the stories of Krishna and Jesus by very selectively reading Krishna's story and then imaginatively retelling it.[19] Although there certainly were stories of miraculously born savior/king god-men before Jesus, the specific elements of Jesus's birth story—the Magi, the inn, and the "tax journey"—seem to originate with Matthew and Luke.

However, biblical scholars also agree that the biblical nativities don't give us historical knowledge of Jesus's birth because there are some historical inaccuracies within the stories them-selves. First, no census ever required the relocation of people to their hometowns, much less the hometown of their ancestor one thousand years removed. (Do you know where you would go? Can you even imagine the logistics?) Although Quirinius did issue a census, it was not of the entire Roman world. (Gali-lee wasn't even under direct Roman rule when this census oc-curred). Besides, Luke says that the census was issued by Au-gustus, not Quirinius, and we know that Augustus never issued a census. Furthermore, there is no record of a slaughter of in-nocents by Herod in Bethlehem, and careful records of Herod were kept by Flavius Josephus. Also, a star that appears and leads people on a journey makes no sense—a star certainly can't stop over a specific location.[20] Finally, Matthew's virgin birth is based on a mistranslation of the passage he mentions, Isaiah 7:14. The Greek translation of that verse, which Mathew had, read "virgin," but that is a mistranslation of the Hebrew word for "young woman" (almah). The Hebrews had a different word for "virgin" (bethulah), but it does not appear in that passage.[21]

But even if we do take the nativity stories at face value, there is no way that the birth of Jesus happened on December 25. There is no way shepherds would be watching their flocks by night, in Palestine, in winter, on one of the shortest days of the year. The sheep would have been housed in barns. So the fact that Jesus's birth is celebrated on December 25 has nothing to do with the Bible. Ironically, however, the date the birth of the "son of God" is celebrated may have everything do with the date the birth of "the sun god" was celebrated.

Jesus's First Birthday Party

Although stories of Jesus's birth circulated among early Christians, early Christians did not celebrate it. They didn't even celebrate their own. Celebrating one's own birth was the kind of self-aggrandizing thing that a Roman emperor would do. It's the kind of thing Egyptian pharaohs do before they hang bakers.[22] Birthday celebrations are what give rul-ers, like Herod, the opportunity to ask for the head of John the Baptist as a birthday present.[23] The earliest Christians celebrated the day of their death but not the day of their birth. Still today, holidays named after saints celebrate the day of their deaths, not their births.

Christians did speculate about the date of Jesus's birth, and the most common theory placed it around the start of spring,

March 25. This was a result of how some believed the Bible should be read. According to them, it didn't estimate. If the Bible says that Moses was 120 when he died, then he was exactly 120, not 119 and 354 days or 120 and one day. This led to the belief that biblical figures lived whole years—their birth date was also their death date. According to the Gospels, Jesus died around Passover.[24] Although the date of Passover fluctuates, based on the Jewish lunar calendar, it was commonly believed that he died in a year in which Passover fell around the spring equinox. (Again, the equinox actually falls around the 21st but was recognized on the 25th.) This would be appropriate since it would place the resurrection of Jesus around the start of spring, and the resurrection was symbolic of the renewal of life, just like spring is. If Jesus died on March 25 and he lived whole years, then he must have been born on March 25 as well.

This was not the only suggested date, however. Probably borrowing from some Egyptian traditions, others believed Jesus's birth to fall on January 6. They also believed that was the day that Jesus was baptized by John the Baptist, and since the Bible said Jesus was 33 at the time, he must have been exactly 33. So January 6 must be his birthday as well. Of course, this poses a problem, since it would also place his death date on January 6, and Passover never, ever, falls that early. So eventually (although some in the Armenian Church still celebrate Jesus's birth on January 6), after later competing with December 25 for Jesus's birth date, January 6 simply came to be recognized as the date of the Epiphany— the date that the Wise Men arrived. Of course, we really have no idea when they would have actually found Jesus at his house in Bethlehem.

However, this still leaves our question unanswered: why do we celebrate Jesus's birth on December 25? The most widely accepted explanation, put simply, is this: the church adopted the existing birth date of the sun god, Sol Invictus, in order to "supplant" him.

Before Constantine, the Roman Empire was not Christian. Constantine himself, along with most of the army and political leaders, worshiped Sol. Constantine became emperor in 306 CE but converted to Christianity[25] and declared Christianity to be the state religion of the empire in 313 CE. Of course, this didn't make everyone in the empire automatically convert and stop celebrating the old religious holidays. After all, who would enforce such a law—all the soldiers who still worshiped Sol? (Think about how many people would actually stop celebrating Christmas if it became illegal today.) A very useful way of dealing with this problem would be to officially declare the sun's birthday to actually be Jesus's birthday. That way all the celebrating that everyone was just going to keep doing anyway would "officially" be in the name of Jesus.

Now it's questionable as to whether or not Constantine actually employed this strategy himself. After all, there is no record of such a declaration at the Council of Nicaea, over which Constantine presided, and the first written recognition of December 25 as Jesus's birthday doesn't come until the year before Constantine's last, 336.[26] However, the church did seem to officially endorse this strategy in 354, when Bishop Liberius of Rome ordered people to recognize Jesus's birth on December 25.[27] With this order, the effort to Christianize December holidays—to make them about the Christ instead of the sun—became official. The goal was to eventually make people think that Jesus was and always had been the reason people celebrate during the early winter season. Pope Gregory I (in 601) laid the church's strategy out quite plainly. As he wrote to Mellitus, his missionary in England, "[Do] not…stop such ancient pagan festivities… adapt them to the rites of the Church, only changing the reason of them from a heathen to a Christian impulse."[28]

This explanation for December 25 is popular because this would not have been the only time the church tried to incorporate aspects of sun worship in order to supplant it. Although Constantine sanctioned Christianity, it was not universal—it needed converts and sun worship was still popular. To compete, Christians adopted sun worship practices into their own. Many (though not all) moved their weekly holy day of worship from the Jewish one they had acquired from their mother religion (which starts at nightfall on Friday and ends at nightfall on Saturday) to Sunday, the holy day of sun worshipers.[29] Apparently, they also adapted the practice of bowing to the sun before entering the temple. Pope Leo was complaining that Christians were still bowing to the sun before entering St. Peter's Basilica as late as the mid-400s. There is even a mural on the Tomb of Julii, from the third century, that depicts Jesus driving the sun chariot across the sky.[30]

Other remnants of this propaganda war survive even today. As the sun, Sol Invictus was depicted as having a glowing orb surrounding his head. This is the origin of the modern halo. In fact, some modern depictions of Jesus are almost indistinguishable from ancient depictions of Sol Invictus. Both include sunbeams emanating from their heads.[31]

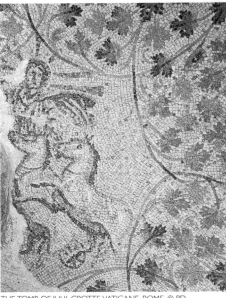

THE TOMB OF JULII. GROTTE VATICANE, ROME. © PD

Sextus Africanus's Competing Idea

Although scholars don't contest the fact that Christianity borrowed many things from ancient sun worship, some do suggest that Christians might have come up with the December 25 date for Jesus's birth independently. What is their argument? It seems that the Christians didn't start adopting sun worship practices until after Constantine's conversion in 313, when Christianity became state-endorsed. Before that, they were more interested in distinguishing themselves. Yet, there is some evidence that a few Christians were celebrating Jesus's birth on December 25 before 313. What evidence? Around 400, Augustine mentions that the Donatists, a rebel Christian group, celebrated Jesus's birth on December 25. Why is a reference made in 400 evidence of pre-313 December 25 celebrations? The Donatists emerged as a Christian group during persecution under Diocletian in 312 and were notorious for stubbornly maintaining their traditions, even rejecting January 6 as Jesus's birthday. So, if they were celebrating Jesus's birth on December 25 in 400, they could likely have been doing so in 312 when the group began, a year before Constantine's conversion when the desire to assimilate pagan traditions emerged. They must have had other reasons for adopting that date—or so the argument goes.

How might they have arrived at this date independently? It has to do with that preference for biblical "whole years" we talked about before. In short, because Jesus died on Passover, instead of placing his birth on that date (to make him exactly 33 years old), that's where they placed his conception, so that he entered and exited the world on the same day. They came to think that the Passover on which Jesus was crucified happened on March 25—so count out exactly nine months later than March 25 and Jesus is born on December 25. Andrew McGowan[32] says two sources, dating from the late 300s, suggest this. Joseph Kelly names Sextus Julius Africanus, a third-century Christian, specifically as someone who proposed this explanation.

Kelly, however, doubts that the December 25 date had the kind of popularity it would have needed to overcome the popularity of the other previously mentioned dates. (Sextus himself was a minor figure.) In my opinion, the "March 25 conception theory" is most likely an ad hoc explanation, developed by fourth-century Christians for why the December 25 date was celebrated after it was adapted from paganism.[33] The ability of the Donatists to preserve their own traditions for 88 years seems unlikely to me. No one is that immune to influence. It's much more likely that either Augustine was mistaken or that they actually did, somewhere along the line, add the celebration to their traditions in the wake of its popularity. For two religions, from the same region and time, to independently establish the birth of their gods to be on the same day is just too coincidental.

But even if the December 25 date for Jesus's birth was established before the church started adopting pagan traditions, it's still the case that December celebrations, including celebrating Sol's birth on December 25, were established and popular. So were the traditions that came with them when the church started celebrating Jesus's birth on December 25. As a result, the church had to compete, and it had a very hard time standing up against, and distinguishing itself from, what people had been doing for centuries. So the church tried to make December celebrations, and in fact, the entire season, about Jesus. It wanted the holiday season and its traditions to become Christ-focused. But as we shall soon see, these efforts were never successful. To quote Christmas historian Steven Nissenbaum, "Christmas has always been an extremely difficult holiday to Christianize."[34]

A War on Saturnalia? You Betcha

To preserve the idea that Christmas is a Christian holiday in *Good Tidings and Great Joy,* Sarah Palin depicts the time when Saturnalia, the sun god's birthday and the church's newly-minted Nativity Feast coexisted as fight for dominance in a kind of winner-take-all-brawl. Christmas emerged victorious, according to Palin, and the other holidays faded away. After acknowledging that the church borrowed the December 25 date from Saturnalia and the solstice, she writes:

> But over time those old pagan celebrations faded into obscurity because they weren't grounded in much of anything but myth, while Christmas gained ever more prominence and meaning. (Does that mean Christians won the "war on Saturnalia"? You bet. And it shows the incredible power of even new traditions to shape culture.)...fast-forward a few years and jump over to a different continent. "Christmas" became an American federal holiday in 1870...[35]

Palin's version of history, however, is woefully inaccurate. Quite a few things happened in the years Palin fast-forwards through that are crucial for determining whether Christmas really is a "Christian holiday."

New traditions don't shape culture as easily as Sarah thinks. When religions compete for dominance, it's usually not winner-take-all. Converting people is not easy. To stay relevant and desirable emerging religions usually take on the practices and traditions of the old, relabeling and repurposing them, and even renaming their gods. This was especially true of Christianity as it rolled north through Europe, adopting and adapting pagan traditions and creating saints out of pagan gods as it went.[36] Making religions compete is a bit like making paint colors mix: if yellow and blue compete for dominance, one doesn't win—you just end up with green.

The same is true for holidays. When two holidays compete, you end up with a single holiday that looks a little like them both. In fact, the church's new Feast of the Nativity didn't even fare that well in the fight. It's not as though, upon its invention, it came fully loaded with Christmas trees, presents, Santa, store ads, and Fox News. It was just the church declaring that Jesus's birth occurred on December 25. And that's fine. But it didn't keep everyone from partying, feasting, drinking, and copulating just as they always had. The Roman government could say everyone was celebrating Jesus's birth, but in reality they weren't. Making Rome "officially Christian" didn't convert all the Romans overnight. The church had just tacked on Jesus's name to the traditional pagan festival.

Now when traditions morph and merge like this, eventually people do forget where they came from, especially if they get a new name. As a result, people did eventually relabel and repurpose the old pagan traditions. They even gave them new explanations. For example, today people think we give gifts because the Wise Men gave gifts to Jesus. In reality, this tradition finds its origin in the Roman New Year Kalends gift-giving exchange. Sarah Palin thinks that "there are so many candles during Christmas" because Jesus "was the light of men,"[37] when in reality we get this tradition from the pagans who lit candles in their homes and windows to drive away the ever-increasing darkness that loomed during the year's shorter days.

So it is true that people eventually came to believe that the reason they were celebrating in December was because "that is when Jesus was born." In fact, they eventually came to believe that was the reason why people had always celebrated in December.[38] But the way they were celebrating was exactly the same way people had always celebrated during that time. So Saturnalia and the solstice didn't fade away into obscurity. Although people stopped referring to them by name, their celebratory practices still lived on and dominated how the holiday was celebrated. And they still do, to this day. Feasting is still popular at Christmas, as is drinking. And the social inversion of Saturnalia survives as charitable giving and "Boxing Day" in the United Kingdom. We will see even more of this as we continue.

Expanding the Nativity Story

The church did try to do more than just tack Jesus's name onto the holidays. In a continuing effort to Christianize the holiday, it expanded the nativity story. How? Well, the four canonical gospels don't tell us much, but there are dozens of non-canonical gospels—written accounts of Jesus's life. The church ignored the fact that it considered them heretical and non-authoritative and harvested them for details about Jesus's birth anyway.

Where did these gospels come from? People desperate for more information about Jesus wrote them in the second, third, and fourth centuries. I've always thought of them as a kind of "fan fiction." People desperate for more information on Star Wars will take a single story from the movie and write an entire novel about it. (For example, there is a whole novel about the Mos Eisley Cantina from *Star Wars Episode IV*.[39]) Likewise, people took single elements of the gospel stories and made up background stories for them. For instance, the *Arabic Infancy Gospel* makes up a story about how Jesus first met the thieves that ended up on either side of him on the cross, one of whom Jesus says will be with him in paradise. According to this heretical gospel, they tried to rob Jesus and his family during their flight to Egypt. The one that showed them mercy and bribed the other to let them go, Jesus says, is the thief that will "go before [him] into paradise." The story even gave them names: Titus and Dumachus. (Titus is the good one.) Other fun stories include Jesus pacifying dragons—dragons!—in *The Gospel of Pseudo-Matthew* and stories of a bratty Jesus as a young boy in *The Coptic Infancy Gospel of Thomas*.

What did these gospels add to the nativity? The Latin Infancy Gospel gives us the tradition that Mary folded her hands in worship before the baby Jesus, as she does now in every crèche. It also names Mary's parents, Anna and Joachim. The Protoevangelium of James gives us the most information. It gives us Mary's age (16) and perpetual virginity. (It explains away Jesus's brothers, mentioned in Mark, by making Joseph an elderly widower). It describes the Christmas star as extremely bright. (Matthew does not). It also gives us the virgin birth—which is different than a virgin conception, mind you. According to the Protoevangelium, Mary suffered no labor. The integrity of her...uh, "nether regions," let's say, remained intact. She was pregnant, and then—poof!—like magic, there was a baby.

The *Protoevangelium* even inserts a doubting-Thomas-type story to criticize those who disbelieve this aspect of the story. A midwife is called and won't "believe that a virgin brought forth" unless she puts "forward [her] finger and test[s] her condition." Lovely. She does. More lovely: God withers her hand because of her doubt. (I think that is my favorite part.) She repents. God relents and restores her hand.

Of course, none of these things are historically accurate, but people gleefully added these details to the nativity story and even to church doctrine in some cases.

Heretical gospels weren't the only places people looked for more information about the nativity, however. They also looked to the Old Testament. Now, let's be clear: nothing in the Old Testament is really specifically about Jesus. It promises a Messiah, sure, and if Jesus is the Messiah, then those passages are about him. (Modern Jewish people would, of course, deny that they are.) However, the Old Testament doesn't tell us anything about the particulars of Jesus's life, much less his birth. But the early Christians wanted it to. So they read it like people today read Nostradamus. They recognize a single familiar element, assume it's about what they want it to be about, and ignore all disconfirming evidence. ("'Hister' sounds like 'Hitler.' Nostradamus must be talking about World War II!")

For example, Isaiah 1:3 says that "the ox knows its owner and the donkey its master's manger." This passage has absolutely nothing to do with Jesus but instead is making a point about the rebellion of Israel generations before Jesus's time. However, since it has the word "manger" in it, the early Christians interjected their own assumptions and—poof!—every crèche now has an ox and a donkey looking at Jesus's manger bed. Isaiah 60:3 says, "Nations shall come to your light, and the kings to the brightness of your dawn." Poof! The Wise Men are now kings. Isaiah 60:6 says, "A multitude of camels shall cover you...they shall bring gold and frankincense and shall proclaim the praise of the Lord." No Myrrh? No matter. The three kings have camels. (Oh, and we only assume there were three kings because the gospels say there were three gifts. Nowhere is anything specific about how many magi there were.[40])

Trying to Christianize Christmas

Expanding the nativity story didn't go that far in the effort to Christianize the holiday, however. The main way the church tried to Christianize Christmas was by expanding the religious elements of the holiday. They added a mass on the evening of the 24th, then a midnight mass, a mass at dawn (Aurora), and then a morning mass, all to emphasize different parts of the nativity story. (Four masses in under 12 hours—loads of fun!) The Epiphany, on January 6, which celebrated the arrival of the Wise Men, is where we get the 12 days of Christmas. Not counting Christmas, there are 12 days between the two dates. Then there's Advent, a time of fasting and praying four weeks before Christmas, and also the Octave of Christmas. Candlemas, on February 2, celebrates Jesus's presentation at the temple. The list is extensive and covers a large portion of the calendar.[41]

The church also added a plethora of Christmas hymns, poems, and songs to their repertoire. During the medieval period (the twelfth, thirteenth, and fourteenth centuries), they wrote and performed plays that educated the illiterate masses about the specifics of the Christmas story.[42] Also around this time, in 1223, Francis of Assisi asked for a statue depicting Jesus in a manger with hay, in an effort to emphasize Jesus's humble humanity in stark contrast with other artists, who depicted him and his family as royalty. Here arises the common depiction of Jesus in a manger, from which the very idea of a crèche (i.e., a nativity scene), is derived.[43]

The most persuasive action the church took when trying to Christianize the holidays happened just before, in the eleventh century, and it was likely unintentional. Of all the masses that one could attend, midnight mass was the most popular. Going was the quickest way to end one's Advent fast. The theme of this mass was Jesus's birth. Tradition held that he was born at midnight—at the dawn of year one, no less. Because it was about Jesus, the Christ, this mass became known in England as "Christ's Mass." Now, say it quickly: "Christmas." Eventually the name caught on and was used to refer to the holiday itself, and then to the whole season.[44]

But of course, this doesn't mean that Christmas was from then on a Christian holiday. For one thing, the fact that the name "Christ" is in the word "Christmas" doesn't mean that our end of the year celebrations are about Christ any more than the fact that the word "sun" is in "Sunday" means that our end of the week worship services are in reverence to the sun. The subject of our celebrations is determined by how we celebrate, not what we call our celebration. And, as we are about to see—eleventh-century "Christmas" celebrations were still primarily secular, as were the ones that followed in later centuries.[45]

Second of all, naming a holiday isn't like licking a donut—it doesn't automatically make it yours. Christians saying that Christmas is a Christian holiday because of its name is a bit like my claiming I own my neighbor's dog because I started calling it "Kyle's dog." Naming something after yourself doesn't make it belong to you or change its behavior. The same was true for Christmas.

The More Things Change, the More They Stay the Same

In fact, the more the church added to the holiday, the more it was still celebrated in the ways it always had been. There may have been times the religious elements almost had equal footing with the secular celebrations, but they never overshadowed or dominated the holiday. More likely it seems, throughout the Middle Ages (just like today for most people) the secular elements were always the primary focus and the religious elements were an afterthought.

This was obviously true in Rome after Constantine. The holiday was Christian in name only. None of the religious traditions had been established, and people celebrated in December like they always had—with raucous customs of feasting, misrule, social inversion, heavy drinking, and wild sex.

When Rome fell, however, the holiday didn't get any more Christian. People perhaps have the idea that everyone was a "good little Christian" in the Middle Ages, but the truth is that even when government and nobility were aligned with the church, it struggled to keep hold of the vast majority of people, like the illiterate peasant masses. Again, the church constantly had to adopt and adapt pagan traditions to stay relevant to people's lives.

So as Christianity, and with it Christmas, moved north into modern-day Germany and England, it absorbed a plethora of barbarian and pagan December traditions that were already established. It was colder in the north and these barbarians, since they couldn't get out as much, liked to bring the outside in. So the traditions of Yule logs and greenery were added, along with candles, ghosts (who they thought roamed the earth during the winter), and even more feasting and drinking. Although church clergy likely didn't participate in such things, they were a small minority. The masses needed a break after the long harvest season and something to distract them from the short days and long nights. "Christmas" was tailored for the job.

Some clergy understood the importance of such celebrations and tolerated them, but others objected. In 743, Bishop Boniface made Pope Zachary aware of raucous celebrations in Rome around St. Peter's Church, where:

> bands of singers parade about the streets in pagan fashion, shouting and chanting sacrilegious songs and loading tables with food day and night, while no one in his own house is willing to lend his neighbor fire or tools or any other convenience...[There are] women with amulets and bracelets of heathen fashion on their arms and legs, offering them for sale to willing buyers. All these things, seen by evil minded and ignorant people, are a cause of reproach.[46]

Pope Zachary ordered such celebrations to cease. Not surprisingly, they didn't.[47]

As the church expanded the holiday's religious elements through the Middle Ages, the secular celebrations grew even more. In the 1200s, Henry III of England and his guests could devour up to 600 oxen at a Christmas feast. In the early 1300s, Edward III would put on non-religious Christmas plays in his court. In the late 1300s, Richard II would have a mummers parade. "The mummers...dressed up as knights, cardinals, and visiting foreign princes. They brought the king gifts, played dice with him (and always let him win), enjoyed much food and drink, danced for a while, and then paraded out."[48] Of course, the common man couldn't celebrate in such grandiose ways, but these royal celebrations set the tone for how Christmas was to be celebrated by everyone. The religious elements weren't completely ignored, nor were religious and secular celebrations seen as incompatible. But gifts, eating, drinking, games, social inversion, costumes, and even sexual activity dominated as the focus of Christmas celebrations.

Of course, such celebrations continue to dominate the holiday even today. You may think it odd to include "sexual activity" as part of this list, but consider this: in Ireland, as late at the early 1800s, midnight mass—usually held outdoors and illuminated by bonfires—was "usually preceded and followed by what a nineteenth-century Irish writer termed 'jovial orgies,' perambulating groups who engaged in heavy drinking that often led to illicit sexual couplings."[49] Oh Holy Night, indeed! It seems that similar practices existed throughout the Middle Ages, and if you think such things have long since fallen out of favor, think about the last office Christmas party you attended.

The effort to Christianize Christmas failed so miserably and the celebrations remained so raucous that by the sixteenth century, around the time of the Protestant Reformation, the Puritans tried to stamp out Christmas altogether. They gave up the war to Christianize Christmas and instead launched a very successful war against it. We will talk more about this when we talk about Myth #3, and we'll see how Christmas eventually made its comebback. However, one quick look around during a modern Christmas season will tell you the basics of how that story goes. Its comeback was one of a primarily secular origin, which was quickly co-opted by capitalistic and consumerist forces. In other words, it remained non-religious.

How This Myth Has Hijacked the Holiday

The idea that Jesus is the reason for the season has hijacked the holidays in a couple of ways. For one, it's used to delegitimize non-religious celebrations of Christmas. "If you aren't focusing on Jesus, you aren't doing it right." And if you are not a Christian, then forget about it. "You're an atheist? You don't have a right to celebrate at all!" Christmas is for Christians only!

This kind of criticism took an even more extreme form in Kirk Cameron's 2014 movie *Saving Christmas*. The movie served as a megaphone for Cameron's opinion about the holidays: that "every inch of Christmas belongs to Jesus." Every Christmas symbol—Christmas trees, house lights, Santa, feasting, buying gifts and even Christmas commercialism itself—is really about Jesus and in honor of him. (According to Cameron, God wants you to be *materialistic* at Christmas because that's when God became "material" himself in the form of Jesus.) So every part of Christmas belongs to Christians: "This is our tree, this is our St. Nicholas..." In interviews, Cameron even went as so far as to claim that all Christmas symbols and traditions are of Christian origin.[50] Therefore, Cameron concludes, not only is it not proper for non-Christians to celebrate, but if Christians don't celebrate like his family—by pulling out all the stops, using the richest butter (yes, he actually used the phrase "richest but-

ter"), and spending everything they can afford on decorations and gifts, they're not doing it right. They are not honoring God enough. They're "that guy"—the "jerk," the scrooge, who "drank the Kool-aid," and is ruining Christmas for everyone, including Jesus.

I mounted a full debunking of Cameron's movie when it came out,[51] but given what we have learned in this chapter, it should be pretty obvious why his arguments are preposterous. First of all, not only is it verifiable historical fact that most Christmas traditions have clearly pagan (non-Christian) origins, it's also quite clear that most holiday traditions have nothing to do with Jesus—they are not "about" him at all. So it makes perfect sense for Christians to simply concentrate on the holiday's few religious elements, if they wish. Second of all, there is nothing wrong or improper with non-Christians celebrating Christmas; there is not even anything new about non-religious Christmas celebrations. Since it was not originally a Christian holiday and never became a holiday celebrated primarily in a Christian way, there is nothing wrong with non-Christians celebrating it.

That's not to say that if you are a non-Christian, you have to celebrate. Even if you are Christian...if you don't want to celebrate Christmas—and there are plenty of good reasons not to—that's fine. Knock yourself out. No one should feel obligated to celebrate.[52] And if you are Christian and want to pull out all the stops and make up stories about how every element of your holiday celebration is really about Jesus—that's fine too. Likewise, if you are a non-Christian and want to have a simple non-materialistic holiday where you give to the poor—more power to you. The point is, no one person should tell any other person that they can't or shouldn't celebrate Christmas, and no one person should tell any other person what form their own personal celebration has to take if it's going to be "authentic," "genuine," or "God pleasing."[53] Even if you are Jewish—if you *want* to celebrate Christmas, go for it. You can make it whatever you want. Christmas belongs to us all, and we each should feel free to make it what we wish and celebrate how we please.

The second way this myth hijacks the holiday is by helping reinforce the myth that we shall address next: the endlessly repeated, near ubiquitous notion that **there is a war on Christmas!**

CHRISTMAS CARDS CIRCA 1890, © PD

THE MANCHESTER REGIMENT OF OLDHAM GREETINGS CARD, 1916 © PD

There Is a War on Christmas

EVERY YEAR, RIGHT AROUND DECEMBER 1, WE'RE repeatedly told "there is a war on Christmas." If there is, however, it's the most unsuccessful war in history. A full 96% of Americans annually celebrate Christmas,[1] and that number shows no signs of moving south. Christmas is even becoming popular in non-Christian and non-religious countries like Vietnam,[2] China,[3] and Japan.[4] The health of our economy is defined by Christmas spending and the Christmas shopping season gets longer every year—we usually see our first Christmas ad in mid-October, and hear our first Christmas music in stores on November 1.[5] And in 2012, Black Friday (the day after Thanksgiving) became Black Thursday. As Jon Stewart put it, "Christmas is so big now, it's eating other holidays. Watch your ass, Halloween! You're next."[6] Nevertheless, every year, we are led to believe that Christmas is under attack—that it's on the verge of extinction:

The secular progressive liberal atheists hate Christmas and every year they wage a war against it. They make us say "Happy Holidays" instead of "Merry Christmas." They unlawfully force the re-moval of court house nativities. They want to turn all Christmas trees into "holiday trees". They ban the colors red and green in schools. They are deter-mined to eliminate Christmas and make it illegal for you to "joyfully and openly celebrate."⁷ We must stop them. If we don't, no one will be able to celebrate Christmas anymore. Keep "Christ" in "Christmas." After all, Jesus is the reason for the season.

Sarah Palin assures us that this war is "not just some figment of the religious right's imagination,"⁸ but it is exactly that. The list of complaints regarding how "liberals" are waging a war on Christmas seems almost endless (and new examples pop up every year), but almost every one of those complaints is either exaggerated (intentionally sensationalized) or just outright false. And while it is true that there are objections to government-funded and endorsed Christmas decorations and celebrations that are overtly religious, such objections constitute a war on Christmas only if the holiday is essentially and only about Jesus—which, as we saw last chapter, it is not. Worse still, the way people have reacted to these complaints is downright dangerous. They threaten everything from your ability to celebrate the holiday as you see fit, to the very foundations of our constitutional democracy.

There Is No War on Christmas

The specific idea that there is a "liberal War on Christmas" did not arise organically. It was invented relatively recently. The earliest claims seem to trace back to 1999, when Peter Brimelow, who is too far right even for *National Review,* founded VDare.com (which was later classified as a hate group), and started complaining about *liberal phrases* like "Happy Holidays" and government Christmas parties being called "A Celebration of Holiday Traditions."⁹

But the claim that there is a war on Christmas—that it is under attack by some "other group" that conservative Christians don't like—is nothing new. For example in the 1920s, Henry Ford, founder of Ford Motors, claimed that the Jews were attacking Christmas in his anti-Semitic tract, "The International Jew."¹⁰ In 1959 it was the communists. The John Birch Society claimed that "One of the techniques now being applied by the Reds to weaken the pillar of religion in our country is the drive to take Christ out of Christmas." (I wonder if this was the first use of that phrase.) Basically, labeling a group you don't like as "anti-Christmas" is an extremely popular and effective way to vilify that group and so it's a common tactic.

Nowhere is this more evident than in Republican politics. Rick Perry cited the War on Christmas when talking about "Obama's war on Religion" in a 2010 campaign ad.[11] In fact the War on Christmas was used by most of the Republican candidates in some form, including Mitt Romney[12] and Newt Gingrich,[13] during the 2012 Republican campaign. But nothing says it better than the lawn sign that a friend of mine, Rev. Lance Schmitz, saw on a suburban lawn in 2011: "Save Christmas, Vote Republican."

Although it was invented by Brimelow, the idea that there is a liberal war on Christmas was most notably popularized by Fox News's Bill O'Reilly and John Gibson in 2005[14]. That year, O'Reilly complained on his show about Walmart greeters saying "Happy Holidays" instead of "Merry Christmas," and John Gibson published *The War on Christmas: How the Liberal Plot to Ban the Sacred Christian Holiday Is Worse than You Thought*.[15] Today, almost every claim about there being such a war ultimately finds its origin on Fox News. These claims include:

- Schools in Plano, Texas; Saginaw Township, Michigan, and Orlando, Florida, banned the colors red and green during Christmastime.[16]
- Ridgeway Elementary School in Dodgeville, Wisconsin; changed the lyrics to "Silent Night," performed in a school play to eliminate all references to religion.[17]
- In 2011 Rhode Island governor Lincoln Chafee (D-RI) called the Capitol's Christmas tree a "holiday tree."[18]
- Denver banned religious floats in its holiday parade.[19]
- Gap doesn't ever use the word Christmas in their ads.[20]
- Walmart, Macy's, and other stores require all their employees to say "Happy Holidays" instead of "Merry Christmas" and never put "Merry Christmas" in their advertisements.

The problem is every one of these claims is either grotesquely exaggerated or just outright false.

- No school has ever banned the colors red and green, and the mentioned schools produced their records to prove it.[21] A similar story popped up in 2013 about a school in Frisco (conflicting reports said it was Waco[22]) but the story was debunked almost as soon as it was reported.[23]
- Ridgeway Elementary didn't change the lyrics to "Silent Night" to eliminate all reference to religion. In reality, a church choir director changed all the lyrics in the play he helped to write to make them easier for kids to learn.[24]

- It's true that Governor Lincoln Chafee (D-RI) didn't call the statehouse tree a "Christmas tree" in 2011. However, he did so in an effort to be more inclusive of Rhode Islanders who celebrate the holiday but are not Christian.[25] "If it's in my house it's a Christmas tree, but when I'm representing all of Rhode Island I have to be respectful of everyone[.]"[26] It was not part of an effort to make the holiday illegal, to try "to put our religion down,"[27] or to force everyone to strip religious aspects from their holiday celebrations. In addition, the previous governor of Rhode Island, a Republican, also called it a holiday tree during the previous eight years,[28] but Fox News never made a peep and no one protested.

- Although the City of Denver did reject a religious parade float, they also rejected many other non-religious floats. It's a small parade and not everyone gets in.[29] The next year, religious floats were allowed.[30]

- Gap indeed does use the word Christmas in its ads and even sells merchandise with "Christmas" on it.[31]

- While it is true that you might hear "Happy Holidays" from employees at Walmart, it's false that it is required. In 2005, Walmart "encouraged" their employees to say "Happy Holidays" instead of "Merry Christmas" in an attempt, they said, to include all their customers, whether they be shopping for Christmas, Thanksgiving, Hanukkah, Kwanzaa, or New Year's."[32] Some Macy's stores did replace "Merry Christmas" with "Happy Holidays" in some of their ads, but the decision to do so was left up to individual store owners—it was not forced.

In 2013, Bill O'Reilly assured us that the War on Christmas was not only real but that conservatives had already won. Why? Because after conservatives complained, things got fixed—employees were no longer "forbidden" from saying Merry Christmas, schools were allowed to "have a Christmas wreath or a Christmas candle or a menorah or whatever," and Rhode Island Governor Lincoln Chafee started calling the state tree a "Christmas tree" again.[33] But most of the things conservatives complained about weren't happening in the first place. Those that were didn't constitute a war on Christmas and only changed because they became a problem as a result of the conservative complaints. O'Reilly created his own problem by complaining, and then when people gave into his complaints, he claimed he had solved a problem.

O'Reilly claiming that he won the War on Christmas is a bit like so-called "anti-vaxxers" claiming that they cured autism by having thimerosal removed from vaccines. Although it had already been proven that thimerosal is safe and does not cause autism, anti-vaxers thought it did. When they complained so loudly that people stopped vaccinating their children (some of whom subsequently died from preventable diseases) thimerosal was removed from vaccines just to appease them.[34] Like O'Reilly, they claimed victory: "See, thimerosal was a problem and we solved it." But of course, they didn't solve a problem. They just made a big enough stink to become a problem themselves and, unfortunately, autism continues to rise.[35]

Something that exposes the hypocrisy of O'Reilly's complaints: the same year that O'Reilly was complaining about the phrase "Happy Holidays" on his show, he himself was selling "holiday ornaments" to hang on your "holiday tree" though his website.[36] Also in 2005, the Bush White House wished everyone a "Happy Holiday Season" in their "holiday card." Truth be told, the phrase "Happy Holidays" predates Fox News's "War on Christmas" by far more than 100 years.[37] It seems to have originally just been shorthand for "Happy Thanksgiving, Merry Christmas, and Happy New Year," and today would include Hanukkah and Kwanzaa. When you think about it, if you are greeting someone but don't know if and which holidays they celebrate, or if you are proclaiming a message that will be seen by multiple people that may celebrate different holidays over a long period of time, it's a "catch all" phrase that makes perfect sense to use. In no way is using it "anti-Christian" or "anti-Christmas."

At the same time, it seems that the "liberal worry" about the use of the word "Christmas"—that it is offensive to the ears of non-Christians—is overblown. This seems to be an instance where political correctness has gone too far. O'Reilly thinks that non-Christians would have to be crazy to be offended by a two-word phrase like "Merry Christmas," adding to the irony that he is so offended by the use of the two-word phrase "Happy Holidays." I think he is right, but for a different reason.

Although the effort to be more inclusive by using the phrase "Happy Holidays" is laudable, the word "Christmas" is no more indicative of Christ and Christianity than the word "Sunday" is indicative of the sun and sun worship. To think "Christmas" is a Christian word commits the etymological fallacy—to think that the present meaning of a word is derived from its origins or even its spelling. As we saw in the last chapter, both words do have a religious origin, but words find their meaning in their connotation and use. And the word "Christmas" has been almost completely detached from its original Christian origin. Recall that December celebrations were originally pagan celebrations that the church tried and failed to Christianize. The church started calling the holiday "Christmas" in the eleventh century, but the celebrations stayed secular and remain so to this day. Consequently, the word "Christmas" conjures mainly non-Christian images, such as Santa, decorated pine trees, gifts, and feasting.

What astounds me, however, is that people don't seem to realize how closed-minded and intolerant they look when they campaign against neutral holiday slogans like "Happy Holidays." Take a scene in the made-for-Christians Christmas movie, Christmas with a Capital C.[38] A local store owner, putting up a "Season's Greetings" banner, defends his decision by saying, "It works for everybody." The protagonist Dan retorts, "It doesn't work for me." The viewer is forced to ask, "So if it doesn't work for you, it just shouldn't be done, everyone else be damned?" I understand that he thinks he is defending his sacred holiday from being attacked, but it looks like pure intolerance. "I know that Walmart is already wall-to-wall Christmas merchandise, decorations, sales and music, but if the next Buddhist who walks through that door doesn't have the phrase 'Merry Christmas' thrown in their face too, I'm not shopping here anymore!"

No one is telling you that you can't say "Merry Christmas"; no one is dictating how you should celebrate the holiday in your private life. Why is the fact that some people or businesses try to avoid saying "Merry Christmas" to people who don't celebrate Christmas such a big deal? I wouldn't wish someone a happy Father's Day unless I knew they were a father. Why would I wish someone a merry Christmas unless I knew they celebrated Christmas?

In short, saying "Merry Christmas" really shouldn't be a big deal—but neither should saying neutral phrases like "Happy Holiday," especially if there are good intentions behind it.

Collateral Damage

Now one might wonder why I'm making such a big deal about the conservative reaction to the imaginary War on Christmas. It's because those reactions are real and have had a negative effect on society. Although some reactions have been fairly innocuous, such as billboards that simply read, "I miss you saying Merry Christmas—Jesus,"[39] others are more menacing.

For example, boycotts have been organized against stores that say "Happy Holidays." In Rhode Island for that "Holiday Tree Lighting," protesters organized carolers to sing "O Christmas Tree" and interrupted a children's chorus to do so.[40] And in 2013, a Salvation Army bell ringer was punched by a Walmart shopper for saying "Happy Holidays" instead of "Merry Christmas."

Worse still, the aforementioned movie, *Christmas with a Capital C*, Sarah Palin's Christmas book *Good Tidings and Great Joy*, and the general Christian response to the War on Christmas promote the stereotype of secularists and atheists as grinchy, amoral curmudgeons who hate America, Christmas, and everything fun and beautiful. ("Angry Atheists with Lawyers" is the title of Palin's first chapter, and "Joe Mc-Scrooge" is the name of the strawman she chooses to represent them.) Atheists are already the most hated and distrusted group in America; they don't need anything else piled on.[41]

Furthermore, these stereotypes about them are blatantly false. It is well-established that morality is possible without God, most seculars and atheists are perfectly moral and good people, and the most popular moral theories in philosophy— deontology and utility—are secular theories. (Immanuel Kant grounded his deontology in reason alone. Jeremy Bentham and John Stuart Mill grounded utility in the notion that one ought simply to produce the most amount of happiness for the most amount of people.) In general, it is incorrect to suggest that one group is more moral than another. Whites aren't more moral than blacks, the rich are not more moral than the poor, and Christians aren't more moral than non-Christians. In the same way, the religious aren't more moral than seculars. There are good and bad eggs in both groups, but I believe the percentages of good and bad people in both are surely the same.

Of course, if you are an atheist but still think you are a good person, Sarah Palin would strongly disagree. But not because of evidence that atheists commit more crimes, are less devoted to their families, or even secretly worship Satan. No, it's because her religion says that humans are deplorable individuals that can't help but act in evil ways unless they are empowered by Christ to act otherwise. As she says, "[without] Christianity...the source of these ever more illusive [sic] values"[42] it's not possible to behave well. "[T]he one thing that can empower [a person] to live virtuously [is] faith in Christ."[43] This is as offensive to today's Jews, Muslims, Hindus, and Buddhists as it is to atheists, and it's historically ignorant to boot. People behaved morally and had values long before Jesus was born or religion was even invented. But Palin's argument is also completely circular. Simply put, someone is claiming that what her religion says is false, and her reply is "No it's not because of something else my religion says is true." You can't prove your religion with your religion.

In fact, Palin's efforts may actually be harming society. They are part of a larger effort to make society more religious, but there is overwhelming evidence to suggest that prevalent religious belief in a society makes that society more dysfunctional.[44] Conversely, the most secular nations in the world produce the happiest (most satisfied and content) individuals.[45]

Because of her belief that morality and a stable, free society are not possible without Christianity (and a government infused with it), Palin gets upset about the one true thing that conservative Christian Christmas warriors say about the War on Christmas: there are legal objections to courthouse nativities and other government Christmas displays and celebrations that are overtly religious. But as we shall now see, it's actually the efforts of Palin and others like her that are the real threat to our democracy and freedom.

Courthouse Crèches, the First Amendment, and the Separation of Church and State

Contrary to Palin's claims, objections to government-funded religious displays don't just come from "angry atheists with lawyers." The first legal action taken against a crèche on government property was launched by three clergymen and one atheist who objected to a crèche erected in Washington, D.C. But such legal actions are real, and conservative objections to them do make sense, once you understand the assumptions of the conservative people behind them, like Palin, Gibson, and Rick Santorum.[46] They think:

Christmas was originally and is primarily a Christian holiday. We celebrate on December 25 because that is when Jesus was born and we give gifts because the Magi did. So any "attack" against any element of Christmas, especially a religious symbol like a nativity, is an attack against Christianity itself, and thus must be opposed. As long as you think it's acceptable for the federal government to recognize Christmas as a federal holiday, you can't object to courthouse nativities. Putting up a nativity is just how the holiday is celebrated.

But once you realize, as we did last chapter, that Christmas is not a Christian holiday—that Jesus is not the reason for the season—it's easier to see objections to courthouse nativities for what they really are: objections to the government endorsing Christianity by endorsing specifically Christian ways of celebrating the holidays.[47] Displaying a nativity is a Christian way of celebrating first recommended by St. Francis of Assisi, who suggested displaying a statue of Jesus in a manger full of hay at Christmas time to emphasize Jesus's humility and humanity. Such objections are not attacking Christmas as a whole, just the fact that some government entities are recognizing it in a specifically religious way. Palin suggests that it's just angry atheists suing the government because they are offended,[48] but offense actually has nothing to do with it. Although they may be offended, the citizens pursuing such legal action are doing so on the grounds that their government has failed to separate church and state as the First Amendment requires.

Of course that won't settle the issue either. The likes of Palin also don't think there should be a separation of church and state. They think Christianity *should* be endorsed by the government. Their suggestion goes something like this:

America was established as a Christian nation. Our Founding Fathers were Christians and the clause "separation of church and state" doesn't even appear in the Constitution. All the First Amendment does is ensure that the government doesn't create a state-mandated religion. But showing favoritism for our founders' religion, Christianity, is perfectly fine. After all, we are one nation "under God," and "In God We Trust" is our national motto and on all of our money.

Let's take this one claim at a time.

It is true that "under God" is in the Pledge of Allegiance, and "In God We Trust" is our national motto and on all of our money, but that's irrelevant to our nation's founding. That wasn't true until the 1950s. Conservatives also don't realize, or fail to mention, another relevant fact: these things were established during an especially irrational time in American politics, the height of McCarthyism and the Red Scare. After World War II, Americans were desperate for a way to distinguish themselves from the "Godless Communists," and so public campaigns began that eventually got "under God" added to the Pledge and "In God We Trust" adopted as the national motto and put on all paper money.[49] Those in favor of church and state separation today object to all of this, just like they object to courthouse nativities.

One might wonder why they didn't object to these things in the 1950s, when they were established, but McCarthyism had established a political environment where practically any diversion from conservative ideals would unjustifiably be labeled as communistic sympathy and could ruin one's political career and public life. Senator Joseph McCarthy, plagued with fears of conspiracy, suggested that communists had infiltrated every aspect of government, and he set out to find them in the now famous, McCarthy hearings. This attitude caught on in the public sphere and in true conspiracy theory style, even an absence of evidence was seen as grounds to believe that a person was a communist sympathizer. ("How else could they hide it so well?") Although it was, in the end, acknowledged to just be a witch hunt, you can see why anyone in the 1950s would have been reluctant to object to "In God We Trust" becoming the national motto. Even a Christian objecting to such a thing on the principle of separating church and state would have been thought to be an atheist communist sympathizer.

It is also true that the phrase "separation of church and state" does not appear in the constitution; however, the specific phrase need not be used in order for the concept of such a separation to be endorsed. This is what the First Amendment does when it says that "Congress shall make no law respecting an establishment of religion, or prohibiting the free exercise thereof." Conservatives suggest that this merely prohibits the establishment of a state religion, but most legal experts disagree.[50]

This is due, in part, to Thomas Jefferson's clarification of the amendment's purpose in an 1801 letter to the Danbury Baptists. They had written to him worried that the religious majority in Connecticut would try to make "their Chief Magistrate... assume the prerogative of Jehovah and make laws to govern the Kingdom of Christ."[51] He replied:

> Believing with you that religion is a matter which lies solely between man and his God, that he owes account to none other for his faith or his worship, that the legislative powers of government reach actions only, and not opinions, I contemplate with sovereign reverence that act of the whole American people which declared that their legislature would "make no law respecting an establishment of religion, or prohibiting the free exercise thereof," thus building a wall of separation between Church and State.[52]

This, in fact, is where we get the phrase.

Of course, Jefferson didn't write the First Amendment himself. He was simply among the founding fathers who agreed upon it. So what was their original intention? This is where things get a bit complicated. The Founding Fathers were an admittedly diverse group. On the one hand, the large majority of them were Protestant Christians. On the other hand, some of the most prominent members (e.g., Benjamin Franklin, Thomas Jefferson) were deists,[53] not Christians. Jefferson, for example, found the history presented by the gospels so "defective and doubtful"[54] and found in them "so much ignorance, so much absurdity, so much untruth, charlatanism, and imposture,"[55] that he published his own version of the gospels, "The Life and Morals of Jesus of Nazareth."[56] It captured the good parts of Jesus's moral philosophy and left out all the miraculous elements.

Despite their religious affiliation and given their experience with religion-infused government, all of the founders likely favored government neutrality when it came to religion. Religions fighting for power and favoritism had led to much bloodshed in their home country of England. And when a specific religion was in control it was not always kind to its dissenters—often killing them—and its laws did not always treat people equally or with dignity. It's also not likely that they had forgotten about the Inquisition. This is why they didn't delegate powers to the government to establish or even favor a religion. They knew that religion-infused government was dangerous and had cost millions of lives.

Conservatives like Palin will, at this point, likely insist that government-infused atheism doesn't fare much better. Stalin and Pol Pot's atheistic regimes murdered millions. "Atheism's track record makes the Spanish Inquisition look like Disneyland in comparison."[57] It's true that Stalin and Pot's regimes murdered millions, but that is not relevant to my point here. We are talking about the intentions of the founding fathers, and they had no example of the effects of atheism-infused government. They were merely guarding against the dangers of religion-infused government.

But this does bring us to a broader point. Those advocating for church and state separation aren't advocating for atheism-infused government. They are advocating for our government to be religiously neutral—to stay out of religion all together. Stalin and Pot didn't stay out of religion—they actively repressed private exercise of traditional religion and in its place established a new one that worshiped the state and its ruler. Perhaps the best example of this is in modern-day North Korea, where according to the Juche Religion, people worship their leader as a god and even believe they will be reunited with him in the afterlife.[58] Those advocating for church–state separation and government religious neutrality would just as strongly object to the policies of Stalin, Pot, and Kim Jong-un as they would to religion-infused government.

It is true, as Palin points out, that John Adams once admitted that "Our Constitution was made only for a moral and religious people. It is wholly inadequate to the government of any other." But the quote's context makes it clear that Adams was merely pointing out the obvious: that no government can enforce the law if everyone starts breaking it—for example, if everyone starts behaving immorally.[59] But that doesn't mean that the government should enforce or endorse religion to keep that from happening. As a Unitarian who rejected the trinity, Jesus's divinity, and acknowledged the abuses of religion,[60] Adams would have likely agreed with Jefferson that "Christianity neither is, nor ever was a part of the common law,"[61] that "[i]n every country and in every age, the priest has been hostile to liberty,"[62] and that "[h]istory…furnishes no example of a priest-ridden people maintaining a free civil government."[63] In fact, John Adams signed the Treaty of Tripoli which declared that "the Government of the United States of America is not, in any sense, founded on the Christian religion."

The founding fathers' motivation for separating church and state was not only influenced by their own experience with religion-infused government, but also their study of the political philosopher John Locke (1632–1704). It is from Locke that they got the idea that humans have a natural right to things like life and liberty.[64] But Locke also famously advocated for the separation of church and state and put forth very persuasive arguments in its favor.[65]

This, of course, has not kept conservatives from trying to claim otherwise—even claiming that the expressly non-Christian founders were in fact Christian after all. In his book *The Jefferson Lies*, David Barton claims to debunk "secular lies" about Jefferson and instead claims that Jefferson let religion infect most of what he did. To establish that he was secular, Barton says, atheists just cherry-pick quotes from Jefferson and take him out of context. Ironically, however, this is what Barton does.

For example, in his chapter "Lie #2: Thomas Jefferson Founded a Secular University," Barton suggests that Jefferson once claimed that *Commentaries on the Laws of England*, a law book by Sir William Blackstone that famously exalted Christian influence on law, was to American lawyers what the Koran is to Muslims.[66] Actually Jefferson was insulting the commentaries, "lamenting" the "opinion" that it was revered like the Koran, suggesting that it was "deprecating law science."[67] Jefferson even decried the use of Blackstone in law schools, suggesting that it had "done more towards the suppression of the liberties of man, than all the million [sic] of men in arms of Bonaparte...."[68] Nearly every page of Barton's book contains a similar blatant and egregious error. It is conservative historical revisionism at its worst.

Barton's book is so bad, in fact, that its publisher, Thomas Nelson, a mega-Christian publishing house, pulled it from the shelves when it "lost confidence" in the text after numerous sources pointed out its factual inaccuracies. The History News Network at George Mason University voted it "the least credible history book in print." Ten conservative Christian professors even published their own book, *Getting Jefferson Right*, which accused Barton of "grossly misrepresenting the nation's third president."[69] So complaints about conservatives trying to turn Jefferson into a Christian are not just "liberal propaganda."

But if religious neutrality was the founder's goal, it was not accomplished. After America's founding, paid congressional chaplains saying Christian prayers, thanksgiving proclamations with Christian language, and encouragement of schools for "religious" education among other things were common. Congress even paid priests to catechize Native Americans. As Constitutional scholar Joseph Story put it, "Probably...the general...sentiment in America was that Christianity ought to receive encouragement from the state...utter indifference [regarding religion]...would have created universal disapprobation."[70] Some might think this is evidence that the founders did not want neutrality, but it really only tells us about the attitude of the largely Christian populace of the time and about how things worked in practice when governing such a populace. After all, even though James Madison in his elder years admitted that he thought paid chaplains and presidentially declared days of prayer were unconstitutional, he (while president) paid chaplains and declared days of prayer.

Courthouse Crèches,
the Fourteenth Amendment, and the
Separation of Church and State

In 2013, I was asked by the London School of Economics to write a few articles on the "American Christmas wars" for their blog.[71] There I argued that American history starts to unquestionably favor the argument against courthouse nativities in the 1940s, when legal precedent was set regarding how the Fourteenth Amendment should be interpreted. Specifically, the Supreme Court interpreted "equal protection of the laws" to entail that citizens must be treated by the government with equal respect and concern—and that it does not do this to non-Christian citizens when it endorses Christianity. In addition, its Due Process Clause made key provisions of the Bill of Rights, including the First Amendment, apply beyond the federal government to state and local governments as well.

My research never revealed when and where the first courthouse crèche was. My guess is that they became popular in the 1950s, at the same time Americans were distinguishing themselves from the godless communists with "In God We Trust." The aforementioned first lawsuit against crèches on publicly owned property was in 1969 (they did win), and the first Supreme Court case regarding Christmas displays was in 1984,[72] with another in 1989.[73] The result? In short, the court ruled that government Christmas displays are unconstitutional if they endorse or convey a religious message. This produced the "Reindeer Rule," which called for equal representation for non-religious Christmas symbols on publically funded government property.

Consequently, to avoid legal battles, many local governments erect secular decorations along with their crèche. The courthouse near my school, King's College, was forced to do this when a student at my school, Justin Vacula,[74] alerted the ACLU of the fact that their display was in violation of the Supreme Court's ruling. Others simply open up a public space for anyone to display their holiday decoration of choice, which has led to some interesting displays such as the Festivus pole made out of beer cans[75] erected next to a crèche in Florida in 2013.[76] Others just pay lip service to the rule, erecting only small Mr. and Mrs. Santa Clauses far behind the crèche. (My local courthouse seems to have shifted to this tactic, after the buzz died down.) Of course still others ignore the ruling entirely and no one objects.

The battle rages on. In 2012, an atheist abandoned his plan to file a lawsuit to get the courthouse nativity removed in Henderson County, Texas, because of death threats leveled against him.[77] That same year, the Freedom from Religion Foundation successfully lobbied to have a crèche removed from public space in Ellwood City, Pennsylvania. But the reason such efforts don't constitute a War on Christmas is because they're not about Christmas. They're about enforcing the Constitution, they're making sure that non-Christian members have "equal protection of the laws," and protecting against the dangers of religion-infused government. None of these efforts will ever entail that a Christian or a church can't put a crèche on their own lawn, nor will they make the holiday less popular to celebrate.

Christmas in School and Merry Christmas Laws

Another aspect of the fictional "War on Christmas" that has appeared in the courts is Christmas in public schools. Classroom displays and parties along with school "Christmas pageants" are likely the most hotly contested. Although I would not object to calling a decorated evergreen in a classroom a "Christmas tree," clearly a nativity scene in a classroom or a school play depicting the birth of Christ is a different matter. Unless they are surrounded by additional secular elements, so as to prevent the endorsement of a religious message, they would be in violation of the Supreme Court's rulings.

Interestingly in 2013, a few Southern states passed[78] or proposed[79] "Merry Christmas Laws" aimed at protecting people who display Christmas scenes and symbols and use the term "Christmas" to describe annual parties or programs at public schools and government buildings. In Missouri, the bill states that "No state or local governmental entity, public building, public park, public school, or public setting or place shall ban or otherwise restrict the practice, mention, celebration, or discussion of any federal holiday." In Texas, "public school students and staff [are allowed] to display religious scenes and symbols on school property—and to freely express holiday greetings."

These laws are poorly motivated and ill-conceived. The arguments in their favor are unsound and, they are likely to be deemed unconstitutional after lengthy court battles at the taxpayers' expense.

Sarah Palin likely thinks that such laws would protect her First Amendment rights, like freedom of speech. She says that is all she was exercising when she used public funds and her power as mayor to erect a nativity on government-owned property in Wasilla, Alaska.[80] Texas Governor Rick Perry suggested, instead, that the laws were protecting his First Amendment right to "freedom of religion."[81] But although the First Amendment does protect the "free exercise" of religion and freedom of speech it does not protect one's desire to use one's capacity as a government employee to proselytize or impose those religious beliefs on others. In short, you're free to believe and say what you want as a private citizen—you can even do so in public—but if you are employed by the state, since there are certain restrictions on what the state can do, there are certain restrictions on what *you* can do when you are functioning in that capacity.

The worry Christian conservatives express about freedom of religion in schools has always been exaggerated. Ask a conservative what a "ban on public school prayer" entails and you would likely be led to believe that a child could be kicked out of school for simply praying out loud—say, asking God for help on an exam he didn't study for.[82] Take for example a story conservatives often repeat about of a five-year-old boy in St. Louis, Missouri, who was picked up by the scruff of his neck and yelled at by his teacher and principal for praying over his lunch. While the story does have an element of truth in it—the story was originally about a student in St. Louis—everything else about it is false. He was actually ten years old (not five), he didn't get picked up by the scruff of his neck (he did get detention), and it was for fighting in the cafeteria (not for praying).[83] In reality, students are actually free to pray whenever they want (unless of course they are disrupting class).[84] In fact, so are teachers. It's just that school employees, when acting in that capacity, since they represent the state in those circumstances, cannot vocally offer up explicitly Christian prayers for all to hear or direct students to pray (say, at the beginning of the school day).

Likewise, the worries about restrictions to Christmas celebrations in public schools are also exaggerated. As previously discussed, most of the "incidents" conservatives complain about never actually happened, and public schoolteachers are perfectly free to celebrate and say they celebrate Christmas at home. It's just that they can't do things like put up a nativity scene in their publicly run and funded classroom or have their students participate in "Operation Christmas Child," an expressly Evangelical program that includes gospel tracts with conversion pledges in the gifts they send.[85]

Another argument you'll hear in favor of government-endorsed religious displays is that "secularism" is just another religion and that not allowing the government to endorse religion just forces the government to endorse the religion of secularism. But "secular" just means "non-religious." It is the absence of religion. A secular government is a non-religious one. To say that secularism is a religion is like saying that "bald" is a hair color or that "not collecting stamps" is a hobby. For the government to be neutral toward religion is not to be *against* religion but to let religion be a private, individual affair.

Governor Perry says that rules against religious displays in schools make religious persons feel like they can't express their faith publicly. But individual public expressions of faith are under no threat. The fact that one can't expressly endorse one's faith to others while serving in the capacity of a state government employee does not mean one's freedom of religion is being oppressed. We are all free to do what we want with religion in our private life. And since Christianity still dominates society, no Christian can have a reasonable fear of persecution.[86] It's just that, if one wants to impose one's religion on others *while at* work, one should become a pastor or work at a private Christian school—not for the government.

All Perry is doing here is feeding a victimization narrative that conservatives often promote to rally their base and to make it seem like they are being persecuted. In fact, all that has happened is that they no longer enjoy complete social dominance. Take, for example, Fox News. Watch for just one day, and you will be led to believe that Christians are an oppressed minority, targeted and victimized by the mainstream media, who dominate the airwaves. Only Fox News provides unbiased news reporting—a mere island's worth, lost in a sea of liberal propaganda flooding the airwaves from the "mainstream media." In reality, of course, 73 percent of the American population is Christian, Christians have always dominated political elections (including every presidential one), and enjoy universal social acceptance. (Unlike an atheist, a Christian would like not be afraid to reveal their religious affiliation in a job interview.) In addition, Fox News has better ratings in almost every time slot than all other news networks combined.[87] They are the mainstream media. As John Stewart put it, they are merely "expressing anger and victimization over the loss of absolute power and reframing it as persecution of real America by minorities, freeloaders and socialists."[88]

David French, Senior Counsel at American Center for Law and Justice, an evangelical legal group, laments that the threat of lawsuits looms over Christians who work at government institutes when they try to put on nativity programs or put up a religious display.[89] But Christian public school teachers feeling nervous about putting up a nativity in their classroom is not a reason to remove the threat of litigation. That's what happens when you do something unlawful—you have to be nervous about the legal consequence. That's what the law is for.

Merry Christmas Laws are designed to protect people who violate the Supreme Court's decision that Christmas displays that clearly endorse Christianity should not be displayed by federal, state, or local governments, or their employees, on publicly owned land. And since the Supreme Court's rulings on governmental endorsements of particular religions are clear and settled, I don't think these laws are going to hold up. It's just going to end up tying the schools up in legal battles and spending money on legal fees that should instead be spent on education.[90] The idea that there is a War on Christmas is indeed costly.

What's the Big Deal?

Why do I care about this so much? Well, Sarah Palin is right about one thing: the battles in the courts about Christmas are an extension of the culture war over the influence of religion on our society and government. This war is real and the stakes are high. To help make her point, she tells two fictional stories about what a college campus might be like in the future if each side in these battles gets its way. The first is where the liberals win: it is a conservative nightmare where all Christians have been banished from campus, atheists have paradoxically put Muslims in charge of everything and the joy of Christmas has been drained from "our public spaces as well as from our minds and hearts."[91] The other is a Palin utopia, where Romney is president, he still has his "fabulous hair,"[92] college Christians are free to put those stinking atheists and their stupid arguments in their place, and the Palins are still free to celebrate Christmas.[93]

She doesn't tell us the broader story of what her ideal society looks like, but you can piece it together from what she says in her book. It's a society in which the Christian majority can ensure the election of Christian politicians who can pass and enforce laws—derived from their understanding of the Bible and church doctrine—that honor America's "Christian heritage." Abortion, premarital sex, adultery, homosexuality, lying, blasphemy, and disobeying your parents are all illegal. Of course, you wouldn't be required to practice Christianity (e.g., go to church). Palin doesn't want a state religion. You'd just have to obey these laws derived from the Christian religion or go to jail. But these politicians certainly could encourage Christianity and use government funds and property to promote Christianity and its ideals—say, by putting up a giant nativity on the court-house lawn "in tribute to the God who gave us life"[94] and a big blinking sign that says "Jesus is the reason for the Season. If you don't keep Christ in Christmas, you ain't doing it right!" After all, by doing so, these Christian government officials would merely be exercising their First Amendment rights to freedom of speech and religion to use your tax dollars to promote their religion. If you don't like it, you can voice your objections and rally the minority to vote against them—and that makes it all okay. When these politicians are once again elected by the majority, they can know that there are a few people who disagree. As long as people are free to complain, they really have nothing to complain about.

Ironically, Palin paints a similar picture when she criticizes the Egyptian people's choice to put the Muslim Brotherhood in power after "the so-called Arab Spring."

> They chose a government that enacted a Sharia-based constitution, oppresses Christians, and imprisons dissenters. Why? Because that level of intolerance is widely represented in Egyptian culture. A recent Pew Poll showed that the vast majority of Egyptians not only support Sharia law (which included suppression of women's rights and independence), they support executing people who convert from Islam…a democracy without respect for individual liberty is just a tyranny of the majority. The right to vote doesn't guarantee virtue. The point is, freedom is the only answer.[95]

And adding to the irony is Palin's use of the phrase "tyranny of the majority."

The phrase comes from the political philosopher John Stuart Mill (1806–1873), who in "On Liberty" identified it as a kind of tyranny that was still possible even in a democracy. Because the majority rules in a democracy, homogenous majority populations can still oppress minority populations, even to the point of enslaving them, and there is nothing the minority can do about it. And that is tyranny just as much as if it were the result of the actions of a tyrannical king. "The tyranny of the majority," Mill thus argues, "is now generally included among the evils against which society requires to be on its guard."[96] So, according to Mill, democracy must be tempered. Limits have to be put on the power of the majority because some things should never be done even if the majority wants them done.

What kind of limits? Mill argues that "the only purpose for which power can be rightfully exercised over any member of a civilized community, against his will, is to prevent harm to others."[97] In other words, the majority should not pass a law refraining anyone from any action, unless that action will harm others. Only by giving everyone the freedom to act as they wish (as long they don't harm others), can we guarantee the greatest amount of happiness for the greatest amount of people. So the majority should not, for example, restrict any non-harm-causing action in the name of some taboo moral or social view that the majority wishes to enforce.

Because he thought speech and merely holding an opinion cannot harm anyone, and that only actions based on them can, Mill was a champion of free speech and opinion. But this also made him a champion of protecting minorities. To protect the freedom of speech and opinion of the minority, it must be protected from the imposition of the ideas and practices of the majority. In a sense, according to Mill, the majority population has a special duty to treat the minority opinion with deference, to give it special leeway. They don't have to adopt the minority view, and they can still argue against it—that's guaranteed by freedom of speech—but the majority cannot use their status as the majority to impose their views on the minority population in any way.

So Mill would, like Palin, object to the Egyptian government as it was run by the Muslim Brotherhood. Mill would be appalled at laws based in religion that merely enforce moral norms and restrict actions that lead to no harm, like laws about sexuality and laws against blasphemy. Any effort by the government to remind everyone that Egypt is a Muslim nation, with a Muslim government and heritage, would be seen as dangerous. Even if all that is true, it would not be showing deference to the minority population but instead would be imposing the ideas and practices of the Muslim majority on them. These are all prime examples of the tyranny of the majority.

Of course (and this is why Palin's use of the phrase is unintentionally ironic), Mill would object to Palin's Christian America utopia for exactly the same reasons. It's a prime example of the tyranny of the majority. Most likely, Palin would retort that Sharia law leads to suppression of women's rights, execution of heretics, and restrictions of individual liberty, and argue that that would never happen with government-infused Christianity. Historically she'd be right, if it weren't for the crusades, the Inquisition, the Salem witch trials, most of European history, America's pre-colonial period (especially the treatment of Native Americans and slaves), and modern Christian-influenced governments like Uganda, which recently passed a law prescribing life in prison for homosexuals at the behest of American Christian missionaries[98]...or pretty much any other time Christianity was infused with government.

Now I'm not saying that things like courthouse nativities will necessarily lead to Palin's tyranny of the Christian majority utopia, but they are exactly the kind of imposition of the majority's ideas and practices that Mill worried about. Any step toward a tyranny of the majority is one step too far.

How This Myth Has Been Used
to Hijack the Holiday

The notion that there is a war on Christmas has been used by the likes of Palin to hijack the holiday as a kind of hostage for their side of the culture war: "If we don't get our way, Christmas will suffer a horrible fate." Of course, they won't be the one to deliver the death blow. They mean that the liberal atheists will kill Christmas if conservative Christians aren't allowed to defend it by infusing Christmas's religious elements into every aspect of public life. Today, a conservative Christian trying to forbid Christmas or even speaking ill of it is unheard of. But this has not always been the case. As we shall discover next chapter, the group that most vehemently opposed Christmas and even tried to eliminate it by preaching against and even outlawing its celebration wasn't liberals, communists, Jews, progressives, or atheists. Instead, it was perhaps the most conservative group of Christians of all: the Puritans.

Our Christmas Traditions Are Old-Fashioned

LET'S BE HONEST; BEFORE PICKING UP THIS BOOK, you probably thought along these lines:

> *Christmas trees, giving gifts to children, stockings and tinsel, Santa Claus and Christmas trees, Jesus in the manger—these traditions all point to one thing that makes Christmas so special: it ties us to the past. By participating in these ancient traditions, we are celebrating in much the same way as our ancestors celebrated Christmas for the last 2000 years. Sure, it has become a bit more commercial lately—the Romans weren't buying Xboxes for their kids—but all the stuff that matters, the traditions I hold so dear, have always been there and they always will be. Everyone loves Christmas; no one will ever stop celebrating the same way they always have.*

By now, however, you probably have your doubts. You're probably second-guessing most of what you thought about Christmas, and you'd be right to do so. Not only have we celebrated Christmas (by that name) for *far less* than two thousand years, and not only do late December celebrations trace back much further (about six thousand years), but the way we celebrate the holidays is in constant flux. It's always changing and likely always will. So most of our favorite traditions, including those listed above, are modern inventions, some less than two hundred years old. Not only weren't the Romans buying Xboxes for their kids—they weren't buying them *anything*. Children's Christmas gifts are a modern invention, as are Santa, stockings, and Christmas trees. Even displaying "Jesus in the manger" is a modern invention, relativity speaking. As we will see, a few of the most ancient traditions do survive, but they are hardly the holiday's focus.

What's more, not everyone always loved Christmas and whole groups of people have stopped celebrating it. Ironically, the most famous group of people to do this was arguably the most conservative and staunch group of Christians in all of history: the Puritans.

Banning Christmas

The Puritans didn't just stop celebrating Christmas. They banned it. They outlawed it. In places where the Puritans had power, taking the day off work on Christmas might cost you your job. In Massachusetts from 1659 to 1681 celebrating Christmas came with a fine of five shillings. In some places it was a criminal offense that could land you in jail. You weren't even allowed to go to church on Christmas Day unless December 25 happened to fall on a Sunday.

To understand the Puritans hostility to Christmas, we have to pick up where we left off regarding the history of Christmas. Recall that even though the church tried to claim Christmas in the 300s and tried to Christianize its celebration throughout the Middle Ages, Christmas was always celebrated primarily in a secular way. It was a time for festivities, dancing, feasting, drinking, and sex...lots and lots of sex. There were even places where jovial orgies preceded and followed Christ's Mass.

These traditions continued right on through to the Protestant Reformation and the first appearance of the Puritans. As you can probably imagine, the Puritans weren't too keen on those sorts of things. The Puritans were also more familiar with the history of Christmas than the average Christian is today. They knew that it found its roots in pagan celebrations, like Saturnalia. They knew there was no biblical commandment to celebrate Christ's birthday or even information regarding when it occurred. They even knew that celebrating birthdays was an idea first endorsed by pagans.

On top of that, there was Christmas mumming, a tradition of cross-dressing—yes you read correctly, cross-dressing—and going from house to house drinking. Then sprinkle on Christmas "caroling," usually done amidst "Rioting and Chambering [fornication] and Wantonness,"[1] which led to a spike in the number of unwed pregnancies just after Christmas. It's all a recipe for Puritan anti-Christmas sermons and statements like this:

> The generality of Christmas-keepers observe that Festival after such a manner as is highly dishonorable to the name of Christ. How few are there comparatively that spend those holidays (as they are called) after a holy manner. But they are consumed in Complications, in Interludes, in playing at Cards, in Revelings, in excess of Wine, in mad Mirth.... (Puritan Rev. Increase Mather, Boston 1687)[2]

> The Feast of Christ's Nativity is spent in Reveling, Dicing, Carding, Masking any and all Licentious Liberty...by Mad Mirth, by long Eating, by hard Drinking, by lewd Gaming, by rude Reveling.... (Puritan Rev. Cotton Mather, Boston 1712)[3]

The Anglicans even joined in:

> Men dishonor Christ more in the twelve days of Christmas, than in all the twelve months besides. (sixteenth-century Anglican Bishop Hugh Latimer)[4]

Now the Puritans did appreciate what Christmas was originally intended to be: a harvest festival. Like the ancients, they too recognized the need to be thankful for the bounty of the harvest and to take the opportunity to fatten up for the winter. After all, they too were an agricultural society who struggled to survive the winter. They just didn't like all the drinking, sex, and debauchery that had come to be associated with it. So they invented their own holiday, one which was far enough from Christmas on the calendar so as to not be confused with it but that still sat at the end of the harvest season when food was plentiful. That's right—Thanksgiving is just Puritan Christmas.[5] It is a somber, simple, debauchery-free version of Christmas invented by Puritans to replace it.[6] Consequently, just about anywhere the Puritans had influence, Christmas was not celebrated.[7]

That's not to say that Christmas was banned and not celebrated anywhere. After all the Puritans didn't control everything. But even after the political power of the Puritans faded, their war on Christmas had lasting effects. For quite some time, Christmas remained an unpopular holiday, at least by today's standards. It certainly wasn't anticipated for months or celebrated for weeks at a time. The entire economy was not defined by it and children didn't even care about it. As actor Josh Gad playing Benjamin Franklin pointed out once on Jon Stewart's *The Daily Show*, in 1789 no one said "Merry Christmas" until December 25. "The celebration of the birth of Christ," Jon pointed out, "lasted a day—like birthdays do!"[8]

As this comedy bit suggests, Puritan influence had waned considerably by the founding of the United States. By that time some people were celebrating Christmas again. More precisely, Christmas's comeback started around 1760. But when it made this comeback, the form it took was similar to the one that the Puritans hated so much. It didn't last for weeks at a time, like it had before, but during the limited time in which it was celebrated, it was once again celebrated as an adult holiday—a time of feasting, drinking, debauchery, and sex. Some songs from the era prove this, like a couple of little-known verses of Yankee Doodle:

> Two and two may go to Bed,
> Two and Two together;
> And if there is not room enough,
> Lie one a top o'to'ther

> Christmas is a coming Boys,
> We'll go to Mother Chase's
> And there we'll get a sugar dram [i.e., rum]
> Sweetened with Melasses [molasses].

> Heigh Ho for our Cape Cod,
> Heigh ho Nantasket,
> Do not let the Boston wags
> Feel your Oyster Basket.[9]

Yes, "Oyster Basket" means exactly what you think it means.

By the early 1800s, a common tradition among some adult men was visiting the houses of their friends, traveling as a group from one to the next to be given food and liberal amounts of alcohol by each house's hostess, and stumble home in a drunken stupor by the end of the day. Again, as "Ben Franklin" observed on *The Daily Show*, if one did choose to celebrate Christmas, it was likely by "stuffing his face, getting drunk, and wallowing in vomit" (December 12, 2011).[10] It was basically like the modern St. Patrick's Day. But Christmas wasn't even *that* popular; it wasn't even a nationally recognized holiday.

The Wonder of Wassailing

One noteworthy tradition of the time was wassailing. If a rich land-owner had servants, which he usually did, on Christmas he was obligated to open up his house to his servants and give them his best food and drink—and I do mean the best, the private stock, "the best the family could afford."[11] If he didn't fulfill that obligation, trouble could be had. This tradition usually involved song and began with one's servants showing up at the door, demanding entrance. It was like a Halloween trick-or-treat on steroids.[12]

> We've come here to claim our right...
> And if you don't open up your door,
> We will lay you flat upon the floor

Once inside, demands of the best food and drink began:

> Come, butler, draw us a bowl of the best
> Then we hope your soul in heaven shall rest
> But if you draw us a bowl of the small [i.e. weak beer],
> Then down will come butler, bowl, and all.13

Once it was provided, good wishes were heaped upon the host and his family:

> Again we assemble, a merry New Year
> To wish to each one of the family here...
> May they of potatoes and herrings have plenty,
> With butter and cheese, and each other dainty...
>
> God send our master a cup of good beer...
> God send our mistress a good Christmas pie...
> With my wassailing bowl I drink to thee[14]

Now none of these songs are familiar, but they do help us make sense of a very familiar song that you, if you are like me, have wondered about since childhood.

> Now, bring us a figgy pudding;
> Now, bring us a figgy pudding;
> Now, bring us a figgy pudding
> and a cup of good cheer
> We won't go until we get some;
> We won't go until we get some;
> We won't go until we get some,
> so bring some out here.

It's a wassailing song! It demands food and alcohol and in return offers up well wishes:

> We wish you a Merry Christmas;
> We wish you a Merry Christmas;
> We wish you a Merry Christmas and a Happy New Year.
> Good tidings we bring to you and your kin;
> Good tidings for Christmas and a Happy New Year.

In his book *The Battle for Christmas*, Stephen Nissenbaum describes the wassailing ritual as a "social safety valve" that allowed the lower classes to let off steam at the expense of their more wealthy social betters and helped solidify the social structure that existed year-round. How? On the one hand, your employer, who bossed you around all year and made you do all his dirty work, can't be all that bad if he is generous at Christmas time. Yet the fact that you are the one begging for food and he is the one providing it helps solidify the notion that he is your superior.

Interestingly, similar Christmas traditions served an almost identical function in the antebellum South. Christmas time on many plantations was a time in which slaves enjoyed significantly greater freedoms. Some would be allowed to cross the white picket fence, perhaps even enter "the big house," where they might fix and enjoy a Christmas meal. Other plantation owners would provide food and gifts for their slaves to enjoy at a Christmas party celebrated at the slave's quarters. The masters themselves might even attend. Some even granted their slaves temporary freedom—the ability to visit friends and family on other plantations—provided, of course, that they returned in the spring when there was again work to do. This too functioned as a social safety valve. The slaves could blow off some steam, and the masters could do their best to endear themselves and make up for past offenses while also solidifying everyone's place in the social hierarchy.

Of course, one should not be fooled by this into thinking that a slave's life was a happy one and that they were complacent or even satisfied with their captivity. The idea that slaves were happy being slaves was propaganda aimed at justifying slavery. (Some still think this today.[15]) In fact, many stories of Christmas generosity were exaggerated to attain this effect. That's not to say that some plantation owners weren't actually generous at Christmas time. They were.[16] But some plantation owners were not, and others would hold back necessities during the year only to give them out as "Christmas presents" in December to create the illusion of generosity.

One common Christmas present given to slaves was alcohol. Christmas would have been the only time that many slaves had access to it. But the express goal of such a gift was often the solidification of the social order itself. The effect on the slaves was often disastrous. The slaves would gorge on the alcohol, make themselves profusely sick, and come to the conclusion: "if this is what freedom was like, I'm better off a slave." Of this practice, Frederick Douglas wrote:

> Their object seems to be, to disgust their slaves with freedom, by plunging them into the lowest depths of dissipation. For instance, the slaveholders not only like to see the slave drink of his own accord, but will adopt various plans to make him drunk. ... Thus when the slave asks for virtuous freedom, the cunning slaveholder, knowing his ignorance, cheats him with a dose of vicious dissipation, artfully labeled with the name of liberty. The most of us used to drink it down, and the result was just what might be supposed: many of us were led to think that there was little to choose between liberty and slavery. We felt, and very properly, too, that we had almost as well be slaves to man as to rum. So, when the holidays ended, we staggered up from the filth of our wallowing, took a long breath, and marched to the field...feeling, upon the whole, rather glad to go, from what our master had deceived us into a belief was freedom, back into the arms of slavery.[17]

These "wassailing-like" traditions continued in the South until slavery was abolished in America around the 1860s. But something happened in the North in the early 1800s that changed the face of Christmas considerably.

Christmas Changes

Unlike the South, the North industrialized. As a result, if you were poor you were less likely to work directly for a wealthy landowner so that it would be unreasonable to believe you would be granted entry into his house for feasting purposes. Instead, it was more likely that you were one of many factory workers who didn't even know what the factory owner looked like much less where he lived. In this way, industrialization clogged up the "social safety valve" Christmas provided, which had kept the relative peace between the classes for a number of years. This was a problem particularly in New York on the island of Manhattan. There the poor were segregated to slums on the southern part of the island and wealthy landowners enjoyed lavish houses on large tracts of land to the north.

But the poor didn't go down without a fight. Recalling the old traditions, many banded together in large groups that trounced through the streets, sometimes dressed in costumes but almost always brandishing instruments and noisemakers to cause as great a disturbance as possible. After making their way to the houses of the wealthy, they would demand entrance regardless of whether they knew the owner. Obviously, the rich did not take kindly to this, and if the poor were let in, they would usually be disruptive as they demanded the household's best food and drink. If the poor didn't get their way, they could react violently by throwing rocks at the house, breaking windows, and even breaking in.

This practice led many of the rich to hire night watchmen, a kind of private security. (Ironically, night watchmen eventually circulated pamphlets encouraging what we would call a "Christmas bonus" to guarantee the safety of the house at Christmastime.) Such efforts were eventually organized by the government, and so we have Christmas revelry, at least somewhat, to thank for modern police forces.

Despite these efforts, Christmastime was not a pleasant time to be rich in cities like New York. And it wasn't just because of wassailing. At Christmas the streets were often filled with the drunken poor, carrying on and causing a ruckus—like carnival—making simply being out on the street a dangerous affair for the sober wealthy. "Customary Christmas license combined with seasonal unemployment made the winter holiday a nosy, drunken, threatening period in the eyes of the respectable."[18]

One such respectable New Yorker was John Pintard, who set out in the early 1800s to invent respectable, sober, upper-class holiday traditions and then popularize them by claiming that he was "restoring something that had been forgotten."[19] These included "open houses" that were open only to his social class, and St. Nicholas Day dinners that he enjoyed with his fellow members of the New-York Historical Society. He claimed that these were Old Dutch traditions, but really he invented them.

Washington Irving was another member of the New-York Historical Society who set out to invent domesticated Christmas traditions with stories that undoubtedly inspired Pintard. In "Bracebridge Hall" old Squire Bracebridge, a then-modern man, recreated the Christmas traditions "of old" by gathering all, the rich and the poor, to join him in feasting and Christmas games, like Lord of Misrule, that "open[ed] every door, and unlock[ed] every heart."[20] In reality, however, such traditions never really existed, which Irving himself admitted in a later edition of the work. It was simply his attempt at creating a brand-new old-fashioned tradition.

Irving was good at inventing history. He did the same in his famous *Knickerbocker's History of New York*,[21] where he described life in New York as one that echoed a life in "New Amsterdam in old Dutch time"[22] that never actually existed. (Ironically, some people today still read Irving's book as real history.) Why would he do this? He belonged to the Knickerbockers, a group of upper-class, early-nineteenth-century New Yorkers who opposed democracy, which they equated with mob rule. In an attempt to create a "cultural counterweight to the commercial bustle and democratic 'misrule' of early-nineteenth-century New York" they wished to forge a "pseudo-Dutch identity for New York,"[23] that was more aristocratic. They were especially bothered by the raucous Christmas traditions. Although they did not succeed in ending democracy, Irving's *Knickerbocker's History* did reinvent and popularize an idea that eventually accomplished what Pintard couldn't: the domestication of Christmas. They turned it into a holiday to be spent at home with one's family.

However, the idea primarily reached the masses not through Irving, but through a poem, a poem that expressed the Christmastime worries of the rich. It became a propaganda tool they used to domesticate Christmas by having it published everywhere and as often as they could. It told the story of a wealthy, land-owning gentry awoken seemingly by the noise of wassailers demanding entry into his house. Upon investigation, however, he discovers that it is not an entire band of dirty lower-class peddlers, but only one. Yet when this lone individual gained entry, he did not demand the home's best food and drink. In fact, demanded nothing. Instead, the dirty little visitor gave—he gave presents to all the children in the household and then left.

As you have perhaps now realized, this poem is "'Twas the Night before Christmas," which was first known as "A Visit from St. Nicholas." Like Irving's history, this poem did not describe an already existing tradition. It invented one. When it was first printed in 1823, no one hung stockings for St.

Nicholas or fooled their children into believing that St. Nicholas came through the chimney. To be sure, there was a mid-seventeenth-century Dutch tradition of St. Nicholas leaving candy and nuts in wooden shoes outside children's doors, but that tradition did not arise organically in American culture by the immigration of Dutch settlers across the Atlantic. None of the Knickerbockers were actually Dutch—they were British. The author of the poem consciously chose and then reconstructed that Dutch ritual. The idea that St. Nicholas in the form of a fur-wearing elf would enter your house through the chimney, drop gifts in the stockings you had hung by the fireplace to dry, and then fly away in a sleigh pulled by magic levitating reindeer was a brand new idea.

Imitating the poem quickly became a fad among those who celebrated. Within a few years, even the poor started to think celebrating Christmas meant spending the day indoors with one's family and passing out gifts. "Finally," the Knickerbockers said, "the poor who celebrate Christmas will stop trying to barge into our houses." The tradition of wassailing faded away in the northern United States. Eventually a Knickerbocker took credit for the poem, Clement Clarke Moore.[24] And the rest is history—now we all buy gifts for our children, in the name of St. Nicholas, at Christmastime, regardless of whether we can afford it.

A Child-Centered Christmas

This switch of Christmas's focus from the poor to children came at a time in which a new "child-centered" philosophy of family living and parenting was gaining prominence. Before this time, a child was regarded as a second-class citizen—someone to be seen and not heard—socially equivalent to the poor. "[Children] were not a separate social group," Nissenbaum points out. "Nor did they act as if they were. Instead, children were lumped together with other members of the lower classes in general, especially servants and apprentices—who, not coincidentally, were generally young people themselves...Class and age were thoroughly intermingled."[25] A key role of children was as an extra set of hands to work around the house, and it was not a parent's obligation to entertain them or even make them happy. The term "maid" today refers to a servant, but then it referred to an "unmarried girl or a young woman" (a "maiden"). The household duties of each were the same.[26]

But around this time a new child-centered parenting philosophy was emerging that made children the focus of almost everything. The domestication of Christmas helped create and sustain this philosophy, and the philosophy helped create and sustain a domesticated Christmas. As Nissenbaum put it:

> The domestication of Christmas was thus related (as both effect and cause) to the creation of domesticity and of "childhood" itself, even to the novel idea that the central purpose of the family was to provide not simply for the instruction of its children but for their happiness as well.[27]

During this time, the purpose of presents to children shifted as well. When Christmas was first being domesticated, the old parenting philosophy dominated, and a gift of a book to one's child would be intended to instruct and teach discipline to a child. Such books even sometimes *warned against* playing with toys. But later as the new parenting philosophy took hold, the purpose of such books became to amuse children with for example, games and fun stories. "[P]leasure was coming to replace discipline as the primary purpose of those presents."[28] In a way, this was the "invention of childhood."[29]

We might even say that although Christmas clearly changed a lot in the first half of the nineteenth century, the primary focus remained the same—social inversion. It's just that this social inversion changed its focus. In the time of wassailing, it had been about letting the poor be king for a day—to let the poor demand the attention of the household and partake of its finest goods. Now it was about letting children—who recently were just a subset of the poor—be king for a day, letting them have their way with the household goods. Simply put, "[a]ge had replaced the social class as the axis along which gifts were given at Christmas."[30]

Christmas Makes a Comeback

So far I have only explained why the celebration of Christmas changed among those who celebrated it. I have not explained why celebrating Christmas became popular again after the Puritan suppression. Although the whole story is complicated, there were three primary influences: Moore's poem, Queen Victoria, and Charles Dickens.

We've already discussed Moore's poem, but its influence cannot be overstated. It accomplished what Pintard and Irving attempted—it created the impression that it depicted a centuries-old tradition, when in fact it had merely invented one. So people who were not yet participating thought they were missing out, and by participating they could tie themselves to a longed-for, bygone era. Consequently, many who had never celebrated Christmas before began doing so. Additionally, this invented tradition appealed to children in a time when they were becoming the average family's focus. When given this leeway, children can be very persuasive in getting what they want. My guess is that children who heard about their friends awaiting a visit from St. Nicholas forced many questions upon parents that the parents could only answer by beginning to participate themselves.

The second influence is Queen Victoria and Prince Albert. In 1714, Queen Anne died with no legitimate heir, allowing an infusion of German blood and tradition from Anne's distant relatives into Windsor Castle. Germany had not suffered under Puritan rule, and so Christmas was not suppressed there. Victoria ascended to the throne at age 18 in 1837, and although Christmas traditions were in the castle before this, it was she and her husband Prince Albert who popularized these Christmas traditions by making them public and domesticated.

Most notably, an illustration of them with their children surrounding a decorated Christmas tree (which can be seen at the beginning of this chapter) was published in *The Illustrated London News* in 1848. Almost overnight the popularity of celebrating Christmas skyrocketed.[31] The public was especially enamored with the young queen, much like it was with Princess Diana and is today with the Duchess of Cambridge. Just like royal women today, Victoria set fashions and trends. Modifying the illustration by removing any signs of royalty made Victoria, Albert and their children look like an all-American family. So when a print of such an illustration was published in the highly regarded American publication *Godey's Lady's Book* in 1850, the popularity of celebrating Christmas in the States rapidly increased as well.

But just before this, an author had already significantly revived the holiday with a Christmas tale the effects of which would long outlast and overshadow even what the royal family could accomplish. Charles Dickens's *A Christmas Carol* was originally published a chapter at a time in 1843, but the hold it took on the public consciousness and the popularity that it enjoyed cannot be overstated. It's estimated that between 20 percent (conservatively) and 50 percent (liberally) of the literate public of his time bought an early copy of Dickens's *A Christmas Carol*. And that's not even considering those who may have bought an unauthorized, plagiarized copy of his work, which were common, or acquired a copy or knowledge of the story in some other way, such as borrowing a copy or attending a public reading. Compare that to today, where reaching only 0.2 percent of the literate public is enough to get a book on the New York Times bestseller list.[32] Of course, Dickens didn't have television to contend with, but consider that only about 35 percent of the American public watched the most-viewed Super Bowl of all time in 2014.[33] *A Christmas Carol* was more popular than the Super Bowl, and perpetually so. You probably don't remember who won the last five Super Bowls, but you do know exactly what Scrooge says to Christmas: "Ba Humbug!"

Although I'll talk more about *A Christmas Carol* in the next chapter, what is important to note now is that at the time in which *A Christmas Carol* was written (1846), Christmas was still not popular. This fact demonstrates how Dickens popularized Christmas. Historian Lee Standiford equates its popularity to the modern Memorial Day, but even that is an overstatement. Memorial Day is a federally recognized holiday during which government offices, banks and such are closed. But during Dickens's time, most businesses, like the butcher shop down the street at the end of his story, were open on Christmas. If a business did close, it's unlikely its employees would receive wages for no work like many do on Memorial Day today. A more apt comparison would be the modern St. Patrick's Day. Most know about it, some celebrate it, but very few get the day off and those who do celebrate usually do so by getting piss drunk. In today's climate where, at Christmastime, most people at least get a few days off of work, and colleges let out for an entire month, it's easy to look at Scrooge's reluctance to close his business as appalling. But truth be told, Cratchit was the odd man out for wanting Scrooge to close his business.[34] It would be equivalent to you asking your boss for a paid vacation on St. Patrick's Day.

So one thing Dickens's story did was popularize the idea of closing shop for Christmas. Standiford mentions a factory owner who, after attending a public reading of *A Christmas Carol*, swore then and there that "Christmas would ever after be a holiday in his shop."[35] Presumably, from that day forward, like Scrooge, he always gave his workers a paid day off at Christmas.

Dickens also popularized the act of celebrating Christmas, and even invented a one-word argument that would instantly convince anyone who didn't to celebrate. Calling someone a "Scrooge" if they don't celebrate Christmas is still an effective way to shame people into celebrating.

Dickens even popularized particular ways of celebrating. Another industrialist, after hearing a public reading, immediately purchased turkeys and gave them to all his employees to enjoy at their Christmas dinner[36] because that is what Scrooge bought Cratchit. In fact, this small element of Dickens story almost toppled London's goose industry. Previously, among the few who celebrated Christmas, goose was the bird of choice for Christmas dinner. After *A Christmas Carol*, everyone had to have a turkey. Dickens left an abundance of uneaten geese in his wake and not enough turkeys to go around.

Like Moore's poem, when we read *A Christmas Carol* we place it in our current cultural context and think that it is documenting an already established tradition. We assume "Scrooge is just a grumpy miser who refuses to conform to societal norms and close his business because he's greedy." In reality, however, the story establishes a tradition, and not until after *A Christmas Carol* did closing your business, giving paid days off or Christmas bonuses, or really celebrating Christmas at all become popular.

So we've seen three influences: Moore, Victoria, and Dickens. Notice, however, that each of these influences is secular. Consequently, even as it rose from the ashes, Christmas remained a secular holiday just as it always had been. Sure, once Christmas resurged, Christians renewed their effort to Christianize it with mantras like "Jesus is the reason for the season" and "Keep Christ in Christmas." But just like before, these efforts were largely ineffectual. Although the truly devout may make Jesus the focus of their holiday celebrations (and, again, I have no argument against that), Christmas celebrations among the general population remain primarily secular to this day.

Think about this: What is the most well-known Christmas story? It's *A Christmas Carol*—a secular story about ghosts and charity.[37] What are the most well known Christmas songs? "White Christmas," "Rudolf the Red Nosed Reindeer," and "Jingle Bells"—all secular. In fact, not a single religious song finds itself in the top 25 most performed Christmas songs.[38] The most popular Christmas movies? *It's a Wonderful Life, Miracle on 34th Street, White Christmas, A Christmas Story*—again, all secular. Secularism has not invasively corrupted and taken over what used to primarily be a solemn religious observance. Christmas was originally secular, and the way it has been celebrated has always been primarily secular. Despite its namesake, Christmas is not and never has been a "Christian holiday."

Christmas Out of Control

The influence of Moore, Victoria, and Dickens explains why more people began celebrating Christmas, but in the early 1800s such celebrations would've only been a one-day or two-day affair, including Christmas Eve. So how did it become the months long, all-encompassing, ubiquitous, expensive, obligatory, and soul-crushing holiday it is today? Although this is a bit simplistic, the primary cause was one thing: capitalism.

The fad of imitating Moore's poem and buying gifts for your children quickly morphed into an obligation. If you didn't buy gifts for your children at Christmas, people thought you were a bad parent. People bought presents that amounted to luxury items, even when they didn't have the money—even during economic depressions. Businesses capitalized on this gift-giving with advertisements for must-have toys that "every child wants for Christmas." Before Santa lived at the North Pole, several businesses even claimed to be Santa Claus's Christmas headquarters.

Then they realized they could make even more money by expanding the gift-giving obligations. Through advertisements, they encouraged husbands to buy gifts for their wives. It would have been improper for wives to buy their husbands, the head of the household, a gift. Gifts flowed down, not up, the social hierarchy. But it didn't take long for business to break through that taboo as well, and soon wives were encouraged with ads to buy for their husbands. Then it was children for their parents. Pretty soon, if you weren't buying a gift for practically everyone you knew, you weren't celebrating Christmas properly.

According to Bruce David Forbes in *Christmas: A Candid History*, one shop owner around 1880 recalled a time when nearly every female customer that entered his store at Christmastime had a list of people for whom she had to buy gifts that was "literally a yard long."[39] Clearly, the average American family couldn't afford to buy expensive gifts for everyone they knew, so entirely new kinds of products emerged on the market, known as "gimcracks," "geegaws," or "doodads." These poorly made, cheap figurines or jewelry were made expressly for the purpose of being affordable gifts to give to friends at Christmas, who would briefly display and then discard them. Eventually the public wised up (to a degree), and now we buy Christmas cards to send to our acquaintances, which we display for a while, and then toss.[40]

One thing we really think is new about Christmas is our frustration with it. We think, "If only we could get back to the good ol' days, when Christmas was pure and unsullied."[41] In reality, however, our frustrations are nothing new. Recall from the introduction, Harriet Beecher Stowe saying in 1850, "There are worlds of money wasted, at [Christmastime], in getting things nobody wants and nobody cares for after they are got." Or take the Sedgwick family experience, as recounted in their letters dated from 1823 and 1835, before Clement Clark Moore even laid claim to his famous St. Nick poem. Sometimes they forgot to buy presents. When they did remember, it was difficult to find the right ones, and often they inadvertently bought the wrong one. Many immediately broke while others were useless baubles. It always seemed that others were getting better gifts, and sometimes it wasn't even clear what a gift was. Having others buy the gifts for you and then paying them back was a common practice, and it became difficult to keep track of who owed whom what. And if the family did do its own shopping after many hints were dropped, it was the woman of the household's responsibility.[42] Our frustrations with the commercialized Christmas are literally as old as the commercialization of Christmas itself.

In fact, they are as old as commercialization itself, because the commercialized Christmas and the commercialized economy grew together. "A commercial Christmas...emerged in tandem with the commercial economy itself, and the two were mutually reinforcing."[43] As Christmas spending continued to grow, our economy came to be defined by it. Christmas spending became the indicator of the economy's health. Businesses appeared whose sole purpose was to sell Christmas merchandise or who had the majority of their profits appear in December. (I don't think it's a coincidence that jewelry stores first appeared in America in Manhattan in the 1880s.[44]) Soon followed the expectation that if the current year's Christmas spending doesn't outdo the previous year's, we are in an economic slump. Thus the pressure to drive up Christmas sales increases every year, along with the veracity and ubiquity of the ads we see. Christmas just keeps getting bigger and bigger.

Interestingly, we owe many of our Christmas traditions to marketing campaigns and hungry capitalists. Rudolph the Red-Nosed Reindeer was invented by Montgomery Ward and first appeared in a free pamphlet given out to kids whose parents shopped at the store.[45] Santa Claus's iconic red and white garb was solidified by a 1930s Coca-Cola ad campaign.[46] Although Santa had worn red and white before, these were not the only colors he could be seen in.[47] But now, if Santa's not wearing

Coca-Cola red and white—he doesn't look like a Coca-Cola ad—then he's not really Santa. We even owe the length of the Christmas shopping season to capitalism. Originally, Thanksgiving fell on the last Thursday of November. But this meant that, occasionally, Thanksgiving would fall on November 30, leaving only 24 days for what had become the Christmas shopping season. Profits plummeted. When this was due to happen again in 1939, retailers implored FDR to make Thanksgiving November's fourth Thursday to extend Christmas shopping by a week. He did, and it's been that way ever since.[48]

How Christmas Trees Became a Crop

Christmas isn't Christmas without a Christmas tree, right? Surely that is an ancient tradition? Nope! The commonly believed history of the Christmas tree is filled with misconceptions:[49]

- The Christmas tree does not date back to the Old Testament. Some think this because the first verses of Jeremiah 10 appear to be a prescription against a heathen practice of cutting down a tree and decorating it with silver and gold. Such trees, however, would have had nothing to do with Christmas, and been nothing like our modern Christmas trees. In fact, the passage is only about how heathen idols (statues) are made. They are carved from a tree; they are not the tree itself.

- The Christmas tree was not invented by Martin Luther (1483–1546).[50] Supposedly, he was walking home on Christmas Eve, found a tree to be beautiful, cut it down, brought it home, and slapped some candles on it. This story is apocryphal, and the 1856 engraving depicting Luther and his family singing songs around a decorated Christmas tree was a fantasy.[51]

- Hessian soldiers did not bring the Christmas tree to America during the American Revolution. As we will see, the American Revolution ended years before the first Christmas tree was displayed in America.

- Neither was it popularized by the aforementioned illustration (1848) of Queen Victoria and Prince Albert, and its Americanized counterpart (1850). Christmas trees were already widely in use by that time.

Those who are a little more historically savvy suppose that the Christmas Tree was introduced to America by a mass immigration of German settlers into Pennsylvania. Although the first

Christmas tree in America may have been seen in a Pennsylvania German household as early as 1812,[52] Christmas trees were not widely in use until 1830, which was about a decade before the mass immigration of German settlers began.[53] So there is no way German immigration could account for the Christmas tree's popularity. What's more—and this is the really surprising part—the Christmas tree became popular in Germany at the same time that it became popular in America.

Don't get me wrong, the Christmas tree did originate in Germany. But the tradition is not that old and it wasn't ubiquitous. It seems to have originated in the early-to mid-1600s, in the Alsatian capital of Strasbourg. People would cut off the top of a fir tree and display it in their house as a part of a very judgmental Christmas ritual in which the "Christkindle" would show up with bonbons for good kids and a demonic punisher in tow called "Hanstrapp" for bad children. (The Christkindle was a young blond girl with candles in her hair that represented the Christ child. More about Hanstrapp when we talk about Myth #5.) But this was a local custom, and didn't make it out of Strasbourg until the mid 1700s. Even then it spread only to a few places. It didn't make its way to Berlin until the 1810s and didn't become popular nationwide in Germany until the 1830s, the same time it was becoming popular in America.[54]

How is this possible? Because like most other Christmas traditions, the idea of a Christmas tree did not spread organically from family to family over the years with love and affection. It was popularized intentionally by people through literature, and literature can easily jump national boundaries, cross the sea, and become known by everyone at the same time. Think about how the appearance of a product and its origin story, such as the "Elf on a Shelf," made a Christmas tradition pop up almost overnight. (More on that when we debunk Myth #6.)

The Christmas tree tradition seems to have exited Strasbourg in 1750 due to the writings of Johann Wolfgang von Goethe, who visited the area and incorporated a Christmas tree in a pivotal scene in his most famous novel, The Sufferings of Young Werther. But we can't attribute the popularity of the Christmas tree to Goethe or really to any single story or author. It was a range of different stories, all appearing in first quarter of the 1800s, which were primarily responsible for spreading the word about Christmas trees.

This literature popularized Christmas trees because it showed that they could service a need—there was a good reason to adopt the Christmas tree as a tradition. As Nissenbaum argues, they provided parents with the ability to make gifts a surprise, control the distribution of gifts, and deal with selfish, spoiled children.

The first Christmas trees were unlike those today. They were the tops of fir trees, displayed on a table for one day only, in the parlor, library, or drawing room, into which children would not have ordinarily been allowed. Before the family's Christmas gift distribution which would not have been an exchange, the small gifts would be placed on the tree. Candles would be lit in its branches, and then the children would be let in, often upon the third ring of a bell. In a Christmas before the invention of wrapping paper, this ritual provided parents the ability to keep presents hidden until it was time for the children to receive them.

Just like today, heaping toys upon children at Christmas had a tendency to turn children into spoiled brats. One custom held that if children could scream "Christmas gift" before their parents on Christmas Day, parents were obligated to produce a gift then and there. A Christmas tree gift distribution would be a way to make children wait, and avoid being woken up by children screaming "Christmas gift" at five in the morning.

In perhaps the most notable story that popularized the Christmas tree in Marian S. Carson's *The Pearl, Or, Affection's Gift*, Christmas Day begins with just such an exchange. Little Mary Selwyn shouts "Christmas gift" at her parents, only to be sorely disappointed. The day goes on, they visit family, play games, have a meal, yet still no Christmas gifts. Mary is crying on the way home because a lack of presents has made this Christmas so "dull." Her mother reprimands her:

> I am sorry...to see that you have so little fortitude in bearing disappointment...every effort that has been made by your kind relatives, to assume you and make you happy has been entirely lost, merely because you could not have every wish gratified.[55]

It's not really until Mary gives up hope and doesn't expect any gifts at all, that her mother surprises her with a party of her friends and then calls them into the drawing room where a gift-filled Christmas tree is waiting for them.

The message was clear: children are not to be spoiled brats, expecting presents and getting upset when they don't get exactly what they want. Instead, they should expect nothing and be genuinely and spontaneously grateful for whatever they get. The newly established Christmas traditions, which made Christmas gifts obligatory, made accomplishing this task impossible, but using a Christmas tree to distribute gifts was seen as a way to do so.[56]

Another fun story about Christmas spoiling children worth mentioning is William Dean Howells' *Christmas Every Day*, which tells the story of a little girl that gets her wish that Christmas would come every day. Pretty soon she is so sick of "disgusting presents" that she throws them out unopened, cluttering the sidewalk in front of her house. The police threaten to arrest her unless she removes them from the sidewalk and eventually the garbage collectors refuse to pick up any more "Christmas trash." In the end, she learns her lesson.[57]

Another problem the Christmas tree helped solve was the commercial Christmas's inauthenticity. As Christmas became more commercial, gifts were bought in stores, and it was impossible for such gifts to be as heartfelt and personal as their handmade forebears. Making store-bought gifts seem more authentic was actually an important role for Santa Claus. This is why he was so often depicted as making the gifts he distributed to children by hand. But a similar problem was faced by the newly formed commercial Christmas itself, which seemed to ring hollow. Stories that included Christmas trees, however, made the trees out to be ancient folk traditions dating back hundreds of years, thus making a Christmas that included one seem more authentic.

One such story, published in 1820 just as Christmas trees were becoming popular, was set in fourteenth-century Germany and suggested that all medieval Germans had Christmas trees, lit up with candles and filled with presents they bought at "shops in the streets," filled with "toys of every kind."[58] Of course, this was preposterous. In the 1300s, Germany contained no Christmas trees, children did not receive Christmas gifts besides perhaps fruits or nuts, and there certainly were no toy stores. But the story still helped make Christmas trees into another "brand-new old-fashioned" tradition. Because people believed they were an old folk tradition, they felt like the commercial Christmas in which they were participating had folk authenticity, and so it was easier to stomach its commercial after-taste. The more things change...

One of my favorite stories that helped to popularize Christmas trees is from *The Token*, edited by Samuel Griswold

Goodrich and tells of a young woman, Lizzy, entertaining gentlemen at her house at the kind of "open house" invented by Pintard, where adult males would visit multiple houses in a day. One of the gentlemen repeats the false claim of Pintard that such visitations were a "fine old custom [of] our Dutch ancestors." Lizzy knows better. Like Pintard, the man was an "interloper who had not a drop of...Dutch blood" in him. This tradition of his was made up, not authentic. Yet the author contrasts these visitations with children playing around a Christmas tree in the next room, creating the impression that celebrating with a Christmas tree is the proper, domesticated, authentic way to celebrate Christmas. Just like Pintard, Lizzy is promoting her preferred way of celebrating by making it seem like something it is not—authentic and old-fashioned.

But how did Christmas trees go from the tops of firs with candles in the parlor to the full-grown, over-decorated, electrically lit evergreens in the living room surrounded by presents we know today? Again, it was capitalism. As capitalism increased and the economy improved, the presents just got bigger and bigger. Soon they were too heavy to fit on a Christmas tree, so they went under it. A bit later, they were so big and there were so many that they overshadowed the tree itself. So the trees got bigger and had to be moved to the floor to keep from touching the ceiling. As the child-centered parenting philosophy took hold, rooms in which the children were not allowed became a thing of the past, making it necessary to hide the presents another way. Enter wrapping paper. The candles in the branches too often caught fire, thus igniting the sale of electric Christmas lights. And bigger trees meant more space for decoration, so Christmas tree decorations were designed and sold posthaste.

The entire Christmas tree market has been in perpetual growth ever since. The first Christmas tree farms likely appeared in 1901 with mass production starting around 1950, and tree farms are now in all 50 states, including Hawaii.[59] It became popular enough for a Christmas tree to first appear in the White House around 1891.[60] At the time, Benjamin Harrison was already calling it "an old Fashioned Christmas Tree."[61] The first Rockefeller Christmas tree was erected in 1933.[62] It was giant compared to the house trees of the time, but of course was miniscule compared to the behemoths that are erected there today.

The Influence of Domestication

Domesticating Christmas—making it a holiday about family and children—had other effects as well. Before it was domesticated, as we've discussed, it was primarily a holiday of feasting, drinking, and sex. But while feasting seems to be compatible with a child-centered holiday, drinking and sex are not. Although such things did not disconnect from the holiday entirely (think, for example, of office Christmas parties), they were deemphasized.

In his third chapter, Nissenbaum summarizes a kind of war of words, often fought in newspapers, between those trying to divorce alcohol from Christmas and those who liked the old drinking tradition. One defender of the drinking tradition was a sheriff who was only offered coffee and never alcohol as he made his Christmas visits. "I've already had breakfast," he insisted. One hostess replied that a newspaper writer by the name of Mr. Stone had recommended coffee as a preferable way to celebrate Christmas. The sheriff decided to visit some hotel bars instead—and who does he see but Mr. Stone himself, eating beef and turkey and washing it down with "large droughts of old Madeira [an alcoholic beverage]."[63] Another defender, Rip Van Dam, depicted Santa in a poem as not only bringing goodies to children, but also goodies to adults like spiced rum. He even fantasizes about jointing Santa in "a drunken orgy:"

> Come then with thy merry eye,
> And let us bouse it [i.e., booze it] till we die!
> Come and o'er my thirsty soul
> Floods of smoking glasses roll[64]

Those opposed to the continued marriage of Christmas and alcohol blamed alcohol for almost every social ill. They eventually won out because the newspapers took their side, often singing the praises of the domesticated Christmas celebrations while drawing attention to examples of societal damage caused by drinking. According to Nissenbaum, "[t]o read the city's newspaper at mid-century is to encounter upbeat editorials about Christmas shopping and the joyous expectations of children juxtaposed with unsettling reports of holiday drunkenness and rioting."[65] Interestingly, this Christmas temperance movement, especially popular among women, was a precursor to the temperance movement that led to prohibition in the 1930s. As early as the late 1840s, largely as a response to Christmas rowdiness, Philadelphia banned the sale of alcohol altogether.[66]

As previously discussed, the domestication of Christmas turned Christmas's focus away from the poor and onto children. Treating one's servants as "king for a day" was replaced with treating one's child as "king for a day." But that didn't mean that charity to the poor disappeared altogether as a Christmas tradition. After all, as we learned in Myth #1, social inversion is one of the oldest holiday traditions. Recall the ancient Mesopotamian tradition of appointing a peasant or criminal as king for a day. Recall the old Saturnalia tradition of the rich serving food to the poor. But the domestication of Christmas did make charity to the poor take on a different form. To be sure, the importance of giving to the poor declined. Since giving to the poor was no longer the primary way that one expressed charity at Christmas, the poor simply got less attention and less money. But the primary way that charity to the poor changed was by becoming something that one did from a distance. Unlike a Christmas wassail, which had fallen out of favor because of industrialization. Once Christmas became domesticated, charity to the poor was almost always something that one did remotely through an organization, to which one would donate money.

We see this kind of giving in *A Christmas Carol*. At the beginning of the book, Scrooge refused to give money to gentlemen asking for donations to the poor. After his conversion, Scrooge catches up with them and promises a large sum of money. But no beggar ever approaches Scrooge, and Scrooge never gives to one directly. His social obligation to such charitable giving is fulfilled simply by giving money to someone else.

Dickens was not the only one to promote this idea. The press, the rich, and even those who were most concerned with helping the poor "all pressed the notion that organized charities provided the most appropriate means for assisting the poor."[67] "Do not give to street beggars," one headline read, discouraging the face-to-face charity of "indiscriminate giving." After all, you might inadvertently give money to an imposter, so "[w]henever you see one of these City pests approaching, button up both pockets...."[68]

Even government programs to help the poor were opposed, despite the fact that the new capitalist economy of the nineteenth century regularly suffered severe economic depressions that created many unwillingly unemployed people. Such programs, it was thought, simply funneled money down to the poor without controlling how it was spent. "How do we know they're not spending it on alcohol, instead of food?" many thought. Only private charitable organizations could make such guarantees.[69]

In addition, private organizations were thought to be more efficient than direct giving. As the *New York Times* touted, "If a man has money, and does not know how he can make the most of it, let him step into the offices of any of these excellent [private charitable] institutions, in whose hands, if you place a dollar, can do what, individually, you could not make five dollars do."[70]

One of the most noteworthy such charities was the Children's Aid Society, founded by Charles Loring Brace, who had concluded that charitable giving to adults was "virtually useless," "like pouring water through a sieve" because adults would often waste the charitable relief on "alcohol or worse." Giving to adults "only created a sense of dependency."[71] Brace was convinced that poor families were "poison" to their own children, more likely to turn them into the societal dregs their parents were. He advocated for and participated in separating children

from poor parents so they could be raised by more affluent families in the West. To his credit, he didn't outright steal these children—he "persuaded" poor parents to give their children away. In all, he managed to "transport some 90,000 boys to new homes and lives in the West."[72] He thought that a life in the "labor starved, Protestant dominated West" would turn these New York vagrants into "honest, hard-working Western Pioneer[s]." Unfortunately, Brace never bothered to track the progress of such children to see if his scheme actually worked.[73]

Giving to charity was uncomfortable, even to children, unless they were deserving—the kind of ideal model of humanity that Dickens's Tiny Tim was. In reality, this was not the case. Many poor children were "newsboys," the boys you see in old films selling papers on the corner, and yelling "read all about it." Parentless and homeless, they were ruffians, street urchins who caused all kinds of trouble. Nevertheless, middle-class Americans were fascinated with newsboys, and so publications *made them* worthy of charity by idealizing them. For example, the newsboy in Elizabeth Oakes Smith's novel *The Newsboy* is made out to be a "miracle of goodness." In reality, he "hardly resembled the kind of real-life newsboy that Charles Loring Brace had to deal with."[74]

Charity to poor children was also a way to assuage the guilt that came with spoiling your own children with gifts they didn't need.[75] Especially in the 1890s, well-to-do Americans began making gift giving to the children of the poor part of their Christmas rituals.[76] Stories about such giving portrayed children as extremely grateful, and they likely were. But the rich seeing the children's "happy faces and joyful voices…[alleviated their] fear that the urban social order was coming apart, that industrial capitalism was leading to social collapse."[77]

In a way, the rich were exploiting the poor through charity, using them to assuage the guilt that the gilded age was heaping upon them. Unfortunately, this was not even close to the most egregious act of such exploitation. Rich New Yorkers began attending large dinners put on for the poor by charitable organizations. Of course, they did not partake themselves. Instead, they went to watch the poor eat from a distance. The likely largest such spectacles were put on, perhaps ironically, by the Salvation Army. Beginning in 1898, they rented out the Madison Square Garden and held a large dinner on its floor where they would feed thousands of poor people at a time. In what is now seen as a disgusting practice, they paid for the event by selling tickets for the Garden's boxes and galleries to New York's more prosperous citizens, who would get all gussied up in their best attire, diamonds and all, and sit voyeuristically watching their poor, hungry fellow New Yorkers greedily eat. As a report in the *New York World* observed:

> Some seem to look upon this feeding of the ravens as a spectacle, and whispered and pointed at poorly clad men and women who ate ravenously, or smiled when a piece of turkey was surreptitiously slipped into a capricious pocket.[78]

But the price of the tickets didn't cover all the costs, so the Salvation Army "hired unemployed men to play the part of street-corner Santa Claus, soliciting passersby for contribu-

tions as they did their Christmas shopping."[79] Yep, it's actually from these nefarious roots that the bell-ringing Santa you see every year comes.

How This Myth Has Hijacked the Holiday

As we discussed in the introduction, there are many aspects of our Christmas celebrations that need to change—traditions that make Christmas work against us instead of for us. But there is nothing we can do about it, we think, because Christmas always has been and always will be the way it is now. This chapter, however, has revealed that this is false. Christmas is in flux; it's always been changing and it always will. The traditions of today don't trace back thousands of years. To give them up would not break ties to our ancient ancestors. By and large, today's traditions were invented recently, often by people trying to bend Christmas to their own advantage. Other traditions, like Christmas trees, were adopted because they were helpful. Yet for some, Christmas trees may have simply become a nuisance.

Christmas and its traditions should make our life better, not worse. So when we identify a Christmas tradition that is causing us more trouble than it is worth, we shouldn't hesitate to get rid of it.

Try to keep this in mind as we continue to the next chapter, where I argue that we would all benefit, as individuals and a society, by significantly changing what we do with our money at Christmastime.

Christmas Spending Is Good for the Economy

IN THE INTRODUCTION, I ASKED THE QUESTION: "WHAT is wrong with Christmas?" In response, many readers probably had some kind of complaint about Christmas shopping and Christmas spending. "I feel obligated. I spend too much. I hate all the shopping." Yet despite the complaints, we are convinced that it's worth it because Christmas spending is essential for the economy. "Christmas," as Sarah Palin put it, "helps to employ millions of people and props up our entire retail economy."[1] This is the myth:

> *Our entire economy depends upon Christmas spending. If this year's Christmas profits aren't larger than last year's Christmas profits, the economy will go into free fall, and we'll all be in big trouble. To keep our economy going, we must spend, spend, spend at Christmas. It's our American duty. If Christmas shopping went away, the entire economy would collapse.*

For obvious reasons, this is exactly what retailers and businesses want you to think. But, of course, it's all a lie. To realize this, one shouldn't need any more evidence than this: there were times before Christmas shopping existed in which the economy did just fine. There are countries around the world today who do not have abundant Christmas shopping, yet their economies thrive (e.g., China, Japan, and India). However, this myth is so entrenched that it's going to take a lot more than that to be convincing. So strap in while we consider the numerous reasons why Christmas spending is not essential to the economy and the many ways it is, in fact, bad for the economy. I hope you will conclude with me that you should likely stop, or at least drastically change, your Christmas spending.

Christmas Just Concentrates Spending

It is true that when Christmas spending is down, retailers and economists freak out and say that it indicates economic disaster. "Doesn't that necessarily mean," one might say, "that Christmas spending is good for the economy and that we have to buy Christmas gifts to keep the economy afloat?" No, it does not.

First of all, the worries are usually exaggerated. Often the retailers and economists are simply upset that Christmas spending is not as high as it was last year or even that the rate of increase simply isn't as high as projected. If the economy was particularly strong last year, a dip this year is not really that worrisome. If the economy was better last year than, say, it has been in the last 20 years, then we are likely still better off this year than we usually are, even if Christmas spending is a bit down.

Second of all, this reasoning involves something logicians call "the causal fallacy." The fact that one thing is correlated with another doesn't necessarily mean one causes the other. In fact, economists know this. The Christmas spending season is merely an indicator of the economy's strength, not a cause of it. If anything, it goes the other way—a strong economy creates heavy Christmas spending by giving people more money to spend.[2] Heavy Christmas spending doesn't create a good economy by giving people extra money to spend.[3] Heavy Christmas spending just indicates that people had extra money to spend. If Christmas spending went away, the economy wouldn't be harmed. We'd just have to find another way to gauge the strength of the economy.

Now, some may think this is crazy. Aren't there billions of dollars spent on Christmas, and wouldn't subtracting those billions from the economy hurt it? Of course, subtracting billions from the economy would hurt the economy. That's Econ 101.

However, the elimination of Christmas spending would not automatically subtract billions from the economy. This argument presents us with a false dichotomy: either we spend that money at Christmas, or we won't spend it at all. When you don't buy a Christmas present, that doesn't make the money you would have spent on that present just disappear from your wallet. The money would still be there, and you'd most likely still spend it, just at a different time. (Even if you saved it, it's still good for the economy, but we'll talk more about saving later.) This is true of everyone. If we all didn't collectively spend the billions that we do at Christmas, we'd most likely just spend it at some other time, and the economy would be equally strong. In general, people don't fail to spend money they have.

We might say that all Christmas does to the economy is make us concentrate our spending into one big burst at the end of the year instead of spreading our spending out through the entire year. But the health of the economy isn't determined by when the money is spent. The good thing about "Christmas spending" isn't the "Christmas" part—it's the "spending" part. As long as the money gets spent, everything is the same. Economically speaking, subtracting Christmas spending would likely have no noticeable economic consequences.

One possible exception, however, is this: eliminating Christmas spending would give us more freedom to spend our money how we see fit. As it is now, buying Christmas presents is seen as a social obligation. Try telling your friends that you are not going to buy Christmas gifts for your kids this year and see what happens. Try telling your parents. Try telling your kids. In 2014, Pope Francis even hinted that this obligation amounts to a kind of "material slavery."[4] Not only are we seemingly forced to buy presents every year, we are expected to buy certain kinds of presents: toys, jewelry, entertainment electronics (e.g., Xboxes and games), etcetera. Things that we want, not that we need, are usually the order of the day. Yet we buy these things as a first order of business as if they are necessities, often even if we have unpaid bills or medical expenses or we have fallen behind on our mortgage.[5] Consequently, eliminating Christmas spending would eliminate this social obligation and free us to spend our money how we need. The social pressure that causes us to spend our first dollars on Xboxes would go away.[6] Of course, we could still buy them if we want, but if there are more pressing matters like a mortgage payment or saving for retirement, we might use the money for that instead. Even though the elimination of Christmas spending would not subtract money from the economy, it might redirect it. We might end up spending more on, say, our mortgages and less on Xboxes.

Would that be a good thing? Some might think not. After all, it's consumer spending—buying goods and services—that drives 70 percent of the Gross Domestic Product (GDP). Economics reporter Jason Hull argues that if everyone started paying off their debt and saving for retirement instead of buying goods and services, the economy would slump significantly. Banks would close, the housing, auto, and restaurant industries would suffer, as would universities, and unemployment would likely rise.[7] It wouldn't be pretty. By forcing us to spend our money on goods and services instead of saving and paying off our debts, maybe Christmas spending *really is* good for the economy.

Not so fast.

As Hull points out, once all of our debts were paid off and we were even able to shore up our savings, the economy would come back even bigger than it was before:

"Once the time of paying off our debt passes, we would ring in a new era of prosperity. Rather than having so much of our income burdened by interest and paying for past purchases, we could free up that income to save for retirement, spending, and giving. We could take more risks and be more entrepreneurial, as we wouldn't have mortgages, car payments, and student loans to worry about if our entrepreneurial ventures did not succeed. The country's net economic power would increase as more money was spent on goods and non-financial services—production rather than monetary intermediaries. We would be back to being able to consume what our country's economic capacity could produce."

Hull is arguing that credit spending is a bit like a drug and coming down off of that drug would be pretty painful. It might take a while. After all, the first money put away for retirement would not get back into the system for quite a few years. But once we were clean and stable—out of rehab, so to speak—we'd be so much better off. In the long term, the freedom to spend our money how we need to, a freedom that would accompany the elimination of Christmas spending obligations, would eventually make our economy thrive even more. (Hull even points out that nearly debt-free societies have existed and they prospered.)[8] By obligating us to spend our first dollars on frivolity instead of paying off our debts and stabilizing ourselves by saving, Christmas spending harms the economy considerably.

In fact, we may not even need to wait for the benefits of eliminating Christmas spending, as Hull suggests. Contrary to Hull's prediction, there may not be any rehab time at all. Why? Hull's argument seems to endorse what is known as "the paradox of thrift," which is, roughly put, the idea that widespread saving through a society is bad for the economy even though, for each individual saver, it is a good economic practice. The assumption is that saving money keeps it from being spent and spending is necessary for the economy to thrive. It's only when that saving eventually gives us more consumer spending power that it is economically beneficial.

But an error seems to underlie such thinking: that saving money subtracts it from the economy. It does not. Unless you are hoarding cash in your mattress, any money you save is being invested in some way. Maybe you have it in a CD or a 401(k) or maybe you use it to buy stocks and bonds. Even if you just keep it in a savings account at your bank, your bank lends that money out to help people buy homes, build business, pay employers, and create jobs. Even when you pay off your mortgage, you are giving money to a bank. The more money banks have available, the lower the interest rates can be, the more such lending can happen, and ultimately, the stronger the economy is.

Instead of a temporary slump, if we all just took the money we would spend this Christmas, and instead of buying presents, invested it, paid off a chunk of our mortgage, or put it into a savings account, we might actually create a gigantic economic boom. There would be a huge uptick in the availability of loans, business expansion, and job creation. (There might be an immediate slump as some Christmas-dependent business went belly up, but they would all be replaced quite quickly.) In a way, saving is just another kind of spending, some argue an even more beneficial kind of spending than consumer spending. By keeping us from saving, Christmas spending may be hurting us both in the long run, and in the short run.

Even our founding fathers seemed to have recognized this. Benjamin Franklin, for example, was a huge advocate of saving. Hence his well-known saying, "A penny saved is a penny earned." Along with many of our Founding Fathers, he would have likely thought that our frivolous Christmas spending weakens the nation. As Stephen Nissenbaum points out, during and after the Revolutionary War, and thus before a consumer Christmas:

...Americans had been taught that indulging in luxury was frivolous—that it was a vice associated with the decadent aristocratic nations of Europe. The American Republic had to be more abstemious than that if it was to survive and prosper. Buying luxury goods amounted, therefore, almost to a subversive political act, the kind of small gesture that could jeopardize the future health of the Republic. Consumer capitalism and civic virtue were not commonly associated with each other in early-nineteenth-century America.[9]

Today, people often think that consumer spending is our obligation as Americans. It decidedly is not.

The Danger of Christmas Spending

So Christmas spending isn't good for the economy. At best, it is merely concentrating our spending at the end of the year. At worst, it keeps our economy from being as good as it could be by keeping us from paying off our existing debts, stabilizing ourselves financially, and making loans more readily available. But is there any way that Christmas spending hurts the economy? Is it possibly setting us up for disaster? Absolutely.

It's important to understand that even if Christmas spending does increase the GDP, that doesn't necessarily mean that it helps to keep the economy in good shape. The GDP is just one factor in determining the strength of an economy. It can be high, but the economy can still be weak. For example, before the recession of 2008, the GDP was quite high, yet the economy was on the verge of collapse. You can't say that an economy is strong if it's on the verge of collapse. By definition, if something is about to collapse, it is weak. After the recession, the GDP recovered to pre-recession numbers by 2011 and actually soared past them by the end of 2012, yet by that same time, the employment rate had only recovered two of the five points it lost in the recession.[10] And an economy that cannot keep people employed cannot be said to be a strong economy. What's my point? The mere fact that an economy has a strong GDP does not necessarily mean that economy is healthy. So even if Christmas spending increases the GDP, that doesn't necessarily mean that it makes our economy stronger.

In what way might Christmas spending make our economy weaker, even if it contributes to the GDP? One way it does so is by turning our economy upside down. Perhaps this is more of a philosophical point than an economic one, but it seems that our economy would be stronger if it primarily supported necessary industries (e.g., agriculture, housing) and services (e.g., construction, our infrastructure) and only secondarily supported non-necessary industries (e.g., jewelry, electronic entertainment). This seems to have been the logic behind our founders' fondness for saving and objection to luxury spending. Christmas, however, has us spending our first dollars on luxury items. As economist Joel Waldfogel points out in his book Scroogenomics: Why You Shouldn't Buy Presents for the Holidays, people's Christmas spending habits have them buying caviar (i.e., luxury items) like they are underwear (i.e., necessities).[11] Our Christmas spending even creates entire industries that survive only because of Christmas shopping, while other more important industries struggle.

I can't help but take this opportunity to lament the fact that we complain about taxes that would go toward repairing bridges and roads, yet we will spend more on Xboxes, jewelry, and other frivolities at Christmas than those taxes would cost us. We spend about $66 billion every year on Christmas,[12] and at the same time people complain about President Obama making a onetime pledge of $50 billion to "rebuild 150,000 miles of roads, 4,000 miles of rail and 150 miles of runways."[13] Unlike Christmas spending, repairing our infrastructure actually would help the economy.[14] Simply put, there are just more important things on which we need to be spending our money.

But one undeniably negative economic effect of Christmas spending is this: it inflates the credit bubble.[15] The ability to buy things on credit gives consumers the ability to quite literally spend money that they do not have. Credit cards have not always been widely used, and an economy can't survive when too much of it is made up of credit spending or when too many people take on more debt than they can pay. We learned that in 2008, when as a nation, we took on more housing debt than we could pay. The same thing can happen as a result of taking on too much credit card debt. (In fact, credit card debt played an overlooked role in the 2008 financial crisis.) Credit card spending may be propping up the economy for now, but it's only on stilts that will give way if we take on too much. Nothing that increases our credit card debt can be said to strengthen the economy. In fact, it weakens it by making it more likely to crash.

However, this is exactly what Christmas spending does.

Decades ago, people used to save up for their Christmas spending in what was called a Christmas club account. But today about two-thirds of holiday spending goes on credit cards. While some people use them as "cash cards," paying off their monthly balance in total and thus accruing no interest, such people are in the minority. Only one-fourth of Christmas credit purchases are paid off by January and only two-thirds by February. Some cards are not even paid off by the next December.[16] Doing so inflates the credit bubble more each year, making it more and more likely that the bubble will burst, moving our economy closer and closer to a collapse. Christmas spending thus weakens our economy.

Christmas spending also weakens a household's economy. Paying four to seven percent interest on a loan that helps you buy a house is financially sound. You need somewhere to live, and if you waited to buy a house until you could afford to buy it outright, you would have no time left to live in it. But paying 30 percent interest on an Xbox, an Elmo doll, or any other frivolous expenditure just doesn't make sense. You don't need these items, and even if you buy them during a Christmas sale, the fact that you pay 30 percent interest on those purchases means that they end up costing you more than if you had just paid cash at the regular price. When used in this way, credit cards just amount to predatory loans that take advantage of people's social situation, in this case, the obligation to buy Christmas gifts they can't afford, to charge them unreasonable interest.

Christmas forces us to, quite literally, spend money we don't have on, as Tyler Durden would say, "shit we don't need."[17] This makes both the national economy and our household economies weaker in numerous ways.

The Waste of Christmas

When "Christmas waste" is mentioned, you might think of the $2.6 billion we spend on wrapping paper,[18] the 30 million trees we cut down to make it, and the two million tons of trash it produces.[19] That is an issue that needs attention. In all honesty, the environmental impact of Christmas probably deserves an entire book. But this chapter is about the economy, and when I refer to "Christmas waste," I'm talking about the economic waste produced by holiday spending. We are literally wasting our money away.

How so? Suppose your extended family is engaging in their annual gift exchange. Perhaps names are drawn and everyone has to buy for a specific individual. Perhaps everyone is assigned to buy a "male" or "female" gift and a "Dirty Santa exchange" commences. What is likely to happen? You will have no idea what to buy, and whatever you get will likely not be something you want. Maybe you can use it, but more than likely it will just end up cluttering your basement or attic. Even if you do like it to some degree, it's very unlikely that you would have bought it yourself. It's just not worth to you what it actually cost to buy it.

This exchange creates what Waldfogel calls "deadweight loss."[20] This is essentially when money is wasted because more money is spent on something than it is worth. Take for example government pork barrel spending. Say that the government spends $1 million building a bridge that only five people use a year. Even if those five people really care about getting to where that bridge takes them, they probably wouldn't be willing to spend more than $10,000 a year to use that bridge. So combined, to those five people, that bridge is worth $50,000. But it is worth zero dollars to everyone else. So the government spent $1 million on something that was really only worth $50,000 to the general public. That is $950,000 worth of deadweight loss. That's how much more the government spent on that project than it was worth.

Even though that $1 million was pumped into the economy by paying people to build the bridge, it obviously would have been better to pay those same people that same amount of money to build something that was actually useful—that was worth more to more people. Ideally, you'd build a bridge that two million people would pay a dollar a year to use, making the worth of the bridge twice its cost. Spending money isn't good in and of itself. It's supposed to be a means to a beneficial end.

But Christmas spending is not—it's like a bridge to nowhere. It creates the same kind of deadweight loss. Think about the last present you got from a friend, a distant relative, your grandmother, or your parents. Chances are unless you told them specifically what to get you, that gift created its deadweight loss. Even if it was something you didn't mind having, likely you would not have spent as much

CHRISTMAS GREETINGS. Fair be all thy Hopes and prosperous thy Life.

yourself to own that gift as they had to spend to give it to you. Perhaps they spent $100 when you would have only spent $10. That's $90 of deadweight loss—$90 that would have created more value had it been spent on something else. That gift wasted $90. Sure, that's money that "went into the economy", but so was the million dollars we spent on the bridge to nowhere. It's not that the money should not have been spent—money does no one any good if it's never used for anything—it's that it should have been spent on something else.

Now, you may not think this is a big deal. How much waste could Christmas create? But as Waldfogel points out, there is more deadweight loss created by Christmas spending each year than the deadweight loss created by all government pork barrel spending combined! Each year the government spends about $17.3 billion on pork barrel projects. If we conservatively estimate that these projects are really only worth about half of what they cost, that is $8.7 billion of deadweight loss each year. Of the $66 billion we spend every year on Christmas, about $12 billion of it is deadweight loss. So, let me do the math real quick…yep, $12 billion is greater than $8.7 billion. Given how upset people get about the government wasting their tax dollars, why aren't people even more upset about the waste of Christmas spending?[21]

1916 CHRISTMAS DOLLS, SEARS CATALOG © PD

Some might argue that the sentimental value of a Christmas gift—the mere fact that it was bought by someone else for you out of love—makes up for the deadweight loss. After all, it's the thought that counts, right? In reality, this excuse doesn't work. For one thing, it's also possible to buy a good gift, one that does not create deadweight loss, out of love, and thus good gifts can have sentimental value too. It would be best if a gift has both sentimental value and economic value. So it's still the case that the money should have been spent on something else.

In addition, how much sentimental value does a Christmas gift really have? Let's be honest. Was it really bought out of love, or obligation? Do you even remember all the gifts you got last year? Do you remember who got them for you? Think about the items in your house. Do you remember which ones were Christmas gifts? Now I don't want to denounce Christmas gifts entirely. Gifts in general can be a wonderful expression of appreciation and understanding and can help form lasting bonds between people. But such gifts, especially at Christmas, are the exception and not the rule. Christmas gifts usually don't have sentimental value, and even if they do, they can still create deadweight loss.

Waldfogel has a few suggestions for reducing Christmas waste. For one, reevaluate your gift-giving obligations. Do you really have to buy a gift? Is there something else you could do instead? You might be surprised how often people find receiving gifts a bit of a chore. But if you can't get around the obligation to give, there are other options.

For one, you could simply pay attention or do more research to figure out what your gift recipient would want. But truth be told, unless they just tell you what to buy, you are likely going to miss the mark. And just having them tell you kind of defeats the purpose. One way that a good gift can form a bond is by indicating that the person buying it for you really understands you and knows what you want. It demonstrates a deep knowledge of their character and interests and makes them feel special to you. If you have to ask them what they want, then you don't know them well, and you might as well have just given them a gift card to buy it on their own.

Waldfogel suggests, if you would have to ask them anyway but can't let go of the obligation to give them a gift, a gift card is a good way to go. They guard against deadweight loss. They provide the gift receiver with the ability to buy what they want, and they are a lot less likely to spend more on something than it is worth to them. But still, if you buy a gift card for the wrong store it may go unused, and sometimes it's hard to use the last few dollars on a gift card. In this way gift cards can still be an avenue to deadweight loss.[22]

The best way to guard against deadweight loss is to give cash. A $100 increase in one's buying power is always worth $100 to the person receiving it. Of course, this is just as bad as asking what someone wants; it displays no intimate knowledge. However, if you are not in a place to have this kind of intimate knowledge but are still obligated to provide a gift, cash is preferable to spending that same amount of money on something that they will not want.

The Good of Gifts?

Even a cash gift can create problems. One hundred dollars is worth a lot more to someone who is poor than someone who is rich. Give $100 to the single mother working two jobs and she is likely to use it on food to feed her family. Give $100 to one of the unbelievably wealthy Koch brothers, and they will likely lose it between the couch cushions. Any amount of money is worth more to someone who is poor than it is to someone who is rich. So if you give money to someone who already has more money than you, you are destroying part of the worth of that money. That money is worth more to you and is more useful in your hands.

This is true of any gift. Take just about any gift that you might buy to give to someone who is wealthier than you. Even if it is a gift that they really want and would have purchased on their own, they can afford to buy that item more easily than you can, and the money that you spent on that gift is more valuable in your hands. Sure, they no longer have to spend 100 of their dollars on that item, but you now have 100 fewer dollars to spend. If you are less wealthy, that $100 is worth more to you.

This is perhaps why buying your boss a gift is often awkward, unnecessary, and frustrating. Unless you are giving something that is handmade or expresses your gratitude toward an employer who is a friend, it probably just creates waste. Buying someone who is wealthier than you something that they could just buy on their own doesn't make economic sense.

This, however, highlights something for which gift giving is really good. If the same amount of money is worth more to you than your wealthy boss, the same amount of money is worth less to you than someone poorer than you. Buying a wanted or needed $100 gift for someone frees up 100 of their dollars so that they can spend it on something else. If they don't have as much money as you, that $100 is worth more to them. In this instance, giving the gift actually helps create value. In a sense, giving a gift to someone is essentially giving them money, and if the recipient values that money more than you, then you have created more value—you have literally made the money worth more.

This highlights the importance of smart gift giving. Only if you buy someone something that they want or need, which they would have bought on their own do you really free up any of their money. If you buy them something they don't want or need, they wouldn't have spent their money on that anyway, and they still have to buy what they want or need with their own money. Say, for example, you buy one of your employees a new wallet because you noticed theirs was in tatters. They were going to buy one on their own, but now they don't have to, so they can spend the $20 they would have spent on something else, like food. If instead you buy them a $20 singing Santa that they would not have bought on their own they still have to spend 20 of their own dollars on a wallet and another $20 on food. In a sense, part of the good of gift giving is that it redistributes wealth from the top to the bottom, where it has more value. By not giving strategically, you defeat that purpose.

Now "redistribution of wealth" is a bad phrase in some circles, but it shouldn't be. What those in such circles usually object to is government mandated redistribution of wealth, which can come in the form of taxes. That is not what I am talking about. Mere redistribution of wealth is actually how all economies function. Buying, selling, and trading are all different ways to redistribute wealth, to make money go from one place to another. All economic philosophies are just different theories about how wealth can be redistributed most effectively, even trickle-down economics. I suppose we could reserve the term "redistribution" for that which is involuntary, and "distribution" for that which is voluntary, but my point would be the same. Gifts are simply an additional way wealth gets voluntarily distributed and exist alongside other ways that wealth is voluntarily distributed in existing economies.

The reason that non-voluntary methods of wealth distribution are usually thought to be needed, above and beyond what happens "naturally" in an unencumbered economic system through buying and selling alone, is because most believe that no economic system is perfect. Ideally, everyone capable of working could work a reasonable number of hours a week and would receive a living wage in return, a wage with which they can at least afford the basic necessities like a place to live, food, clothes, and health care. Unfortunately, it seems difficult to achieve these results. There are never enough jobs to go around, and it can become necessary for many people to work multiple jobs just to make a living wage. Redistribution of wealth can help prevent this.

Moreover, in many economies, money collects at the top in the hands of a wealthy few, creating a large income disparity that destroys monetary value. Since any amount of money is worth more to the poor, putting more money in the hands of the rich destroys its worth. That $1000 a billionaire wouldn't even miss could feed 10 of the poorest people for years. Consider the unregulated free-market capitalism—with no taxes, no labor laws, and no minimum wage—that led to the Gilded Age. Gilded Age railroader Cornelius Vanderbilt II had so much money that he embossed gold into the wallpaper of his house, The Breakers, a Gilded Age mansion in Rhode Island.[23] Meanwhile, the immigrants building his railroads were earning pennies a day and often dying on the job. Think of what they could have done with the money he spent gilding his wallpaper. Today even though statistics show that families tend to blow large inheritances in two to three generations and supposedly the Vanderbilts were no exception,[24] it's still the case that more and more wealth is in the hands of fewer and fewer of the richest people. In January 2014, the top 1 percent possessed 46 percent of the world's wealth, and the poorest half of the world's population had a net worth equal to the richest 84 people in the world.[25] This is why many feel that increased taxation to fund programs like welfare, Social Security, Medicare, and Medicaid are needed. Since economic systems don't seem to do this on their own, taxes for such programs forcibly take wealth from the top and use it to provide services to those at the bottom. Like Robin Hood, they steal from the rich and give to the poor. Although the full historical story is more complicated, the income tax first introduced in 1916 did exactly that and helped end the Gilded Age.

I don't want to get into a debate about taxes and government programs. These things forcibly take money from some and give it to others, and regardless of economic inequality, that may be wrong. Even though redistributing wealth from the rich to the poor does create value, it may be immoral to do so by the force of law. But that is what is so great about gift-giving. It's voluntary. When done right, it redistributes wealth and creates value, yet it is done on a completely voluntary basis.

We, in fact, already have a great example of such gift-giving done on a grand scale—the Bill and Melinda Gates Foundation.[26] Bill Gates, who is consistently one of the top two or three richest people in the world,[27] voluntarily donates huge amounts of his money to his foundation, which supports initiatives on everything from agricultural development to vaccine delivery, from family planning to water sanitation. Gates realizes the money needed to provide the world's poor with basic necessities is sitting in the pockets of people so rich that they would barely miss it. Gates provides a model of voluntary redistribution that, if followed broadly, would go a long way toward alleviating many of the world's problems.

Gates has encouraged other billionaires to follow his example, but we can too. And, although no single middle-class individual can do as much good as Bill Gates, they can participate in something that is just as beneficial. Instead of damaging our economy like it does now, Christmas gift-giving can become a force for economic good in the same way if we simply replace our inefficient gift-giving habits with annual habits of charity. So, instead of buying a gift for your boss, donate to a worthwhile charity in their name or give them the opportunity to donate to the charity of their choice. Instead of buying your children more toys than they need or could ever play with, buy fewer toys and give the extra money to a charity of your choice. Better yet, make a Christmas tradition of doing charity work with your family. And I also suggest using charitynavigator.org to find a charity that will use your money wisely and efficiently!

Of course, some will object that such a change would betray our Christmas traditions but, as we have learned, Christmas used to serve this function. Before the church's influence, the rich participating in Saturnalia served food to the poor. Before the invention of the commercial Christmas, rich landowners gave their best food and drink to their servants. By giving back to the poor at Christmas time, we will actually be participating in the most ancient of Christmas traditions—one of the few that really does trace back thousands of years.

But of course, when you do it, don't make the mistake the Salvation Army made in its early days. Don't amuse yourself with the need of others; don't bathe yourself in their gratefulness. Don't draw attention to the fact that you are doing it (unless you are encouraging others to do the same). Just do it because it is the right thing to do.

What a Scrooge! What a Grinch!

Of course, this will not be easy. The social obligation to celebrate Christmas in the traditional way, especially by buying gifts, is overwhelming. Imagine again telling your friends or family that you won't be buying gifts for your children this season. Then break the news to your kids. It won't be pretty. Just consider

Bill Maher, who simply observed that we should stop "spending money you don't have to give people you don't like stuff they don't want." Could advice get any reasonable? Yet, just like him, if you were to suggest the same, you'd be called a "Grinch," or perhaps worse: a "Scrooge."[28]

One way to fight this social pressure is to realize, and maybe even point out, that this criticism is actually true—but not in a bad way. Embracing the Christmas economic philosophy I have suggested in this chapter actually embraces the lessons of the two famous stories containing these characters and makes one more like the reformed Scrooge and Grinch that exist at the end of them. Let's quickly look at the stories to see why.

First, let's look at How the Grinch Stole Christmas.[29] The Grinch did steal all the Christmas presents from Whoville, and I am suggesting that we should considerably reduce the number of presents we buy. So, on the surface, it seems that the comparison is apt. But let's look a little deeper to see if the comparison really is appropriate. After he steals all of the Whovillians' presents, the Grinch turns his ear towards Whoville expecting to hear cries of disappointment. But instead:

> Every Who down in Whoville, the tall and the small,
> Was singing! Without any presents at all!
> He HADN'T stopped Christmas from coming! IT CAME!
> Somehow or other, it came just the same!
> "It came without ribbons! It came without tags!"
> "It came without packages, boxes or bags!"

The Grinch was surprised to find that even without presents, the Whos celebrated Christmas anyway—and they had a great time doing it. The lesson he learned?

> And he puzzled three hours, till his puzzler was sore.
> Then the Grinch thought of something he hadn't before!
> "Maybe Christmas," he thought, "doesn't come from a store."
> "Maybe Christmas...perhaps...means a little bit more!"
> And what happened then? Well...in Whoville they say,
> That the Grinch's small heart grew three sizes that day!

In other words, he learned that Christmas isn't—or shouldn't be—about presents.

So yes, when the Grinch was evil, he stole everyone's presents; but when he cured himself of that evil, he realized presents are not what Christmas is about. Christmas "doesn't come from a store." So, someone who thinks my suggestion that we should reduce the number Christmas presents we buy is "anti-Christmas" is actually endorsing the evil Grinch's view—the view that Christmas is about presents. Like the evil Grinch, that person thinks that taking Christmas presents away will ruin Christmas. What I am suggesting is that Christmas is about more than presents—that eliminating or reducing them won't ruin Christmas because Christmas is bigger than that. It's about so much more. All I'm suggesting is that we take the lesson of Dr. Seuss's story to heart and apply it.

Does this attitude make me a Scrooge? Let's look at Charles Dickens's tale. The first thing a close look at A Christmas Carol reveals is that Scrooge is not as wealthy as people usually make him out to be. He certainly is not diving into a safe full of gold like Scrooge McDuck does in the Disney adaptation. He owns a meager counting house with one single employee and lives in a dreary house in which most of the rooms have been rented out to businesses:

> He lived in chambers which had once belonged to his deceased partner. They were a gloomy suite of rooms, in a lowering pile of building up a yard, where it had so little business to be.... It was old enough now, and dreary enough, for nobody lived in it but Scrooge, the other rooms being all let out as offices.[30]

Similarly, Bob Cratchit is not poor; his family is not splitting a single bean for a Christmas meal. He is employed, and not by a factory or a mine. His wife doesn't even have to work. While Ebenezer is perhaps what we would today call "upper" middle class, Cratchit would most likely be "mid" middle class—a white-collar worker, like a bank teller. Unlike most working-class people of his day, who worked in factories, he had an office next to his boss, whose face and name he knew, and he likely would not have been fired during hard times.[31]

We learn from the Ghost of Christmas Past that Scrooge actually came from poverty. Consequently, like my grandparents who survived the depression, he wisely scrimped and saved to make sure he could get by. What Scrooge had failed to recognize—and one thing the ghosts teach him—was that he had finally made it. He no longer had to be such a penny pincher. Although he was not rich, he could afford to give some back.

To whom does Scrooge give back? Most notably, he gives to Cratchit—a turkey for Christmas dinner, a raise in his salary, and some coal for the fire. Scrooge learns the value of downward wealth distribution to those just underneath his social class with whom he interacts on a daily basis.[32]

But *A Christmas Carol* also contains a lesson about giving to the poor. Recall the scene in the first chapter when two of Scrooge's social betters come to his counting house collecting for the poor.

> "At this festive season of the year, Mr. Scrooge," said the gentleman, taking up a pen, "it is more than usually desirable that we should make some slight provision for the Poor and Destitute, who suffer greatly at the present time. Many thousands are in want of common necessaries; hundreds of thousands are in want of common comforts, sir."[33]

Although Scrooge himself is not that rich, he does voice a sentiment that was common among the rich of Dickens's time. He expresses a sarcastic worry that these gentlemen's collection efforts must mean that all the programs for the poor he supports with his taxes—the prisons, the union workhouses—must no longer be in operation. The gentlemen assure him that they are in operation; they are collecting additional funds because such programs "scarcely furnish Christian cheer of mind or body to the multitude...."[34] Scrooge refuses to give, and when the gentlemen point out that many would rather die than go to the aforementioned establishment that Scrooge supports with his taxes, Scrooge insists that "they had better do it, and decrease the surplus population."[35]

His words are thrown back at him later on in the story by the Ghost of Christmas Present, when Scrooge meets Tiny Tim:

> "Spirit," said Scrooge, with an interest he had never felt before, "tell me if Tiny Tim will live." "I see a vacant seat," replied the Ghost, "in the poor chimney-corner, and a crutch without an owner, carefully preserved. If these shadows remain unaltered by the Future, the child will die." "No, no," said Scrooge. "Oh, no, kind Spirit! Say he will be spared!" "If these shadows remain unaltered by the Future, none other of my race," returned the Ghost, "will find him here. What then? If he be like to die, he had better do it, and decrease the surplus population."[36]

Later Scrooge notices what look like claws protruding from the Spirit's robe that turn out to be the hands of two "wretched, abject, frightful, hideous, miserable" children:

> "Spirit, are they yours?" Scrooge could say no more.

> "They are Man's," said the Spirit, looking down upon them. "And they cling to me, appealing from their fathers. This boy is Ignorance. This girl is Want. Beware them both, and all of their degree, but most of all beware this boy, for on his brow I see that written which is Doom, unless the writing be erased. Deny it!" cried the Spirit, stretching out its hand towards the city. "Slander those who tell it ye. Admit it for your factious purposes, and make it worse. And abide the end."

> "Have they no refuge or resource?" cried Scrooge.

> "Are there no prisons?" said the Spirit, turning on him for the last time with his own words. "Are there no workhouses?"[37]

Dickens himself was an adamant critic of unchecked capitalism and a fierce proponent for the poor. He lived in a time before child labor laws, minimum wages, 40-hour work weeks, and many other worker protections that we take for granted. In the pure unregulated capitalistic society in which he lived, unemployment and poverty were rampant, and people who did work often worked too many hours for only pennies a day while the rich enjoyed lavish wealth. The gap between the rich and poor was enormous, and there was a lot of social unrest as a result. According to Dickens, it was everyone's responsibility to reconcile these ills. As the ghost of Scrooge's old business partner Marley tells him, after Scrooge says he was a "good man of business":

> Business[?].... Mankind was my business. The common welfare was my business; charity, mercy, forbearance, and benevolence, were, all, my business. The dealings of my trade were but a drop of water in the comprehensive ocean of my business![38]

At the end of the story, Scrooge adopts this philosophy. He sees the two gentlemen and pledges to their charity an amount of money that is undisclosed but makes the gentlemen gawk in amazement.

> "Lord bless me!" cried the gentleman, as if his breath were taken away. "My dear Mr. Scrooge, are you serious?"

"If you please," said Scrooge. "Not a farthing less. A great many back-payments are included in it, I assure you...."

"My dear sir," said the other, shaking hands with him. "I don't know what to say to such munifi[cence]."[39]

Yet Scrooge does not learn to give gifts to his family; he learns that Christmas is a time for spending with one's family, as he comes to accept his nephew's invitation to Christmas dinner. But he does not give them gifts. Instead, Scrooge learns to give gifts to the poor.

And so, it turns out, to heed my advice does make one more like Scrooge, but not the Christmas-hating Scrooge at the beginning of the story. Giving fewer gifts to one's own family and more gifts to charity makes one like the reformed Scrooge, who thinks that Christmas is for spending time with your family and for showing generosity and charity to the poor. That is a label I would proudly embrace.[40]

How This Myth Has Hijacked the Holiday

AD FROM EVENING POST, DECEMBER 1935. IMAGE COURTESY OF THE NATIONAL LIBRARY OF NEW ZEALAND.

The myth that Christmas spending is good for the economy has hijacked the holiday by making us feel obligated to spend. Regardless of whether a gift is really needed, regardless of whether we can afford it, regardless of whether it threatens to spoil our children, we feel we must spend, spend, spend because it's good for the economy. It's not. At best the effect of Christmas spending is economically neutral; in reality, Christmas spending is most likely bad for the economy. It turns the economy upside down, inflates the credit bubble and creates deadweight loss. There is so much more good we could be doing with the money we spend at Christmas—everything from repairing our infrastructure to feeding the poor. It's up to us to change.

Some may want to blame business and retailers for the commercialization of Christmas and the obligation to buy gifts. After all, they are the ones running Christmas ads in October, playing Christmas music in November, and opening up their stores on Thanksgiving. But they wouldn't do these things if they were not profitable. (And we can't blame them for trying to make money. That is what businesses do.) And these things are profitable because of the way that we respond to them. We buy the things ads tell us to buy; we spend more when we hear Christmas music; and we line up on Thanksgiving for those door buster sales. You may think that the only way you can afford all the Christmas gifts you have to buy—but do you really have to buy them?

The myth that Christmas spending is good for the economy goes a long way in driving this behavior. But so does the idea that we must buy gifts for our children at Christmas in the name of Santa Claus. After all, wasn't that what the goodly St. Nicholas did—on whom Santa is based? Well, it turns out, that's a myth too. Not only did St. Nicholas likely not give gifts to children, but neither is he the historical ground of the Santa myth...and who Santa really is, *is gonna blow your socks off*!

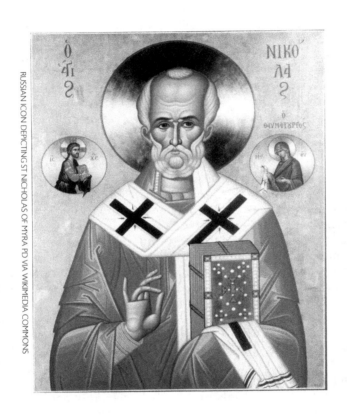

Santa Claus Is St. Nicholas

IN DECEMBER OF 2013, ALISHA HARRIS WROTE AN article for *Slate.com* in which she argued that Santa Claus should no longer be thought of, or portrayed, as white.[1] As an African American, Alisha was confused and made uncomfortable by a white Santa as a child—after all, he didn't look like any Santa displayed in her house. Instead, she suggested we change Santa from a white male to something more neutral and universally lovable—like a penguin.[2] Fox News's Megyn Kelly was having none of it.[3] She assured the world's children that "Santa just is white" and argued that fact shouldn't—and couldn't—be changed. Santa is white, she insisted, because (like Jesus) the historical St. Nicholas is white and "You can't take facts, and then try to change them to fit some sort of a political agenda or sensitivity agenda."[4] Later Bill O'Reilly came to Megyn's aid by presenting a history of Santa that traced back to St. Nicholas, and declaring the revered saint was indeed white.[5]

Ironically, the picture of St. Nicholas that Bill showed had brown skin.[6] As we will see shortly, this is likely more historically accurate.[7] Neither Jesus nor Nicholas would have been white. But this is not the only misconception that Megyn and Bill's arguments fed. Like most, they think:

Santa Claus is just an Americanization of an historical figure: the Turkish Bishop, St. Nicholas of Myra. The historical figure was renowned for his generosity, especially to children, and delivered gifts to them often. After he died, others continued the tradition in

his name, delivering gifts to children on Christmas.
The tradition changed forms over the years, and once
it reached America we commercialized it. But it all
traces back to the original "Santa Claus": the his-
torical figure St. Nicholas.

As I am sure you have guessed by now, everything in bold above is false. And it's not just that Santa Claus is not based wholly on St. Nicholas; he is not based on him *at all*. It's not, of course, that they have nothing in common—they do have a little bit. But that's only because they are both based on another fictional character. And that's not the entire story either—many of the historical assumptions about St. Nicholas in the bolded paragraph are likely false as well. Given my research, not one iota of it is true.

It's worth noting, however, that research about Santa is difficult to do. The origins of myths and traditions are hard to find because speculation about them is *not* hard to find. When people don't know where a tradition comes from, they invent their own explanation; it gets passed down through the generations, and eventually it's in a book as fact—and this is especially true for Santa. There are, for example, many different explanations of why Santa drops through chimneys, all incompatible, but all from fairly reliable sources. Then there is the difficulty presented by the wide variety of traditions that exist. Today, Santa has a uniform look because we have a mass media system that sells us one image. Before mass media, however, "Santa" traveled mainly by oral tradition, and changed roles, looks, and names radically, depending on which community he found himself in.

For this reason, in writing this chapter, I was very careful to lay out the reasons for my conclusions and the confidence level that I have (or don't have) in them. You may not agree with all my conclusions, but you will undoubtedly agree that the history of Santa Claus is absolutely like nothing you previously assumed—or could have imagined.

Santa Claus Is Not St. Nicholas

The assumption that Santa Claus "is" St. Nicholas is nearly universal. After all, "St. Nick" is just another of Santa's names. But when you stop to think about it, the suggestion doesn't make much sense. Go read "'Twas the Night before Christmas," and ask yourself: *What historical saint ever wore fur, looked like a ped-*

dler, and entered houses through chimneys? What saint ever had twinkly eyes, merry dimples, rosy cheeks and a cherry nose? What saint was known for being chubby and plump and shaking like a bowl full of jelly? What historical saint was an elf—yes, in the poem, St. Nick is a tiny elf—and was whisked around the sky in a tiny sleigh like a hurricane by flying reindeer named after elemental powers like thunder (Donder) and lightning (Blitzen)? As Phyllis Siefker asks, "Why weren't they named Faith, Hope, and Charity? Why wasn't Santa's ride one of righteousness, tranquility, and somber hope, instead of a wild comet ride, an unleashing of powers with undertones of chaos?"[8] We know that the St. Nick of the poem eventually became known as Santa Claus, but the similarities between the historical St. Nicholas and the St. Nick of the poem don't go much beyond the name. So tracing Santa Claus back to the historical St. Nicholas doesn't offer much in terms of an explanation.

ST. NICHOLAS PROVIDING DOWRIES, BICCI DI LORENZO © PD

Of course, you might be thinking, what about the gift-giving in the poem? Wasn't St. Nicholas a gift-giver too? Maybe you even know "the story of the three daughters." A poor father with three daughters was going to have to sell his daughters into prostitution because he could not afford their dowry. The wealthy St. Nicholas got wind and slipped a bag of gold into the father's house. When the father proved trustworthy by using it as a dowry to marry off the oldest daughter, Nick did it again. The father caught him the third time, but Nick made him promise not to tell anyone it was him. (I guess he broke his promise.)

But the problem with appealing to this story is, despite the fact that it has no supernatural elements, we really have no good reason for thinking anything remotely like this happened to the historical St. Nicholas. Truth be told, even according to the Catholic Church, all we "know" about St. Nicholas is that *he was a Bishop, from Myra (in modern Turkey), in the fourth century*.[9] That's it! All other tales and stories of St. Nicholas, including the one above, are almost universally agreed to be folklore.

Why? Numerous reasons, but one is that Nicholas's stories can be found in non-Christian myths that predate him. For example, Nicholas supposedly remained chaste all his life (though celibacy was not required of Catholic clergy until about the 1100s). He also supposedly gave away all his worldly possessions, saved a condemned man from death by intervening in his trial, and sometimes appeared in two locations at once. But all of these things were also supposedly true of the Pythagorean philosopher Apollonius, according to the Greek writer Philostratus, who wrote a century before Nicholas would have been born. There is even a story about Apollonius providing dowries for three daughters of a poor father. Nicholas's version of the story is "Christianized" a bit—concern for the daughters is shown, not just the father—but it is very clearly the same story, with a few added elements.[10] Obviously, Philostratus is the source of these stories, not St. Nicholas's life.

This hasn't stopped numerous people from writing about what St. Nicholas's life would have been like. The most recent is William Bennett's book *The True Saint Nicholas*.[11] But it is only speculation based on what we know regarding the time and place in which he would have lived. So the historical St. Nicholas still remains a mystery and thus provides us with no good explanation for Santa Claus.

To make matters worse, we may not "know" anything about St Nicholas at all. There is no good reason for thinking that St. Nicholas actually, historically, existed. In fact, we have pretty good reason for thinking that he didn't. The first historical mention of him is in 440—about a hundred years after his supposed death. If that mention had laid out some historical facts, or maybe a Nicholas epistle or treatise, then the historicity of Nicholas would be in good shape. But it didn't. Instead, it was loaded with miraculous stories that we know are legend.[12] The first biography of Nicholas doesn't show up until the 700s, and we have no idea where the author got his information.[13] And then there is the fact that multiple locations have simultaneously claimed to have his remains.[14] That would be pretty hard if Nicholas actually had remains, but if he didn't, because he never existed, that wouldn't be too surprising.[15] Not to mention that the forgery of documents and relics (including the bones of non-existent saints) was quite common in the Middle Ages.

There is one "tack" in history with Nicholas's name on it. Tradition holds that he attended the Council of Nicaea in 325, but it doesn't look like this is actually true. Copies of the "roll" they took exist, but only three of the eleven bear Nicholas's name.[16] So he was either there and his name was removed, or he wasn't there and his name was later added. Which is it?

Well, when the church "preserved" writings throughout the Middle Ages, they did so by having monks copy them. It was quite common for monks to add things they thought "should" be included to what they were copying. (For example, it is well known that they added information about Jesus into the works of the Jewish historian Flavius Josephus; for some reason, this Jewish historian didn't include the fact that Jesus was the messiah in his lone paragraph about Jesus.[17]) If a monk copying the Council of Nicaea roll in the Middle Ages knew Nicholas lore, happened to put the dates together, and realized that Nicholas "should" have been at the Council of Nicaea, that monk would not have thought twice about adding his name. So this seems likely—certainly more likely than Nicholas's name being inexplicably removed from the roll.

There is a story that supposedly accounts for why Nicholas's name was removed. It suggests that, while at the council, Nicholas struck another bishop—Arius—for professing (what were soon to be) unorthodox views about Jesus's divinity. Consequently, Nicholas was defrocked and thus taken off the roll. Now, if this story predated knowledge of the discrepancies in the roll, it might hold some water. But records of the council were kept, and no official record of this incident exists. In fact, the story is relatively new.[18] So it seems much more likely that it was concocted as a just-so story to explain away Nicholas's absence from the roll. In addition, it is unlikely Nicholas would have been left to keep his hand after striking someone in the emperor's presence, but Nicholas is not known for a missing hand.[19]

That St. Nicholas never existed would not be a novel realization. Numerous saints, who were recognized before the Catholic Church developed an official "saint recognition" system, have been determined to have never existed. This is the result of the Bollandists, a Jesuit group of scholars, who were set with the task of authenticating ancient saints. In 1969, based on their findings, the Catholic Church dropped more than 40 saints from their calendar and declared that the feast days of 90 or so saints were optional.[20] It is impossible to find a compiled list that delineates which saints the Bollandists declared "non-historical" and which they declared "mostly-mythical." My guess is that the "dropped/optional" divide reflects something along those lines. But even the world's "Largest List of Saints" is almost silent on the subject, and only mentions a couple of defrocked saints by name.[21] Two "biggies," St. Christopher and St. Valentine, were dropped and, from what I can tell, are thought to have never existed—although their "cults" were not completely repressed and became confined to specific locals. (Others' cults, like St. Ursula's, were repressed.[22]) St. Nicholas's feast was declared optional, but Catholics are very careful to clarify that they still think he exists.[23] From what I can tell, this is merely because he is so popular, not because of any solid evidence.

Fictional saints are common because, before the official system was put in place, popular opinion determined sainthood—and the populace loved to make saints. In addition, the church often liked to "saint" existing pagan gods. We will see more on this shortly. In fact, we will see good reason to suspect that St. Nicholas was invented in exactly this way—by a pagan god, with a very similar name, being appropriated and sainted.

But the thing is, even if St. Nicholas really existed, and even if the three daughters story was attributed to him because he was a generous guy—he didn't give gifts annually, ride in a sleigh, have a giant white beard and a red suit, smoke a pipe, wear fur, live at the North Pole, or own flying livestock. At best, Nicholas and Santa Claus have two things in common: part of their name, and generosity. So, again, tracing Santa back to the "historical" St. Nicholas does little in terms of explaining the jolly old elf.

St. Nicholas Gets a Few More Tricks

We've just seen really good reason for thinking that St. Nicholas never existed. But the people of the Middle Ages didn't know any better, and Nicholas was one of the most popular saints ever. Not only was he the patron saint of sailors, but also of children, merchants, pawnbrokers, penitent thieves, archers, and prostitutes (yes, prostitutes have a saint...and it's "Santa Claus"). Of course, none of the stories that make him a patron are authentic; Nicholas was just a magnet for miraculous stories. But pretty soon, people believed that he would return from heaven on December 6, the supposed anniversary of his death, to deliver gifts, often riding on a white horse or donkey. Now we are getting somewhere! This sounds a bit more like Santa Claus. But why did people start believing these things about Nicholas? From where did these traditions come?

We find the answer in paganism. Converting pagans wasn't easy. Even if you converted their leaders, the general pagan population would continue their old festivals and worship their old gods. ("God bless those pagans."[24]) So, just like it did with Christmas, the Catholic Church turned to the old "adopt and adapt" method. Pagan gods were turned into Christian saints so that praying to them could be "Christian." Demeter became St. Demetrios, Mars became St. Martin. The list is extensive. This is one reason why so many Catholic saints have been declared

non-historical. But finding overlap between St. Nicholas and pagan gods will not only help answer our questions about the origin of Santa. The more similarities we find, the more reason we will have for thinking that Nicholas is just a Catholic appropriation of a pagan god, instead of an historical figure.

One such overlap we have already seen is the stories of Apollonius. Another great example is found in Nicholas's seafaring miracles. He is the patron saint of sailors, and was said to have rescued sailors from all sorts of trials: walking on water, calming storms, and even appearing on board and helping with sailing duties. But these miracles mirror, quite precisely, those of the sea gods Poseidon, Neptune, and the Teutonic (German) god Hold Nickar.[25] Temples to these gods (and the clergy that ran them) were even appropriated by the church and renamed for Nicholas.

Looking for parallels to St. Nicholas's more "Santa-like" qualities, we find the Norse god Odin. The Norse were warriors, and Odin was too—a great warrior, with a great big white beard. The Norse also lived up north where it was cold, and when they locked themselves inside during blizzards in December, it would sound like all hell was breaking loose outside—and that is what they believed. The sounds they heard were Odin, returning to earth, with dead warriors in tow, rampaging through the countryside. (These beliefs would eventually help create Halloween.) And as they did this, Odin rode an eight-legged white horse named Sleipnir.[26]

This may account for St. Nicholas's December visiting, but what about the gift giving? One of the spirits believed to accompany Odin was a goddess, often called Berchta. She would visit your house bestowing either blessings or curses. Homeowners would leave out food, and oats for her horse, to influence her decision. In Scandinavia, the traditions combined and become more concrete; Julebuk, who was said to be Odin, would visit and deliver actual physical presents to the children (not just a "blessing" on the household). This all went down at New Years, but when the northerners adopted the Roman calendar, the whole shebang got moved to December 6.[27] This, of course, would later become St. Nicholas Day, which commemorates his death. (Notice that the date we observe St. Nicholas's death does not trace back to a historical record of when he died, but instead finds its origin in pagan practices—yet another reason to doubt his historical existence.) On this day, Nicholas would eventually be believed to return to earth to decide whether children were good enough to deserve his gifts. The children, of course, would leave out oats for his horse to influence his decision—a clear precursor to milk and cookies.

As far as I can tell, the December visiting didn't get tacked onto Nicholas lore until the 1100s, when a group of French nuns decided to give gifts to children on December 6 in St. Nicholas's name.[28] Now, why did they do this? Gift giving has been a part of holiday celebrations since the beginning (at least two thousand years before Christ), and it was a particularly big part of the Roman Kalends (New Year's) celebrations. So the nuns may have simply been giving their saint something "holidayish" to do. Or perhaps they got the idea from Apollonius's three daughters story, which seems to have been attached to St. Nicholas lore in the 700s.[29] The answer might also be found in the aforementioned Hold Nickar, who was also believed to annually distribute blessings to his worshipers during the winter solstice.[30] It's hard to tell.

Presuming that Santa finds some of his origins in the St. Nicholas lore, however, we now have some good ideas as to where Santa gets the gift giving and the December visiting. And an eight-legged white horse at least gives us a starting point for explaining eight tiny reindeer. But this still only accounts for a few of Santa's attributes. And, in all honesty, we still may not know where St. Nicholas comes from. The first mention of St. Nicholas is in the fifth century, but the Norse and their gods weren't being Christianized until about the eighth century. Fortunately there is much more to the story—and it just gets crazier.

Santa's Naughty Side

Do a Google image search for "Santa postcards" and you will stumble across some very odd pictures indeed—pictures of old European postcards depicting the "jolly" old saint Nicholas, holding children down, tying them to trees, whipping the hell out of them with birch rods, or even stuffing terrified children into sacks. John Grossman has a wonderful collection of them in his book *Christmas Curiosities: Odd, Dark, and Forgotten Christmas*.[31]

In Europe, St. Nick was a punisher. As you can see on the next page, this image survived through at least the early 1900s: the top postcard is from the 1890s, the bottom from 1907.

I've heard of getting coal in your stocking for being bad, but this is ridiculous! Sorry for the cliché—although I guess the ominous threats do make a bit more sense now. "No crying. No pouting! He sees you at all times! He'll know if you've been bad, so be good for goodness sake!" The song doesn't make much sense if the worst thing that can happen is a lump of coal. But if *Santa's gonna beat your ass...*

How did St. Nicholas get into whipping and sack stuffing? It's a bit complicated! At first this might seem unrelated, but hear me out.

The story starts with one of the first gods that ancient people worshiped. (History about religious traditions that go back this far are hard to verify, but this god may have even been the very first.) Evidence of human belief in this god goes back 50,000 years (long before Abraham would have been born), and he appears in one of the very first written stories, the *Epic of Gilgamesh*. It is a god Phyllis Siefker calls "the Wild Man."[32] The Wild Man was an untamed half-man half-beast creature that was believed to live in the wild. The half beast part of him was usually a goat, which meant that he often had horns, hairy legs, and hoofs. He was also believed to have grandiose powers

A Merry Christmas

over nature (thunder and lightning were often associated with him) and powers over fertility, which gave him powers over the bountifulness of crops and even the fertility of people.

In fact, it was believed that the Wild Man was "one" with nature. Now, when winter arrived every year, it seemed that the earth was dying, and the ancients would have had no way of knowing whether it would revive again. But, it seems, the ancients reasoned that if the Wild Man were to die and be revived—given his "oneness" with nature— such an act would ensure that nature itself would be revived and that spring would return. Thus a custom was developed. First, the Wild Man would be captured, often using a young girl as bait—he was a fertility god after all. He would be chained up and lead out of the wild and in through the streets of the town or village, to the square. Once there, he would be killed. Then a "healer" would come along and revive him. Everyone would celebrate, for that meant that spring would return. Lastly, the Wild Man would be set free, back into the wild.

Of course, the Wild Man didn't really exist and no

"healer" back then had the ability to revive anything. What was actually happening is that someone would dress up as the Wild Man—donning furs, horns, and such—and go hide in the forest. The townspeople would pretend to capture him, chain him up, and put on this big show parading him through town. It's unclear how many of the adults were in on the act, but I'm sure the children were scared to death. The sounds of the chains alone, rattling through town, must have been horrifying. We don't know how widespread this practice was, or how far back it dates. But we do know that both the parents and children of those who did participate (regardless of whether they knew it was just a person in dress up) did believe in the power of the play. To them, these events really did ensure the return of spring.

These traditions were often very sexual. This makes sense, given the ritual's association with spring. The Wild Man would carry a phallus or pitchfork, or some other sign of fertility, threatening townsfolk with it or with sexual gestures. Often, he would have sex with the young girl right in the town's square—sometimes playacting, other times literally. Then he would be killed—again, sometimes playacting, other times literally. If he was playacting, his resurrection was easy to accomplish. But if he was literally killed, it was his offspring, now residing in the pregnant girl, that was thought to represent his "revival."

According to Siefker, the Wild Man seems to show up in the origins of almost every religion in the world: Egyptian, Babylonian, Roman.[33] My favorite example is from Greece. You are probably familiar with Pan, the little horned god with goat legs who plays the flute. Given my description, you can probably figure out for yourself that Pan finds his origins in the Wild Man; but what you likely don't know is that Pan was originally the only god the Greeks had. He was "the All." It was later that the Greeks personified the different aspects of the All, and created other gods, like Eros and Apollo, and Pan got moved down the list. But Pan was the original.[34]

And this is just the beginning of the Wild Man's seeming influence and effect on society. The Mesopotamian, Persian, and Babylonian traditions that we talked about while debunking Myth #1, of killing a king to ensure the return of spring, likely find their origin here. Almost every society has some kind of dying/resurrecting god: the Greek Osiris, the Babylonian Tammuz, and later the Christian Jesus. They are all likely influenced by the Wild Man tradition. The Wild Man may have also gone on to become Robin Hood, Harlequin, and even the "fool on Parade." In fact, the very idea of a parade likely finds its origins in the Wild Man tradition. But what seems most established is that the Wild Man also became Santa Claus, and probably St. Nicholas too.

Santa's Wild Side

We see the most obvious connection between Santa Claus and the Wild Man in the north. The annual visits of Odin, Berchta, and Julebuk most likely find their origin in the annual appearance of the Wild Man. Recall, it was believed that Julebuk actually appeared physically, bestowing gifts upon children. In reality, someone annually dressed up as Julebuk by donning a horned mask[35]—clearly reminiscent of the Wild Man tradition, in which someone would annually don furs and horns to play the part of the Wild Man. Since these traditions got laid upon St. Nicholas, and Nicholas later became Santa Claus, the connection between the Wild Man and Santa is pretty clear. But that story is also a bit too simple.

As we have seen, the Wild Man tradition did influence and branch off into other things, but it also survived—pretty much in its original form—throughout the Middle Ages (and even

DIE ANSICHTSKARTE ZEIGT DEM KIND DER NIKOLO FÜR BRAVE KINDER, WER NIKOLO UND KRAMPUS SIND, DER KRAMPUS HOLT DIE KLEINEN ZÜNDER.

THIS POSTCARD, FROM 1899, ABOVE, DEPICTS ST. NICHOLAS WITH THE CHRIST CHILD (IN WINGS) AND HIS "HELPER" (AT THE DOOR) IN TOW. NOTICE THE BOYS HIDING UNDER THE TABLE: THEY'VE BEEN BAD. COURTESY, THE WINTERTHUR LIBRARY: THE JOHN AND CAROLYN GROSSMAN COLLECTION.

into the 1900s, in a few isolated places). As you can imagine, this did not sit well with Catholic clergy who were trying to convert pagans. And the people were not only worshiping this god, but they would dress up like him and parade around. The church tried to outlaw such practices, but it didn't work. Even when they converted the leaders of the community, the populace still followed the old gods and partook in the old traditions. But, if you can't beat 'em, join 'em, right? So the church again turned to the old "adopt and adapt" method.

One way they attempted this was by equating the Wild Man with Satan. Up through the 500s, when Satan was given a physical form in art, he was usually depicted as a fallen angel.His appearance differed from other angels not at all, apart from the fact that he was, literally, falling. He was also occasionally depicted as a serpent, or dragon. But he wasn't depicted as we think of him today until the early 600s, when Pope Gregory officially equated the appearance of Satan with the appearance of the Wild Man. Ever since, Satan has been depicted as a horned, furry goat-legged beast with a pitchfork. But not even this really kept people from worshiping and dressing up like the Wild Man character. The populace often didn't "really" convert, and usually weren't too concerned with what the church said the Wild Man really was. And to stay in the populace's good graces, priests, who were often converts from the same pagan religions, would indulge their "followers" and allow them to partake in the old practices.

In fact, the Wild Man even got a boost from the church's efforts to supplant village plays. Disgusted by the debauchery of medieval village plays, the church put on its own plays that depicted Bible stories and the myths of saints, hoping to draw public attention away from the secular. But just like today, when the church attempts to seem hip and relevant by adopting popular forms of entertainment—think "Christian Rock"— the public thought the plays were lame and ignored them. To spruce them up, the church added comic relief in the form of the devil, who would often enter the stage spouting his comedic catch phrase, "Ho, Ho, Hoh." Although he was "the bad guy," the public loved him. (Compare this to how The Joker and Darth Vader are often people's favorite character, despite the fact that they're the bad guys.) The plays became more popular, but so did the Wild Man/Devil.

But the most relevant way the church tried to depose the Wild Man was by making him the slave (or "sidekick") of a saint.[36] Recall that, in the Middle Ages, it came to be believed that St. Nicholas would return to earth on the anniversary of his death, December 6. But, although his visits would involve gifts, his main role in the Middle Ages was as a disciplinarian.[37] In many traditions, he would show up at your door and quiz you on your religious knowledge; if you failed you were punished, and if you passed he would give you a small gift.[38] And parents wouldn't just pretend that St. Nicholas dropped by while the kids were asleep. Nicholas (that is, someone dressed up like Nicholas) would physically appear at your house. And if you weren't up to snuff, you might get your just deserts right there. Again, it's unclear whether the parents were "in on it"—most of them were illiterate and only knew what the church told them. If the church sent someone and said it was Saint Nicholas, they would probably have believed it. Regardless, the children were scared out of their gourd. Clearly, the current "Mall Santa" is a remnant of this dress up tradition, and the ancient Wild Man parades were a precursor. Today, someone dressed as St. Nicholas still appears at people's houses in Europe.

But in what way would St. Nicholas punish you? In tow, held back by chains, Nicholas would have a "companion"—a sidekick—a demonic "goat-man," complete with horns, hooves, and furry legs and body. It was the Wild Man! What better way to "depose" this ancient Pagan god?

If you displeased the saint, he would release the chains and let the Wild Man dispense his punishments on you. What punishments? The pre-World War I post cards on this page, from Monte Beauchamp's 2004 book *The Devil in Design*, give us some ideas. Not only would he whip naughty chil-

dren with his birch rods, but he might also pick them up by the ears. He could also stuff them into the bottomless basket he carried on his back. And, perhaps worst of all, he might add the naughty children to his chains and lead them away to hell! As you can imagine, a visit from St. Nicholas and his helper was not always something to which children looked forward.

So, it seems that in this December 6 tradition, two myths came together—the St. Nicholas myth, and the Wild Man myth—to form one tradition. But looks can be deceiving. The Wild Man predates St. Nicholas, and St. Nicholas is hardly ever seen without him. The Wild Man's first appearances with St. Nicholas are very early—so early that some, like Siefker, claim when St. Nicholas first appeared, he already had the Wild Man in tow. Regardless, as the tradition continued, the two were often inter-

In case you need more evidence that Krampus is based on the Wild Man, you can see Krampus' ties to the old fertility god on which he is based in these postcards.
FROM THE DEVIL IN DESIGN: THE KRAMPUS POSTCARDS ©2004 BY MONTE BEAUCHAMP.
USED WITH SPECIAL PERMISSION.

changeable and continually took on each other's characteristics. So much so that, in Germany, the Wild Man character was often called Nicholas, and "Old Nick" became another German name for the devil. Is it just a coincidence that St. Nicholas is the only saint that people dress up as and pretend to be, like people used to do with the Wild Man? It's hard to tell if two traditions became one, or if one tradition became two.

So here we see one final reason to suspect that St. Nicholas was not historical, but instead was, just like so many other saints, an appropriated pagan god. Long before St. Nicholas was around, the Wild Man actually had names. He was often called "Claus," and depending on his look or purpose, other descriptions were added. If he were more human, he would be called "man Claus." "Ru Claus" was the "rough Claus."[39] The Wild Man tradition was popular in Germany, and St. Nicholas was first mentioned in the 400s, about a century into the "Christianization" of the German peoples. And in Germany, "Nick" is not short for "Nicholas." They usually don't use the first part of the name, they use the last. Today, if you lived in Germany, and your name was "Nicholas," your nickname would probably be "Claus." (It's hard to realize why with an American accent. Pronounce it like "louse"—"Ru Clouse" and "Nick-Clouse.") In fact, according to Siefker, the wild man was often called Nocholas in some places in Germany. So, if you sainted the Wild Man, who was named "Claus," and called him by his full name—as you would likely do, since he is now a saint—you would call him "St. Nicholas." (This also explains why Germans sometimes call the devil "Old Nick"—for that purpose, they choose to use the first part of the Wild Man's name.)

But regardless of whether Nicholas was a historical saint who gained a servant, or he was just a "sainted Wild Man," he and the Wild Man remained the best of friends throughout the Middle Ages. They separated into distinct characters, but where you found one, you almost always found the other. And this provides us with a few more answers about Santa's origins. We now know the origin of Santa's bottomless sack of presents—it used to hold children—and from where the "lump of coal" punishment tradition comes. We also see the beginning of Santa being dressed in fur, since the Wild Man was covered in goat fur. We even heard the faint echo of Santa's catch phrase, "Ho, Ho, Ho." But these are all things that belonged to the Wild Man; how did they get transferred to Santa Claus?

How the Wild Man Became Santa Claus

The short answer is that St. Nicholas and the Wild Man combined, once again, into one character that shared attributes of both. This new character was human, like Nicholas, but wore fur, carried switches, and doled out punishment like the Wild Man. The Wild Man, as Nicholas's companion, had many names—"Hans Trapp," "Knecht Ruprecht," "Black Peter"[40] and my favorite "Krampus"—but Saint Nicholas just had the one name. So the name this new character took was "St. Nicholas" (or sometimes "Furry Nicholas"). And it was this character, after it became a bit more humanized, that become Santa Claus.

But, again, that short answer is far too simple.

For one, St. Nicholas did acquire other names—like the moniker "Kris Kringle." That was due to German Protestants trying to replace St. Nicholas as a holiday gift-giver, because he was a Catholic symbol. They thought the "Christ Child," or "Christkindel," would be more appropriate, and they moved the gift giving to Christmas Eve. The Christ Child was most often depicted as a young woman wearing a wreath of candles (an actual baby wouldn't be very effective as a gift giver), but the Christ Child's function was the same as Nicholas's and s/he would also be accompanied by some version of the Wild Man. But the Christ Child was too boring; people started throwing St. Nicholas into the mix again and he eventually took back the leading role. Finally, the Christ Child was just "phased out" of the tradition, leaving St. Nicholas with a new date to deliver gifts (December 24) and a new name, Kris Kringle.[41]

Now, the combination of the Wild Man and St. Nicholas helps explain why, in Europe, you sometimes see depictions of "St. Nicholas" beating the hell out of kids. So that's covered. But it doesn't really help explain the American Santa Claus that much. Our Santa doesn't beat people, and has a wealth of other attributes: chimney sliding, flying reindeer, living at the North Pole, etcetera. In addition, it doesn't really explain the Santa Claus Lie. After all, kids in the Middle Ages "saw" St. Nicholas show up, at their house. We just lie about that.

We find the beginnings of an explanation for these things in the Protestant Reformation. As we just saw with the Christ Child, Protestant reformers didn't have much love for the Catholic St. Nicholas. One such group of reformers was composed of Germans who settled in Pennsylvania. They didn't hate Christmas like the Puritans did, and they also, apparently, had a love for scaring their children into obedience. Thus, they created their own punishing Christmas visitor, named "Belsnickel."[42] If the European "Mean Nicholas" is St. Nicholas with some of the Wild Man's attributes, then Belsnickel is the Wild Man with some of St. Nicholas's attributes. As Belsnickel, the Wild Man took on some of St. Nick's human features and duties (like gift giving), and even part of his name. Among many of his other names was "Pelznichol," which literally means "Furry Nicholas." But even though his switches turned into a whip, and his rattling chains turned into huge bells, he remained the black beastly punisher he once was, bag, furs, and all. And, just like his predecessors, he would make actual physical appearances in people's houses.[43]

> ...Pelznichol, whip in hand, went from house to house with cookies and chestnuts, rewarding well-behaved children and frightening and whipping those who had been naughty. Their appearance varied, but they were always black faced and bell-jingling, dressed in animal skins or patches, and carrying a whip or bag...He [was] the precursor of the holy old elfe "Christkindel" or "St. Nicholas,...it is no sooner dark than [his] bell is heard flitting from house to house.... He would toss nuts on the floor, and when children tried to pick them up, he would strike their backs or hands with his whip.[44]

But how did Pelznichol become Santa Claus? How did his giant clanging bells become ringing sleigh bells? The setting for the explanation is already familiar. Recall from Myth #3 that, when Christmas made its comeback, an important Christmas tradition was wassailing, where servants would invade the homes of their masters and sing songs of well-wishing in exchange for the household's best food and drink.[45] After industrialization, and the widening of the gap between the rich and poor, this tradition took the form of the poor getting drunk, banding together, and wandering around demanding entrance into the houses of wealthy landowning strangers—and if they were refused entrance, things could get nasty. This was especially a problem in New York, and so some wealthy New Yorkers—among them Clement Clark Moore, John Pintard, and Washington Irving—set out to domesticate Christmas, turning it into a family-oriented holiday about staying indoors with your family.

Their efforts included, recall, the *invention* of domestic Christmas traditions that never existed but that they claimed

were authentically Dutch. One Dutch tradition that did exist was the St. Nicholas tradition, and they tried to introduce it to America as well. For example, St. Nicholas appears many times in Washington Irving's *Knickerbocker's History of New York*—a fictional pseudo-Dutch history of New York published on St. Nicholas's holiday (December 6). John Pintard also commissioned a broadside of St. Nicholas in 1810. But their Nicholas was too much like the original—too saintly—a staunch figure donning robes and brandishing a switch. So, although their work made Americans aware of St. Nicholas, it did not have much influence in establishing St. Nicholas as an annual December visitor outside their circle of friends (like the New-York Historical Society, or those that identified themselves as the Knickerbockers).

It was Clement Clark Moore's effort that succeeded in that regard and that turned Pelznichol into Santa. Recall that in his poem "A Visit from St. Nicholas" (which we know today as "'Twas the Night Before Christmas"), Moore intentionally drew parallels between St. Nicholas and the poverty-stricken people who showed up at his door at Christmas demanding libations and shouting threats. To contrast them, however, Moore has Nicholas demand nothing and threaten no punishments. Instead, he merely rewards children, expecting nothing in return, and then leaves. This new St. Nicholas was appealing both to the rich and the poor alike, especially given the new child-centered family philosophy that was arising, and this poem catching on domesticated the holiday as those like Moore wished.

Interestingly, the authorship of the poem is contested. Descendants of the Dutch author Henry Livingston Jr. claimed that they recalled him reading that poem at Christmas long before it was first published in the *Troy Sentinel* in 1823. In my opinion, Joe Nickel[46] and Seth Kaller[47] have decidedly settled this dispute in favor of Moore, and I won't rehash their points here.[48] But one important point in this debate helps us explain Santa's origins. If the poem had been written by Livingston, the poem would be decidedly more Dutch. But, as I pointed out at the beginning of this chapter, the St. Nicholas of the poem is nothing like the staunch religious saint that visited Dutch children in the mid-seventeenth century. Instead, the poem reads more like it is written by someone who is pretending to be Dutch because doing so was in line with their own political agenda. The author is borrowing Dutch traditions that he doesn't fully understand and that he gladly tweaks and adds to, to make the story into what he needs it to be. This describes Moore to a tee. Like his friend Pintard, and especially Washington Irving, Moore was very interested in inventing a pseudo-Dutch history for New York that would have made it more aristocratic.

So where did Moore get the elements that he added to the Dutch story?

Some of them were pulled almost directly from Irving's *Knickerbocker's History*, that we discussed in Myth #3, which (as I've mentioned) tried to invent exactly such a pseudo-Dutch history for New York. In it, Irving describes St. Nicholas as riding over the tops of trees in a wagon, smoking a pipe, and laying a finger beside his nose. These were additions by Irving. The Dutch St. Nicholas rode a horse, not in a wagon, and did not smoke.

The *finger aside his nose* gesture, that both Irving and Moore describe, was—at the time—a gesture that indicated the need to keep a secret.[49] "Let's keep this between the two of us." This may be were the Santa Claus lie originated. "We don't have a St. Nicholas actually to show up at the door like he used to," people likely reasoned. "We'll just tell the kids that he came while they were sleeping." (We'll talk more about that lie next chapter.)

Interestingly, Moore turned St. Nicholas's pipe into a "stump of a pipe" which clearly identified the St. Nicholas of the poem as lower class. At the time, the rich and well-to-do smoked pipes with long stems. The poor would buy the same pipes—they weren't expensive—but in defiance, they would break off most of the stem. Think of it like a fashion statement, like bending the bill of a brand new hat, or ripping or stonewashing a brand new pair of jeans. They didn't want to be like those rich bastards smoking a long pipe, and so they shortened theirs.

Moore wanted St. Nicholas to be lower class because he wanted him to reflect and yet redefine the poor ruffians who tried to get into his house every Christmas. But why was St. Nicholas so dirty? Why does he have a pack? Why is he dressed in fur from his head to his foot? Why is he a jolly old elf? And why is he fat and rosy?

He likely was fat and rosy because, according to Moore, he was modeled after a "portly, rubicund Dutchman" from his neighborhood.[50] He may have been an elf simply because the chimney was the only way he could get in without breaking into a house like Moore owned, and he had to be small enough to fit down the chimney. And this may be why he was dirty, too. But being dirty was something that he had in common with the Pennsylvania Germans' Belsnickel, as were his two most distinguishing characteristics, the fact that he was covered in fur, from head to foot, and the fact that he had a sack full of goodies to give to kids.[51] The Dutch St. Nicholas had neither of these attributes.)It's not clear to me whether he was familiar with the Belsnickel tradition through his heritage, or just through exposure, but it seems that it greatly influenced Moore's depiction of St. Nicholas's appearance.

If so, the most direct descendent of Santa Claus is Belsnickel, who finds his origins in the Wild Man. But Santa may have gotten some of his other attributes from other descendants of the Wild Man too. Recall the Wild Man was half goat, and was in charge of the forces of nature, like thunder and lightning. The Norse thunder god Thor rode a flying chariot that was pulled by magical goats named Gnasher and Cracker—that is, "thunder and lightning." Thor seems to have been partly derived from the Wild Man, and it is from Thor that Irving (who I believe was the first to do so) likely got the idea to give St. Nicholas a flying wagon. Also, "Donder and Blizten" is German for "Thunder and Lightning."[52] Moore likely got the idea for naming the reindeer from the Norse tradition, stole those two names, and then made up the rest.[53]

But how did we go from goats to tiny reindeer in the first place? Vincent Yzermans suggests that the sleigh and reindeer came from the lore of the Laplanders, who turned St. Nicholas into a shaman who they believed flew in sleighs drawn by flying reindeer.[54] Siefker, however, points out that the Laplanders' most important Christmas visitor was Stalo (another variation of the Wild Man). He had a sleigh, but it was pulled by Laplandish lemmings, and he was certainly not benevolent—

terrifying Laplanders through the twentieth century.[55] Lemmings are tiny, however; so maybe some combination of the two traditions produced "tiny reindeer pulling a tiny sleigh." The idea of a chimney entry could have come from any number of places,[56] but, again, another explanation for Santa's tininess could be that he had to be small enough to slip down the chimney. Who knows? Britain's Father Christmas, another offshoot of the Wild Man, had ten children who were led around by *Cupid*, and among them was Gambol the *dancer*.[57] So that could account for two more reindeer names. But all in all, although his name was St. Nicholas, the gift giver in the poem had almost nothing in common with the Christian saint. Instead he was mostly inspired by Wild Men of the past.

The Americanization of "St. Nick"

Of course, the St. Nick of the poem lacks many of our modern Santa Claus's attributes. He is an elf, not a full-grown person, and he only leaves small presents in stockings—nothing big, and nothing under the tree. And his name is not "Santa Claus," it's St. Nick. What's more, the poem says nothing about a red and white suit, the North Pole, Rudolph or Mrs. Claus. So from where did these traditions come?

It is commonly said that the name "St. Nicholas" became "Santa Claus" as a result of Americans butchering the Dutch pronunciation of what the Dutch called "St. Nicholas"—Sinterklass (translated "Saint Claus")—into "Santa Claus." That might be right. However, it's worth noting that, even if that is true, it happened long before Moore's famous poem. A year before the first publication of *A Visit from St. Nicholas* in 1822, another poem in *The Children's Friend* referred to him as "Olde Santeclaus." Another poem in the *New York Spectator* referred to him as "Sancte Claus," in 1810, and yet another (in *Rivingston's Gazetteer*) referred to him as "St. a Claus" in 1773.[58] It would be more accurate however, I think, to say that the names "Sinter-klass," "Saint Nicholas," and "Santa Claus" are all just different ways of expressing the original German concept of a saintly Wild Man: the "Saint Claus."

Some of the other traditions are easier to track down. His stature as a full-grown, rotund person owes the most to his depictions in *Harpers Weekly*. Thomas Nast was the main influence. His first depiction of Santa as full grown was in 1857.[59] Nast's full-grown Santa was delivering presents to Union soldiers in 1863, and was most lovable in 1881, when Nast de-

THOMAS NAST'S MOST FAMOUS DEPICTION OF SANTA AS A
FULL GROWN PERSON (NOT AN ELF) IN 1881. © PD

picted him as a full-grown man complete with a long pipe and
a white beard.

In the same year, Santa got married. Mrs. Claus was added
in 1881 by Margaret Eytinge's poem "Mistress Santa Claus"
and she was popularized in 1889 by Katherine Lee Bates's
poem "Goody Santa Claus on a Sleigh Ride." She saves the day
by knitting a stocking that won't hold its gifts.

Before 1931, Santa's fur suit had been red and white at
times, but that was only one of many color combinations that
he donned. In 1931, however, Coca-Cola launched an ad campaign that replaced Santa's pipe with a Coca-Cola bottle, and
solidified the color of Santa's suit into red and white—the colors of their company logo. From then on, if the plastic Santa on
your lawn didn't have a red fur suit, with white cuffs—it wasn't
Santa Claus![60]

Rudolph was added to the reindeer in a children's book marketing campaign by Montgomery Ward in 1939: "Shop at Mont-

gomery Ward, get a free copy of the children's booklet, 'Rudolph the Red Nosed Reindeer.'" It was almost an instant hit. In the gift department, Santa expanded beyond stuffing stockings due to capitalism. As Christmas grew in popularity, and businesses discovered there were profits to be had, they convinced us that we had to have more and more and bigger and bigger presents. They couldn't fit in the stocking anymore, so they had to go on, and then eventually under, the Christmas tree.

Why is Santa believed to live in the North Pole? Some claim that Thomas Nast was responsible, by depicting him as living there—for example, sitting atop a "Christmas box" bearing the address "North Pole" and spying on kids with a giant telescope from that location. Nast supposedly did this to make Santa a "citizen of the world."[61] But I am pretty sure that the tradition goes back further than that. The Norse believed that evil came not from "down below," but from "up north", where everything is nasty and cold. They believed that their version of the devil, who they also called Old Nick, was from the north. In addition, recall that the Laplanders live even further north than the Norse; it is likely that their Christmas visitor Stalo, evil as he was, was also believed to live at the North Pole.

The Wild Man Lives On

But Santa Claus is not the only surviving heir of the wild man. In places in Europe, St. Nicholas (not Santa Claus) still visits houses in person, and often has a version of the Wild Man in tow. (Just like before, it is this helper who is responsible for carrying out punishment.) In Austria, the helper's name is Krampus; he is especially terrible (and wonderful)—and has recently enjoyed a comeback.

Krampus is portrayed by young men wearing heavy fur from head to foot, hanging giant cow bells from their body, and donning horrific-looking horned masks. Today we would call them "demon" or "devil" masks, but of course we think they look like the devil only because the Wild Man was equated with the devil by Pope Gregory in the 600s. In reality, these are likely the most authentic modern representations of the ancient Wild Man. On *Krampusnacht* ("Krampus Night," December 5) these men will visit homes and businesses (sometimes with, sometimes without, St. Nicholas) and participate in *Krampuslauf* (a Krampus parade). Do a Google or YouTube search for any of these terms, or just "Krampus Austria." You won't be disappointed.[62]

After I became fascinated with Krampus in 2008, I started seeing him pop up, over and over, in American pop culture.

The first year I taught a course on Christmas, in 2009, the December issue of *National Geographic* had a short article about the Austrian Krampus and Krampus visited Stephen Colbert on Comedy Central's *The Colbert Report*.[63] In 2011, Anthony Bourdain helped create a Krampus animated short which was posted to YouTube.[64] In 2012, the artist and author Brom wrote a novel, with wonderful illustrations, in which Krampus kills and takes over for Santa Claus.[65] Also in 2012, Krampus's cousin Belsnickel appeared on NBC's *The Office*.[66] In 2013, *National Geographic* did a longer article,[67] Krampus was on the TV show *Grim*,[68] and the *Christian Science Monitor* did a piece about Krampus, mentioning the trend of "Krampus parties" that raise money for charity. (I think this would be a wonderful way to employ the lessons of last chapter, and reemphasize charitable giving at the holidays.[69]) Also in 2013, an episode of Seth MacFarlane's show *American Dad* stared Krampus. It did a wonderful job of pointing out that Krampus is not an evil character. Krampus only threatens to punish *wicked* children, and only so that they will turn from their evil ways. As the episode suggests, Krampus would be much more effective at this than Santa.[70]

References to Krampus was so plentiful in 2014, they deserve their own paragraph. The NCIS Christmas episode ("House Rules") had a cyber-terrorist villain named Krampus and Krampus hosted *Adult Swim*'s Christmas special marathon ("Kristmas with Krampus: An Adult Swim Krampathon"). *Last Gasp* did a short piece on how Krampusfests are popping up

Left: This very year for Krampuslauf, dozens of young men will dress up as Krampus and parade through the streets; some will be dragging the very fires of hell behind them to remind you where they might take you if you've been bad.
Right: The modern Krampus usually wields whips for punishing bad children (and parade onlookers) and giant bells to announce his presence. Like Santa's sleigh bells, Krampus's bells are derivative of the sounds the chains of the Wild Man would make during his parade through town. ARTIST: KING STIMIE.

Brom's novel, *Krampus: The Yule Lord*, includes brilliant renditions of its main characters, including this one of Krampus himself— complete with switches and a magic bottomless sack. For more, I highly recommend a visit to www.bromart.com.

From *Krampus: The Yule Lord* © 2012 Brom. Used with permission.

in the United States (in Los Angeles, San Francisco and Salt Lake City)[71] and the Austrian actor Christoph Waltz explained Krampus to Jimmy Fallon on *The Tonight Show* of December 16th. *The New York Times* (Munich Journal) did a piece on the resurrection of the Krampus tradition in Bavaria[72] and Michael Dougherty announced plans for a Christmas 2015 Krampus horror movie.[73]

The wonderfully ironic thing is both the demonic Krampus and jolly old elf Santa Claus find their origins in the same place: an ancient fur-wearing fertility god.

(In fact, just before the publication of this book, I learned of five major Krampus movies that either already exist or are in the works. There is Jason Hull's *Krampus: The Christmas Devil* (2013), Grant Harvey's *A Christmas Horror Story* (2015), Michael Daugherty's *Krampus* (2015), Kevin Smith's *Anti-Claus* (2016?) and Jason Hull's Krampus: *The Devil Returns* (2016)—which is apparently as sequel to aforementioned "*The Christmas Devil*".)

How This Myth Has Hijacked the Holiday

In this chapter, we've explained the "historical how"—the historical explanation for how we came to believe the myth that Santa is St. Nicholas. And we also now know, historically speaking, why we trick our children into believing that a giant fat man with a white beard in a red suit will visit on Christmas Eve, traveling from the North Pole, pulled by flying reindeer in a sleigh, delivering loads of presents upon the condition that the children behave. It is most likely not because of the influence of an historical Catholic saint. Instead, it is likely because of the influence of an ancient pagan god that often went by the name "Claus." And we fool our children into believing that he literally exists and visits while they are asleep because a poem about him, that depicted him secretly delivering presents to children, caught on like a fad in the early 1800s.

That fad practically became a religion. Nothing has hijacked the modern holidays more than the Santa Claus lie. Try telling someone that you tell your children the truth about Santa, and see what happens. You'll get the same reaction you'd get if you told a Christian that you don't believe in God. About the same amount of guilt would be laid upon you too—guilt, ironically, for *not* telling a lie. But this leads us to another question: has Santa hijacked the holiday in another way? Has he made Christmas worse? I believe he has. And how this chapter's myth—that Santa is St. Nicholas—has hijacked the holiday worst of all is by feeding and supporting next chapter's myth: that the Santa Claus lie is harmless.

"Luckies are easy on my throat"

There are no finer tobaccos than those used in Luckies, and Luckies' exclusive process is your throat protection against irritation...against cough

The Santa Claus
Lie Is Harmless

EVERY DECEMBER PARENTS ALL OVER THE WORLD convince their children that a large fat man in a red suit with rosy cheeks and a white beard will come bounding down the chimney to fill their stockings and place presents under the tree—but only if they're good and only if they're sleeping. In reality, of course, regardless of how they behave, they are rewarded. Ironically, spoiled brats seem to be most handsomely compensated. But this isn't just a fun game where we play pretend. We tell our children this entity really exists. He physically invades our house. And we encourage our children to believe this, literally, for as long as we can.

To keep them believing we retell his stories and twist ourselves into logical knots trying to explain how it is all possible. We assuage doubts with magical explanations and even concoct false evidence to convince them. We'll eat the cookies the children leave out or even leave boot prints from the chimney to the tree. The government's even in on it; your kid can track Santa's progress using NORAD at www.noradsanta.org. There is almost no length to which we won't go.

There's even an unspoken agreement between all parents not to ruin other children's naïveté. If a child ever earnestly asks for the truth, we have to just flat out lie: "Yes, Virginia, there is a Santa Claus." This agreement, arguably, has more force than many laws. You can lose your job for violating it[1] or even be forced to apologize on television for contradicting it.[2] It even enjoys a more protected status than religious belief.[3] In 2010, when the American Atheists posted a billboard outside the Lincoln Tunnel, depicting the nativity with the text "You know it's a myth. This season, celebrate reason," many didn't like it—but no one argued against their right to put up the billboard in the first place. But suppose I wanted to erect billboard depicting Santa Claus that simply read: "Stop lying to your children." Would anyone defend my freedom of speech? Would an agency even sell me space? If they did, would I not get death threats? Ironically, the thing that is most taboo to say is one of the few things that we all agree is true: "Santa doesn't exist."

We discovered last chapter where this tradition of lying to our children about Santa comes from. But it is generally held that this tradition is perfectly harmless.

....

Believing in Santa Claus, and eventually learning the truth, is simply a childhood rite of passage. Every child should believe it, every child does believe it, and there's nothing wrong and no harm in keeping them believing for as long as we can. In fact, it can even be good for children as the lie promotes imagination and creative play.

I am about to embark on the monumental task of convincing you that all of that is false, that indeed the Santa Claus lie is harmful, both to children and society, and should be avoided. I will not be arguing that we should eliminate the Santa Claus myth or remove it from Christmas; I will simply be arguing that we should stop encouraging our children to believe the myth is literally true—tricking them into believing that Santa Claus literally exists. To do this I am going to argue that (a) it is morally wrong because it's a lie, (b) that it constitutes bad parenting, (c) that it is damaging to children's critical thinking skills, and (d) that it doesn't encourage imagination. Along the way I'll address Francis Church's "Yes, Virginia" and I'll end by responding to a plethora of objections that have been lobbed at me ever since I first defended my argument publicly.[4]

Don't Fool Yourself—It's a Lie

Some parents insist that the Santa lie is not a lie at all. "Santa exists," I've heard adults profess, "he's my husband." But of course no one's husband lives at the North Pole, owns flying livestock, commands an army of woodworking elves, or has all-encompassing knowledge regarding the moral standing of every child in the world. So either those parents are lying about Santa's existence or they are lying about their husbands' address, live-stock, position on master–slave relations and cognitive abilities. Others might suggest that Santa exists because he is "the spirit of generosity that lives in us all." Of course, if this is what they told their children Santa actually was, they would not be lying. But they don't because it is impossible for an attitude, like generosity, to physically bound down the chimney, shake like a bowl full of jelly, and deliver presents—and that is the role they want Santa to play.

Others suggest that they aren't lying because they merely withhold the truth. "We just read *'Twas the Night* on Christ-mas Eve, label the gifts from Santa, place them under the tree, and let the kids draw their own conclusion." But, although this isn't technically a lie (i.e., a verbal utterance that is known by the speaker to be untrue), it is a form of deception. And the rea-son lying is wrong is because it is a form of deception. Of course parents know this. A teenager who says he was just hanging with friends at a party but leaves out the part where they were drinking alcohol is not technically lying; but he is engaged in a form of deception that his parents find morally reprehensible. "I didn't lie; I just didn't tell the whole truth" doesn't morally pardon parents any more than it does their children.

Now don't get me wrong, I'm not saying that lying is always wrong. Clearly some lies are justified. If an axe-wielding mur-derer shows up at your door looking for your friend, the mor-ally right thing to do would be to lie and say that your friend is at the police department across the street. In this case, the ends do justify the means. There are, what philosopher Plato called, "noble lies." I personally don't think the one he proposed to preserve the peace of his just society was one, but noble lies do exist. So the only question is, is the Santa Claus lie a noble lie? Well, it sure doesn't seem so. I mean, we shouldn't fool our-selves– we're not saving lives here.

Some might defend the Santa Lie in the name of creating a fun and exciting childhood Christmas experience. But even if the lie does accomplish this, it only does so by tricking children into believing what we think they want to believe—and usually we don't regard such acts as noble. We wouldn't like it if our government kept atrocities it committed from us, even though we might want to believe that our home nation is blameless. Cult leaders encourage false beliefs (and their followers usu-ally believe them) because they think it's better for them. But, again, we don't think that's noble. In general, we shouldn't lie to help people just believe what they want. Certainly, as a professor, I would be shortchanging my students if I led them to think that it was acceptable to believe whatever they wanted simply because they wanted to. I should be developing their skills for ascertaining the truth and accepting it. If you can just believe whatever you want, what's the purpose of education?

I'm only objecting to encouraging literal belief in Santa's reality and that's not what creates most of the fun and excitement. That honor goes to the presents. Give a child a choice between literally believing that St. Nicholas will arrive at their household and put candy and nuts in their shoe, or receiving lots of giant presents from their parents with full knowledge that Santa is not real, and what do you think they would choose? What would be more exciting? And if you really want some "Christmas awe"—how about including last chapter's hero, Krampus? In no way is literal belief in Santa necessary for possessing the "Christmas spirit." After all, we get that phrase from Dickens; wouldn't it be better if the Christmas spirit in children included them being generous—say, by giving to the poor—instead of being greedy?

Other parents may justify the lie in the name of the fun that they have watching their children on Christmas morning. But it could also be fun to trick your children into believing that you have magic beans that will grow into a beanstalk that reaches into the sky. However, if parents you knew actually did that to their children, you would think that they were cruel. As far as I know, "it's fun" has never been a legitimate excuse for an immoral action.

Can the Santa Claus lie be justified in the name of creating an illusion of security for children? Only if that lie is necessary for such an illusion, but clearly that is not the case. Parents accomplished this goal for years without Santa Claus and they still can today. Besides, how exactly does the Santa lie create an illusion of security? Awe and wonder and some warm fuzzy feelings, maybe. But how does the idea that someone will invade your house in the middle of the night make one feel more secure? Even if it is to bring presents, if Santa can get in, why not the bogeyman? Why not anyone? The Santa lie made the children of one of my colleagues feel so insecure that they expressed the desire for Santa Claus to simply leave the presents on the front porch instead of invading the house. A student of mine recalled being very unsettled every Christmas Eve because they knew their parents left the door unlocked for Santa Claus because they didn't have a chimney. Clearly, a sense of security is no excuse for the Santa lie.

It's Just Bad Parenting

The Santa Claus lie is not good parental practice for numerous reasons. To start, Santa steals your thunder. You earned the money, you bought the presents. Your children should be thanking *you*, not Santa. Not only do your children need to learn to show appreciation to real persons when they deserve it (instead of mythical creatures), they need to learn that fulfilling their wishes takes effort, sacrifice, and money.[5]

Another significant worry is the consequence of children finding out the truth. If you lie to them about Santa, the moment of them discovering the truth is inevitable. And that moment is not just the time at which "Santa dies," but the moment when the child realizes that they have been lied to systematically by the people they trust most in the world: their parents. I surveyed my friends, relatives and students for stories about this defining moment. Here are my five favorites:

Mary Beth was nine. The kids at school were making fun of her for believing in Santa. She asked her mother, who finally admitted the truth. "I remember, I was upset—not so much because there was not [a] Santa, but because my mother had lied to me. That is why I was so mad at the kids at school—it implied that my mother had lied to me. When I found out that she had, I was livid!"

Becky's friend grew up with her belief in Santa as a huge part of her childhood. Her parents kept her believing as long as they could. When she finally found out the truth, she was extremely upset. She essentially felt like a gullible idiot for falling for it for so long, and was very upset at her parents for taking advantage of her gullibility.

Caleb's mom was eleven and it was Christmas Eve. As always, her father told her that Santa wouldn't come unless she was asleep, so she hurried to bed. She was awoken by a noise and, thinking it was Santa, she took a peek—only to see her father setting out presents. She was so upset about the fact that he had lied to her for so long, she vowed then and there that, when she had kids, she would not teach them to believe in Santa. She remained true to her word. She and her father continue to have trust issues to this day.

Julie believed until she was 10. To keep it going, every Christmas Eve her brothers told her that the red light on the radio tower was Rudolph's nose. Her parents used other false evidence, like partially consumed milk and cookies. They even had Santa answer the note she would leave for him. On her tenth Christmas, in answer to her suspicions about Santa's reality, her brother told her to hide behind the couch on Christmas Eve—and she saw her parents doing Santa's job. "I was SHOCKED! I was upset for days, and I wouldn't talk to my parents. I didn't even want to open my presents."

Jay got into an argument at school with his best friend about Santa. He defended Santa's existence profusely, and eventually the entire class was involved. Jay's main argument was that Santa must exist because his mother told him he did, and his mother would not lie to him. To settle the issue, Jay sought out the classroom encyclopedia. Upon reading the words, "Santa Claus: A fictional character..." in front of the whole class, he looked up at his teacher, wanting her to tell him it wasn't true. "But I could tell by her slumped shoulders and the look in her eye she couldn't. I remember that moment like it was yesterday. I was so embarrassed because my ignorance was revealed in such public display, in front of all my friends. I had said my mother would never lie to me, but clearly she had. Mrs. Stubblefield was apologetic, but I realized that she was in on the deception too. I, seriously, still get upset when I talk about it."[6]

I will grant you that the Santa Claus lie might be fun for some,[7] but most children would rather not be the butt of everyone's joke, or, as another of my students said he felt, the target of a "grand conspiracy." They want the truth. They're curious about the world, want to know about it, and trust their parents to provide them with accurate information. When we tell them the Santa Claus lie, we betray that trust.

I'm not saying, of course, that every child reacts this way.[8] (Although you would likely be surprised at how many of the stories I collected were negative.) I'm simply saying that this reaction is a risk that's not worth taking. Even if the chances are low, the benefits simply aren't worth it. I wouldn't do any action that had a chance of crippling my child, even if the chances were low, unless there were no other options. But clearly, in the case of the Santa lie, there are other options.

In fact, you'd be surprised how many parents have contacted me, thrilled that someone is finally defending their practice in public. (Others, like one emailer, Jade, tell me my argument finally convinced their spouse and got them their first apology in four years!) No Santa Parents are everywhere; they just keep quiet to avoid ridicule.

The Santa lie may also damage a child's moral compass. Too often, it is spoiled rich children, who don't always behave so well, that come back after Christmas break spinning grade-school tales of Santa's most lavish rewards. I specifically remember, as a child, being genuinely confused regarding how a certain member of my class, who everyone agreed was a bully, had been so handsomely rewarded by Santa Claus. In my case, I was old enough that this made me question Santa's existence, not my sense of right and wrong but not all children will draw that conclusion.

Finally, the Santa Claus lie encourages bad parenting because it is a parental crutch that encourages behavior for the wrong reasons. Although this has less to do with literal belief, and more to do with the conditions for rewards that the literal belief establishes, the Santa lie establishes a bad precedent when it comes to motivating children's behavior.

Now, don't get me wrong: kids do need to face consequences for their actions. We learn to be virtuous by imitating virtuous behavior.[9] Ideally, a child will do what it is right simply because it is right. They will value goodness for its own sake. But to teach them this, it's perfectly acceptable to encourage such behavior through positive reinforcement (e.g., praising and even rewarding it immediately upon seeing it) and to punish bad behavior when it occurs.

But the Santa Claus lie does neither of these things. Not only does it delay its consequences until long after the behavior it is supposed to reward, but it does not punish misbehavior nor does it reward virtuous behavior. It simply rewards a lack of misbehavior. When a child is throwing a tantrum in a store, and his parents tell him if he doesn't stop Santa won't be bringing him any gifts, they are not threatening punishment for misbehavior. Even if his parents follow through on their threat, the child is still in the same state as he was before. He simply won't receive extra rewards on top of what he already has. And if he does stop, he will not be rewarded for virtuous behavior, but simply for not misbehaving, the bare minimum of what he should be doing.

In my classes, I don't give bonus points for merely attending class, the bare minimum of what a student should be doing. I take off points for missing class; I punish misbehavior. If I didn't, students would stop coming to class. Worse yet, they might come to class but do no work because their bonus points for doing the minimum effort would allow them to pass the class. Rewards should be reserved for work above and beyond what is required, not given out as a reward for simply not misbehaving. Yet this is exactly what the Santa lie does.

Of course, in practice, parents never follow through on their threats anyway. Regardless of their behavior, children get the gifts that they would have gotten. In reality, however, regardless of whether we tell the Santa lie or not, children should think the gifts they receive are given merely because they are loved, not because they didn't misbehave.

I'm not alone in my assessment. Even defenders of the Santa lie, like child psychologist Melinda Wenner Moyer, agree that the lie's disciplinarian aspect should be avoided.[10]

> Though lying can be an awfully convenient parenting crutch—Sorry, sweetheart, but the police might arrest you if I let you have more candy so we better not—it's generally best to keep it to a minimum, both to develop trust between yourself and your child and to lead by example...[but] sometimes, parents use Santa inappropriately, such as when they force their terrified kids to sit on Santa's lap or when they use him primarily as a disciplinary threat—If you keep throwing pens at your sister, Santa will leave coal in your stocking.[11]

Although some parents don't use the Santa lie this way, they are in the vast minority. Consider, for example, the "Elf on the Shelf," a recent fad that has become attached to the Santa lie. Parents put this elf up on the shelf where it can "watch" the children, and they say that it reports back to Santa every night regarding their behavior. As one of my students told me about their older brother and his wife's Elf on the Shelf, "All they have to do is remind the kids that the elf is watching, and the fights and tantrums stop and they are perfectly behaved." The Elf on the Shelf is simply an extension of how we use the Santa Claus lie, taken to its logical end—a constant reminder that simply being minimally decent will earn lavish rewards.

What's more, if we motivate children to not misbehave with lavish rewards, what happens to these children when they grow up and realize that it is actually misbehavior that is usually rewarded? What happens when they learn that lying and cheating usually have much more grandiose payoffs than being honest and virtuous? I'm not saying that the Santa Claus lie is solely responsible for all corruption in politics, business, and Wall Street. But I'm not saying it's innocent in that regard, either.

Even if reward doesn't become the prime motivating factor for their actions, it's undeniable that the Santa lie threatens to make our children greedy. They expect the gifts. They often gripe more about what they didn't get than they are thankful for what they did. Although I think that the gifts that children get should not be conditional upon their behavior, we should do all we can to encourage them to be thankful regardless. The Santa lie encourages the exact opposite.

Santa Makes Us Stupid

David Hume (1711–1776) rightly observed that "A wise man... proportions his belief to the evidence."[12] William Clifford (1845–1879) argued that "it is wrong always, everywhere, and for anyone, to believe anything upon insufficient evidence."[13] Although evidence might not always be available—making a guess, in some circumstances, is permissible if it is necessary—the general sentiment is correct. It is important to have good reasons for what one believes. As contemporary philosopher Ted Schick points out:

> Without good [reasons], humans have no hope of understanding [anything]...Without good [reasons], our beliefs are simply arbitrary, with no more claim to knowledge than the random choice of a playing card [and] our beliefs lose their value in a world where beliefs are a dime a dozen.[14]

As I tell my students, if you don't learn to formulate good reasons for your beliefs, you'd be better off deciding what to believe by just flipping a coin. At least that way, half of the time, you'd get it right.

Credulity is the tendency to readily believe something that is false, and is often equated with mental laziness. Credulous people often fall prey to marketing scams and hustles (e.g., pyramid schemes), are tricked into believing in pseudoscience (e.g., creationism), wasting money on ineffectual "alternative medicines" (e.g., homeopathy),[15] or buying into conspiracy theories (e.g., 9/11 Truthers). You might believe such thinking is uncommon, but more than half of Americans believe in spiritual healing (55 percent)—not to mention creationism (42 percent), ESP (41 percent), ghosts (32 percent), telepathy (31 percent), UFOs (24 percent), clairvoyance (26 percent), communication with the dead (21 percent), astrology (25 percent), witches (21 percent), and reincarnation (20 percent).[16] A full 18 percent of Americans think the sun revolves around the earth![17] How many people do you know who believed (or still believe?) that Obama is a Muslim and not a US citizen? How many believed that the world was going to end in 2012? To those who value and are adept at evaluating evidence—"critical thinkers" they are often called—such things are obviously nonsense. But to those who do not have such skills—the credulous—the evidence for these things can sound convincing.

Critical thinking skills do not come automatically. They must be taught and reinforced. The natural human state is one of credulity. Our senses, memory, and intuitive reasoning often lead us astray, and yet we have a propensity to trust them uncritically.[18] For example, we trust what our eyes see, and even trust eyewitness testimony, yet it's been established that our senses are notoriously unreliable and that eyewitness testimony leads to false convictions more often than any other evidence.[19] We trust our memories despite the fact that we continually, willingly and unwillingly, add and subtract details to them.[20] And we trust our intuitionally derived conclusions despite the fact that, quite often, we are simply engaged in motivated biased reasoning.[21] The critical thinker understands all this and learns to employ the kind of careful reasoning that guards against the limits and powers of our senses, memory, and intuitive reasoning and comes to accept conclusions grounded on solid evidence.

The credulous, on the other hand, don't value evidence. They think it is acceptable to believe without evidence, even when evidence can be had—sometimes, even ignoring evidence to the contrary. They'll encourage one to "avoid thinking and just believe" or will concoct bad reasons and faulty evidence and find them convincing. And when pressed to provide explanations for what they believe, they will often appeal to ignorance: "You can't one hundred percent prove it's false, so it's true." They will even suggest that it works "by magic" or some unconventional science unknown to the experts.

What does all this have to do with Santa? Perhaps nothing encourages credulity more than parents promoting the Santa Claus lie.

First of all, parents often concoct faulty evidence in favor of Santa's existence and tell children to find it convincing. This includes traditional staples, like half-devoured milk and cookies, and more extreme examples like having a neighbor dress up like Santa and capturing him in a Polaroid in the act of delivering presents. One student of mine recalled such an event from his childhood. He carried the picture around for an entire year professing it as Santa proof to all of his classmates. He of course was traumatically embarrassed when the truth was exposed.

One example from this category lights up, like a neon sign, how protecting Santa belief promotes credulity in children. It's a mocumentary on DVD called "Search for Santa."[22] Actors pretending to be archeologists, physicists and explorers present "convincing evidence" for Santa's existence: a newly discovered sleigh runner in the desert that's been there for eight hundred years, a blurry video that captures a frame of Santa's image near a chimney on Christmas eve,[23] and an expedition to the "magnetic north pole" where they fail to find Santa's workshop, but do come across reindeer that don't leave footprints in the snow.

Its purpose? You show it to your kids to squeeze another year of Santa belief out of them. As one reviewer on Amazon.com said, it is "the perfect film to show a child questioning the existence of Santa Claus. 'Search for Santa' is guaranteed to add a few more years to your child's wonder about Old Saint Nick." Of course it's a farce, but it mirrors exactly real documentaries that engage, encourage, and take advantage of viewers' credulity. It's the same kind of thing you might see on the History Channel that argues that the Nazis had alien technology, or on Animal Planet that argues that Bigfoot is real, or on TBN that argues that the Shroud of Turin is the actual burial shroud of Christ. A few lessons in basic critical thinking will expose the reasoning of these documentaries as fundamentally flawed, and if you want your child to be a critical thinker, you should avoid them—or, better yet, you should sit down and debunk one with them. Yet parents will show "Search for Santa" and tell them that it presents convincing evidence. The actors even specifically equate "gut feeling" with "scientific evidence"; what could be more poisonous to a budding mind just learning how to reason?

Next parents will invent explanations for how Santa can pull it all off—explanations that defy all logic and scientific fact but that parents encourage children to believe nonetheless. Worse yet, when children are smart enough to express doubt about such explanations, parents encourage fallacious reasoning in an attempt to keep the Santa lie alive. "You can't prove that it's not true, so it must be!" But the fact that something can't be disproven is no reason to believe that it's true. This is called "appealing to ignorance," and it's one of the hardest bits of credulous reasoning to dislodge. It doesn't need encouragement.

Worse still, parents will skip all attempts at explanation and simply appeal to magic. But to explain something by magic is to not explain it at all. Explanations must increase our understanding and not raise unanswerable questions. You can't appeal to the inexplicable to explain the unexplained. Magic is an unexplainable force that works in unknown ways. How does it work? Where does it come from? Among critical thinkers, it is well known that, as an explanation, "it's magic" is equivalent to no explanation at all. Yet it often is the explanation of choice among the credulous. By encouraging children to embrace magic explanations, parents encourage children to find a staple of credulous reasoning acceptable.

If this fails, parents will encourage children to "just believe anyway." After all, "Don't you want to believe in Santa? Isn't it more fun? Isn't it more comforting? If you don't, you won't get presents." But by doing this parents are endorsing the notion that is the groundwork of all credulous thinking: the idea that what one believes should simply be what one wants to be true. Not only is such an approach to belief formation irrational, it sets one up for disaster. Having true beliefs is important because we base our actions on our beliefs. If we don't believe true things, our actions are less likely to be successful. In fact, few things are more dangerous to a young mind than the idea that it is acceptable to believe whatever you want simply because you want to. Such an idea is even antithetical to the very notion of getting an education. "Why bother," a young person is likely to think, "if it's alright to just believe what I want to? I can do that from home." It's no wonder so many children think that school is a waste of time.

"But they're just kids," I can hear some saying. "What's the big deal? Are you expecting four-year-olds to be critical thinkers? Just let them believe whatever they want. What's the harm?"

There are a number of things to say in response.

First of all, the fact that they are just kids actually makes my point all the more important. A person's youngest years are their most formative years. It is children who are most impressionable. The lessons we learn as children stick with us more than any others. Every bad critical thinking lesson a child learns will be exponentially harder to unlearn when they get older. I recall one college freshman student of mine, who believed in Santa until she was 10, who still believed that magicians like Criss Angel had real magic powers. I'm not sure even showing her an interview with Criss, where he "comes clean," dislodged the belief.

Second of all, I am not expecting four-year-olds to be critical thinkers. I'm merely saying that we should teach them critical thinking lessons, endorse such reasoning, and encourage it by displaying it, from the very beginning. You don't wait until a child can speak to try to teach them how to speak, and you should never encourage them to speak poorly. Even though studies show that "baby talk"—which is slower, elongates vowels, and draws attention to itself with a higher pitch—is better for a child's language development, studies also show that ungrammatical baby talk is harmful. Saying "Where coat?" instead of "Where is your coat?" stunts your child's grammatical skills.[24] In the same way, you shouldn't wait until a child can think critically to try to teach them to think critically. You should be encouraging such thinking as soon as you can. For example, although you don't want to ruin the fun by telling them how magic tricks work, you should never encourage them to believe that magicians actually have magic powers.

In 2013, I participated in a discussion on Huffington Post Live, regarding whether and how long literal belief in Santa should be encouraged.[25] One parent said that she tries to keep it going for as long as she can, by whatever means necessary, and if she could send her children to college still believing, she would. Why? Because she sees the moment a child no longer believes in Santa as the moment they are no longer a child. They lose that childhood innocence that makes childhood so dear. She would be horrified if a four-year-old came to realize the truth, or if a child never believed in the first place.

Yet if this was her approach to anything else in her child's development, everyone would agree that she was a deplorable parent. What if her baby starts walking early? Is she going to push her down because she doesn't want her to grow up too fast? Say her child starts talking early. Is she going to tape her mouth shut? Of course not. Regarding everything else, early development is something we encourage and celebrate. Why should it be different with critical thinking skills or the abandonment of naiveté? Critical thinking skills are simply adult thinking skills; why don't we celebrate when a child displays them early? "Little Johney figured out that Santa doesn't exist when he was four. I'm so proud of him! He's a little genius!"

But what's the danger of a little credulity in society? I could go on and on about how credulity regarding medicine leads to alternative medicines that literally cost people their lives, about how credulity regarding science is damaging the nation's economy and environment, how credulity infused in religion and politics threatens our education and is pushing our nation back toward the dark ages. But I don't think I could put it more succinctly or persuasively than Hank Stuever did in *Tensel: A Search for America's Christmas Present*:

> If a child has concluded...that it's impossible for a man in a flying sleigh to make it all the way around the world in one night, delivering elf-made replicas of all the stuff you see in Target and Best Buy, then that's a child I would be happy to steer toward a voting booth when she's 18. That's an American in search of facts. If, however, she goes on pretending to believe well into her teens (I encountered more than one such teenager in Frisco) because it makes her parents (and God) feel sweet and happy, then I become worried. That becomes an American willing to spend $100,000 on her "special day" wedding or who will believe without hard evidence that other countries harbor weapons of mass destruction when they don't.[26]

I'm not saying that we shouldn't expose our children to myth or fairy tales. Unlike Richard Dawkins, I don't think that reading Harry Potter is likely to have an "insidious effect on [a child's] rationality...."[27] But encouraging a child to believe that Harry Potter is real would. If a child asks if Harry Potter is real, you say, "No, it's just a fun story." So why do we do the exact opposite with Santa? I'm not saying we should get rid of the Santa myth. I'm not even saying you shouldn't put presents under the tree with Santa's name on them. I'm simply saying we should treat it like every other myth and not encourage our children to believe that it is literally true. If you do put presents from Santa under the tree, admit to your children from the start that it is just a game you are playing. Or at the least, when they are old enough to know the difference between reality and fiction, tell them the truth when they ask: "Santa's not real. We are just pretending Santa is real because it is fun."

You may think the "admitting but pretending" approach is impossible, but many parents have admitted to me that they do exactly this. Lisa, for example, couldn't bring herself to lie about Santa and so, instead, they just "played the [S]anta game and had a ball." Ironically, the only problem this caused was conflict with her non-immediate family who, ironically, objected to not lying. But, she recounts, "all our children tell us now how much they appreciate how we did Christmas and our oldest is continuing our tradition with her own daughter."

Sorry, Virginia

Of course, we can't talk about the Santa Claus lie without talking about "Yes Virginia, There Is a Santa Claus"—Francis Church's reply to eight-year-old Virginia O'Hanlon's question about Santa Claus, first printed in *The New York Sun* in 1897.[28] In actuality, despite its reputation, it's a not-so-well-thought-out reply to a child's question—so it really doesn't deserve to be taken too seriously. But since it is the most reprinted editorial in history (and many apparently think merely mentioning its title refutes the entirety of my arguments), I am obligated to respond to it in detail.[29]

Little Virginia O'Hanlon was seriously seeking the truth about Santa Claus, and so she wrote to *The New York Sun*:

I am 8 years old. Some of my little friends say there is no Santa Claus. Papa says, "If you see it in The Sun, it's so." Please tell me the truth, is there a Santa Claus?[30]

The people Virginia trusted most in the world, her parents, refused to tell her the truth, and so she had to seek it from The New York Sun in the form of advice from a stranger. Like her parents, Francis Church violates her trust by writing a reply in which he tells her an outright lie: "There is a Santa Claus."

Now, it might seem that he is not lying. A cursory reading suggests that he equates Santa with an abstract idea, like "love and generosity and devotion," and such things clearly do exist. And of course, if Church had said that "Santa doesn't literally exist; it's just a nice story that champions generosity," I'd have no objection. Of course no one would have ever reprinted his article had he said that, but at least he would not have been trying to deceive Virginia. But a more careful reading reveals that this is not his intention. These abstractions are examples of what, like Santa, can exist without being seen, but Church isn't suggesting that Santa is a mere abstract idea. Santa is actually more like fairies, which also can't be seen but do physically exist (and are apparently dancing on your lawn). In a paragraph that is often left out of modern renditions, he says:

> Not believe in Santa Claus! You might as well not believe in fairies! You might get your papa to hire men to watch in all the chimneys on Christmas Eve to catch Santa Claus, but even if they did not see Santa Claus coming down, what would that prove? Nobody sees Santa Claus, but that is no sign that there is no Santa Claus. The most real things in the world are those that neither children nor men can see. Did you ever see fairies dancing on the lawn? Of course not, but that's no proof that they are not there. Nobody can conceive or imagine all the wonders there are unseen and unseeable in the world.

So Santa is not just an abstract idea that exists in the hearts of humanity, but is something as real as fairies—which, for some odd reason, Church also champions. (Notice how unconvincing you would find his arguments if he were presenting them in favor of literal belief in fairies.)

This paragraph also helps me prove my previous point because Church is encouraging Virginia to be credulous. In reality, the mere fact that you can't see something is evidence that it is not there, and unless other evidence is presented in favor of that thing, the default rational position is disbelief. This is true even for love, generosity, and devotion; we believe in these things because we see people expressing love, being generous, and showing devotion.[31] If we did not have such evidence, we would not be justified in believing they exist. A basic rule of critical thinking is that, when it comes to existential matters (i.e., questions regarding existence) the burden of proof is on the believer. If you say, for example, that a teapot is orbiting the sun between Earth and Mars, I am justified in doubting you unless you can provide evidence—say, by showing me the teapot using a telescope. And if you excuse away evidence against your position, that's called an "ad hoc rationalization," and it makes your belief unfalsifiable and consequently irrational.[32] One would do this if, after failing to see the teapot, you insist that it's just too small for any telescope to see. Likewise, Church does this when he says that watching for Santa and not seeing him would not prove anything because he can't be seen. Critical thinkers know that this is a telltale sign of an irrational belief.

Of course, Church does not present evidence for Santa, but instead tries to motivate her belief in a different way.

Alas! how dreary would be the world if there were no Santa Claus. It would be as dreary as if there were no VIRGINIAS. There would be no childlike faith then, no poetry, no romance to make tolerable this existence. We should have no enjoyment, except in sense and sight. The eternal light with which childhood fills the world would be extinguished.... Only faith, fancy, poetry, love, romance, can push aside that curtain and view and picture the supernal beauty and glory beyond.

In short, Church suggests, either Santa exists or we must do without everything that makes tolerable our mortal existence. But here, Church makes two mistakes.

First, Church is suggesting that the positive consequences of believing something are a good reason to believe it, all evidence be damned. But, of course, even if poetry and romance can't exist without Santa, that is not good reason to believe in Santa. Again, a critical thinker proportions her belief according to the evidence, not according to what is more comforting or fun. She cares about believing what is true and realizes that wishful thinking leads you astray. Thus "Yes, Virginia" is, yet again, a prime example of how encouraging belief in Santa encourages credulity.

Second, Church presents us here with a false dichotomy. He presents only two options when there in fact are more. It's either Santa or a meaningless existence? That's preposterous. Humanity enjoyed poetry and romance abundantly long before the Santa Claus lie started in the early 1800s, and we still will once the tradition fades into the past. To be fair, Church likely intends to defend the kind of faith necessary for belief in Santa, suggesting that without it we have nothing to make tolerable this mortal existence. But this too is plainly false. First of all, in no way is faith required for poetry and romance. I need not believe anything without sufficient evidence in order to, say, enjoy poetry or fall in love. But more importantly, the kind of faith that Santa Claus requires actually makes the world a worse place. How?

Virginia's friends who no longer believe in Santa aren't merely "affected by the skepticism of a skeptical age" and refusing to "believe except [in what] they see." Likely, when they merely couldn't see Santa Claus, they did believe. But now they have evidence to the contrary: their parents' confession, catching them in the act, or the realization that visiting all children in one night is not possible. To believe in Santa would require them to ignore this sufficient evidence to the contrary and just keep believing anyway. We might call this kind of faith "blind faith"—because one is blind to the evidence. This is actually one of the most dangerous things on the planet.

It is blind faith that enables fundamentalist terrorists to ignore the evidence from their own scriptures that killing innocents is wrong. It is blind faith that allows "anti-vaxxers" to believe, despite overwhelming evidence that proves otherwise, that vaccines cause autism—an idea that has caused outbreaks of preventable diseases all over the world.[33] Blind faith is, in fact, required for belief in any alternative medicine, which has actually cost humanity thousands of lives.[34] It is blind faith that enables creationists to ignore all scientific evidence, still believe the world is only six thousand years old, and thus promote this idea and petition to get creationism taught in public school science classrooms. It's no coincidence that America lags behind the rest of the world in accepting science's most important theory in biology: evolution.[35] It's blind faith that allows Mormons to believe that the Garden of Eden is in Jackson County, Missouri, and that black skin is punishment for sin; it's blind faith that allows Scientologists to believe, literally, L. Ron Hubbard's science fiction story about the intergalactic lord Xenu. This is even the kind of faith that Hindus exercise when they bathe in the river Ganges believing it is not polluted. They believe it is the goddess Ganga and thus unpollutable—despite the tests that show its bacteria count to be 10,000% higher than safe bathing water standards.[36]

Some may think that parents want to encourage blind faith in their children because they want them to believe in God, but most theologians don't think that belief in God requires blind faith—faith despite sufficient evidence to the contrary. Although there is no proof that God does exist, they maintain that there is also not proof that he does not—the evidence is a wash. To believe in God merely requires "simple faith," belief without evidence, which they suggest is perfectly acceptable.[37]

In fact, if parents want their children to believe in God, avoiding belief in Santa might be the safest bet. As Tennille tells her story:

When I was real young I was told to believe in this Santa.... My mom tried real hard to get us to believe in him, but... one year my mother made a goof and wrapped a Barbie for my brother. I knew that this all awesome Santa would not make such a mistake and my mom explained that she was

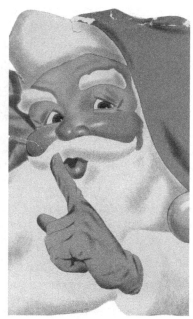

VINTAGE SANTA GREETING CARDS, © PD

THE COMING OF SANTA CLAUS, ENGRAVING BY THOMAS NAST, 1872, © PD.

in fact Santa. I was mad because she tried so hard to lie to me and it made me wonder what else she lied to me about.... Unfortunately it also lead [sic] to my questioning of God. It made sense now why I did not always get what I asked for for Christmas because Santa did not exist, so when I prayed to God and things did not come true I figured my mother made him up too. It made a very big impact because I spent years being mad at God when I could have had faith and lightened my load...

But regardless of whether you want to encourage faith in your children, Church's reply to Virginia is not a successful defense of encouraging children to literally believe in Santa Claus. Instead, it actually reinforces my argument by making clear that encouraging literal belief in Santa involves immoral deception that violates a child's trust and encourages credulity.

The Santa Lie Doesn't Encourage Imagination

Accredited professionals have defended the Santa lie in the name of imagination. For example, in her article "What if Santa died? Childhood myths and development," Lynda Breen points to studies that suggest benefits like "family bonding and pro-social behaviour," including sharing" and "enhanced fantastical thinking, expansion of the internal object world and purposeful play."[38] In her Slate.com article "The Santa Lie: Is the Christmas Con Hurting our Kids?",[39] Melinda Moyer argues:

What Kris Kringle does...is feed the imagination [and a] type of imaginative play that sparks creativity, social understanding and even—strange as it may sound—scientific reasoning [with].... Fantasy play [that] forces kids to think through hypothetical or counterfactual scenarios, which bolsters their reasoning skills.[40]

I definitely don't doubt the results of these studies, nor (obviously) do I question the benefits of imagination. But there are still two things wrong with using such research to defend the Santa Claus lie. First, even if the Santa Claus lie has these benefits, it's not the only thing that does. There are other ways to promote family bonding, purposeful play, and imagination that don't require deception, violate your child's trust, and risk their moral and rational development.[41] In fact, even Breen acknowledges the threat to trust that the Santa Claus lie poses. She simply suggests that the costs and benefits should be weighed by each parent. All I am suggesting is that it would be best for us all to err on the side of caution. If Santa was the only way to attain these benefits, then maybe lying about him would be worth the risk—but he's not.

More importantly, it's not the lie that's doing the work; it's not tricking a child into literally believing that there is a fat flying gift giver named Santa Claus that generates the mentioned benefits. I'm only objecting to promoting the literal belief. If instead of lying to your children, you admit to them that it's just a story that you are going to pretend is true because it's fun, then I have no complaints. But that is all that is needed to accomplish all the things the research points to: family bonding, pro-social behavior, sharing, fantastical-thinking, imagination, and so forth. In fact, encouraging literal belief in Santa actually stifles imagination. Think about it. Does the Muslim *imagine* that Muhammad's rode his horse Barack (Al Boraq) at lightning speed from Mecca to Jerusalem to then ascend into heaven? Does a Christian *imagine* that Jesus rose from the dead? No, of course not. They genuinely believe these things. To imagine something is true, you have to know that it is false but pretend it is true anyway. When we encourage our children to literally believe in Santa Claus, we rob them of the option of pretending Santa is real, and thus of the opportunity to use their imagination.

Imagination is wonderful. If my son is running around the house with a towel tied around his neck claiming he can fly because he is Superman, I will do nothing do discourage it. But literal belief can be dangerous. If he climbed on the roof and did that, I would tell him quite promptly that he wasn't really Superman. Of course, literal belief in Santa is not such an immediate threat—but it's still dangerous.

Responding to Twelve Common Objections

Criticisms of Santa Claus are more socially taboo than criticisms of religion. Since I started defending my position publicly, advocates of the Santa lie (or "ASLs," as I sometimes call them) have raised countless objections—some in print and some directed at me personally. So, to close out this chapter, I'd like to consider some arguments that ASL's have lobbed at me in objection to my conclusion that we should avoid the Santa Claus lie. In honor of the 12 days of Christmas, I'll consider the twelve most common objections I've heard.

OBJECTION 1

It's okay for kids to literally believe that Santa exists...because he does!

Honestly, this objection doesn't really deserve a response, but it's recently found a champion in Hollywood writer and philosophy student Eric Kaplan. In his book, *Does Santa Exist?: A Philosophical Investigation* he argues that Santa does exist—as a "face" of "the limitless," what Kabbalists (of which Kaplan is one) call their conception of God.[42] And in a *New York Times* piece for the Stone, Kaplan argued that we can convince ourselves that Santa exists, even if initially we think he doesn't, because (unlike Santa) selves don't really exist—so they can be shaped into whatever we want, even Santa believers.[43]

I've already reviewed Kaplan's work elsewhere,[44] but here it will suffice to just say this: Kaplan's arguments are simply a thinly vailed attempt to defend his version of Kabballah—a mystical pseudoscientific version of Judaism. So unless you are a Kabbalist, you should not be impressed. You should agree with his claim that Santa exists only if, by "Santa exists," you mean what he (but seemingly no one else) means by that phrase: "there is a gentle face of the limitless." And that's being generous; that's assuming that phrase actually means anything to begin with. In my opinion, a 43-year-old adult using his own variety of mystic pseudoscience to defend Santa's existence only helps prove my point that literal belief in Santa promotes credulity.

OBJECTION 2

It is every child's right to believe in Santa Claus!

So Jewish, Buddhist, and Islamic parents are violating their children's rights? And what about all children born before 1800? And what does this right amount to? Children have a right to be fooled into believing a comfortable lie? That's silly. When pressed, defenders of this objection admit that they simply see it as a "rite of passage" because "every child believes." Ironically, this parallels the way children often excuse their own behavior. "Everyone is doing it." My response is the parent's: "If everyone jumped off a bridge, would you do it too?" The fact that everyone is participating in something does not make it acceptable.

OBJECTION 3

You are just a killjoy who hates
Christmas and children
and wants to spoil all of their fun.

This is what logicians call an "ad hominem"—a personal attack. Those who employ this fallacy are trying to draw attention away from the argument they can't refute by criticizing the arguer himself. Even if what they say about the arguer is true, that doesn't affect the cogency or strength of the argument. Arguments stand and fall on their own merits. Although an argument might *sound more persuasive* coming out of different people's mouths, an argument's strength or cogency is just a matter of its form and content, and that doesn't change from speaker to speaker. Besides, this criticism isn't true. I love Christmas and children. In fact I'm looking out for them. I'm simply arguing that there are better ways to have fun at Christmas that don't involve risking a child's moral and rational development.

OBJECTION 4

So according to you I'm a terrible parent
because I teach my children to believe in Santa.
Who are you to judge?
It's just a matter of parental preference.

No, I'm not saying you are a terrible parent. Whether or not you are a good parent depends on multiple factors, and I have no idea how you size up. And, in all honesty, if you love your kids and do your best, you're probably a good parent regardless of whether you participate in the Santa Claus lie. But not everything is a matter of preference and some parental practices are worse than others. All I'm saying is that if you want to be the best parent you can be, you should probably consider giving up the Santa Claus lie.

OBJECTION 5

So if I don't listen to you, my children are going
to turn out to be credulous moral monsters?
I believed in Santa and I turned out just fine.

I'm sure you did. After all, I believed in Santa and now I teach critical thinking and am not a moral monster. But I am not arguing that literal belief in Santa Claus guarantees anything.

I'm suggesting that what we do to encourage it promotes credulity and can warp a child's sense of right and wrong. It increases the risk of such damage. Anecdotal counter-examples where it didn't have such effects doesn't prove otherwise. After all, my grandfather Johney Bryan survived World War Two, but that doesn't mean that fighting in World War Two wasn't risky. Even if the majority of Santa-believing children don't turn out like this, their moral and intellectual skills are still not worth the risk.

OBJECTION 6

Where is your scientific evidence that the Santa lie promotes credulity?

I'd love some, but Santa is such a sacred cow, no one has ever bothered to do the research. There has been research on the tooth fairy showing that a child's literal belief in that fictional creature makes them more likely to confabulate memories—memories, specifically, of magical or supernatural events surrounding the event of their tooth loss.[45] I don't see why literal belief in Santa wouldn't do the same thing or why such a thing wouldn't promote credulity. It could only encourage belief in other magical or supernatural phenomena. But even if there is no such scientific evidence, scientific arguments are not the only kind that exist—and I have already given many arguments for thinking that the Santa Claus lie promotes credulity. Besides, just like I don't need a series of studies to know that exposing my child to improper grammar will negatively affect his language skills, I don't need them to know that exposing my child to uncritical thinking will make him less likely to be a critical thinker.

OBJECTION 7

So I guess we should just never lie to our children and introduce them to the dog eat dog nature of the real world and let them be eaten alive as soon as we can.

This sarcastic remark is what logicians call a "strawman argument" which restates an argument in a weak way to make it easier to attack. Clearly, the fact that certain lies are unacceptable doesn't mean that all lies are unacceptable. The fact that we should tell our children the truth about one thing (e.g., Santa) doesn't mean that we should tell them the truth about everything (e.g., the family's finances). My argument only applies to the Santa Claus lie.

OBJECTION 8

I encourage my children to believe in Santa, and keep them believing for as long as I can, because it makes them happy, just like it made me happy when I was a kid. We all believe in things that don't really make sense because they make us feel happy and comfortable.

Of course, this objection fails because it is unacceptable to just believe whatever makes you happy. This is a hallmark of credulity. But I am appalled by how often I hear this objection, by how many parents think it's perfectly fine, even for adults, to believe something is true simply because you want it to be—because it's comforting or because it's fun.[46] This objection actually helps me make my point because these parents usually admit that their parents kept them believing in the Santa Claus lie for as long as possible too. This is not scientific proof, but the more I hear from parents, the more I'm struck by how many adults who believed in Santa for too long still have childish belief-forming habits—and the more I'm convinced that the Santa Claus lie is a major contributing factor.

OBJECTION 9

If it's not okay to teach your children to believe in an imaginary being like Santa, why is it okay to make them believe in an imaginary being like God?

It wouldn't be, if we all knew that God didn't exist with the same certainty that we know that Santa doesn't exist. Of course, those who believe in God don't think they are teaching their children to believe in something imaginary, so this objection doesn't stick. But notice that, if you didn't believe in God you wouldn't teach your children to believe in him. So why would it be different with Santa? I'm simply suggesting that, when you know that something doesn't exist, don't teach your children that it does. Since everyone knows that Santa doesn't exist, no one should be teaching children that he exists.

If you tell your kids the Santa story isn't true, they will realize that other adults (like their teachers) are lying to them. This will make them wonder what other lies adults are telling, and thus they will think that adults always lie. This would be more damaging to their critical thinking skills than belief in Santa.

First of all, if we tell the Santa lie, the realization that all adults are lying about Santa is inevitable, because the realization that the Santa story isn't true is inevitable. So, if you really think that the realization that the Santa story is a lie (combined with the realization that almost all adults promote it) will lead children to the objectionable realization that adults always lie, then you have a really good reason to abandon the Santa Claus lie. The only way to keep children from realizing that adults are lying to them about Santa is to not lie to them about Santa.

In my opinion, however, while it is good for children to trust their parents, it's also good for them be skeptical of authority— to learn that authorities can be wrong and will lie to manipulate them. Telling them the truth about Santa, but that other adults will lie to them about it, is a great way to accomplish this. Of course, if we all eliminate the Santa lie, we will have to find another way. But in the meantime, you don't have to feel bad about telling your kids the truth about Santa. You will be teaching them a worthwhile lesson.

OBJECTION 11

But I don't want my child causing trouble at school, ruining it for other children, and other parents hating me because my child ruined their Christmas. And I don't want my child being made fun of.

First of all, it's kids who believe for too long that are often made fun of. Being in on the secret before their classmates is usually enjoyable for kids. They feel like they are "one up" on them. Regardless, other children's naïveté is not your duty to protect. The Santa liars don't get a default favored status just because their web of deception is easy to burst. You are under no obligation to protect their religious beliefs and you are under no obligation to protect their Santa beliefs. But if you are worried about upsetting your friends who are Santa liars, just instruct your child regarding how to respond. I suggest, when asked if they believe in Santa, have them reply with "At our house, Santa is just pretend."

OBJECTION 12

I use the lie to teach children critical thinking principles by encouraging them to figure it out for themselves. We play the game, and I don't tell them one way or the other, and when they ask I guide them through a question-and-answer process that leads them to conclude for themselves that Santa isn't real.

I'm not sure I really object to this. Again, I have no objection to playing the "Santa game"—pretending with your children that Santa exists—as long as you never encourage them to literally believe it, don't lie to them when they ask, and encourage them to figure it out for themselves.

I suppose things could go wrong. I've collected some stories from parents whose kids won't stop believing Santa exists even though they are told otherwise. A colleague of mine once admitted that, as a little girl, she refused to stop believing even when she found out the truth. The aforementioned Tennille couldn't get her son to accept the truth, after she told him, because everyone at school said Santa was real. Kids sometimes just refuse to listen to their parents.

At the least, such an approach is undeniably better than trying to keep kids believing as long as you can with lies, tricks, fake evidence, and magic explanations. The main thing I am worried about is promoting credulity in kids. So if you are avoiding those things, and using the Santa lie to fight credulity, I'd say you are on the right track.

How This Myth Has Hijacked the Holidays

We saw last chapter the historical explanation for how the Santa Claus lie took over the holidays. In this chapter we have seen how the myth that it is harmless actually puts us all in harm's way. Not only is it an immoral lie, but it's bad parenting and threatens to make us stupid and greedy. Yet nothing seems more entrenched and immutable than the Santa Claus lie. How could it ever change? How could any of it change? It is to that myth, that Christmas cannot change, that we will turn in the next and final chapter.

TITLE PAGE ILLUSTRATIONS BY JOHN LEECH FROM CHARLES DICKENS: A CHRISTMAS CAROL. LONDON: CHAPMAN & HALL, 1843. FIRST EDITION. .

Christmas Can't Change

I BEGAN THIS BOOK BY ASKING "WHAT IS WRONG with Christmas?" By merely answering this question, we all tacitly admitted that Christmas, at least in some respect, needs to change. But Christmas is such a cultural juggernaut that we likely also thought changing Christmas was an impossible task:

Christmas is immune to change. It's always been the same and it always will. Any effort by a lone individual or a group to change the way the Christmas is celebrated is destined to fail.

Of course this is a myth, but I don't need to spend this final chapter convincing you that it is; we've already seen this myth debunked. In Myth #1, we saw how "king for a day" celebrations morphed into Saturnalia, how Sol Invictus's birthday became Jesus's birthday, how the church added a plethora of observances and traditions in an attempt to Christianize the holiday, and how it remained primarily secular in the way it was celebrated and acquired even more secular elements. In Myth #3 we saw how the Puritans almost stamped out Christmas, how it made a secular wassailing comeback, and then changed into a domesticated commercial orgy of spending. And don't forget all the ways the Wildman/St. Nicholas/Santa tradition changed throughout the years. Christmas definitely can change, has changed, and will change. The only question is: as it continues to change, will it change for the better or for the worse?

In fact, in the Netherlands, change is already on the way—and it seems to be for the better. There is a movement to change the way they celebrate Christmas by abolishing a character called Black Peter (their version of Krampus). Those in the movement see the tradition as racist since those who dress up as Black Peter traditionally don "blackface" makeup. (That's why he's called Black Peter.) Given the problematic history and connotations of white people appearing in blackface, this seems right. Regardless of its origins or the motivations of those who portray Black Peter, unless the tradition can be drastically changed it seems it should be abandoned. Interestingly, elementary schools in the Dutch city of The Hauge (which includes over 160 schools) apparently agree. In 2015, they announced that they will be replacing Black Peter with "visually neutral Santa servants" by "phasing out the use of blackface, curly hair wigs and red painted lips..."[1]

So, just as we have seen in our exploration of Christmas history, both individuals and groups can be effective at changing the holiday. Ironically, however, we have not seen a single example of anyone publishing a book filled with arguments about what is wrong with Christmas and making suggestions regarding the way it should change. And we certainly haven't seen any such effort be effective. Even when you're Pope Zachary, and you don't like the rowdy way Christmas is being celebrated in Rome, you can gripe about it and offer decrees for it to stop until you're blue in the face, but it's not going to have any effect. So I'm under no illusions here. I don't think the publication of this book is going to start a mass Christmas revolution and change the way everyone celebrates Christmas.

And that shouldn't be too surprising. Although I'm sure you, dear reader, are an exception to this rule, arguments are usually ineffective in changing people's minds and behavior. In fact, when people are presented with facts contrary to the views they hold, especially when those views are emotional or controversial, people usually don't proportion their beliefs to the evidence and change their views. In fact, they most often double down and become even more firmly convinced that their original opinion is right.[2] So despite my best efforts, and regardless of how watertight my arguments are, they are likely not going to be persuasive to most people. But that's okay, they don't have to be. Although arguments are not always immediately persuasive, they can trigger social change.

By the beginning of the nineteenth century, after the influence of the Puritan ruler Oliver Cromwell had diminished, interest in old Christmas traditions began to grow. This set the stage for books about Christmas celebrations to be published, like Thomas Harvey's 1837 study of Christmas customs entitled *The Book of Christmas: The Customs, Ceremonies, Traditions, Superstitions and Fun of the Season*. Of course, you have never heard of it, and I doubt it convinced many to start celebrating, but you have heard of a work that followed a few years later that did: *A Christmas Carol*. I was unable to prove that Dickens read Harvey's *The Book of Christmas* (although I think it likely[3]), but Harvey's book set the stage for something that would change people's minds about Christmas, a heartfelt emotional story that pulled on the heartstrings. The public was once again ready for Christmas, Harvey told them how to do it, and Dickens motivated them to celebrate.

I'm hoping that *The Myths That Stole Christmas* will play the role in changing Christmas that *The Book of Christmas* played in reviving it. I think the public is ready for change. Enough people are dissatisfied with what Christmas has become. And like Harvey's book, my book tells us how to do it—how we can change. But, as we discussed in Myth #3, even if my book is a best seller, it will still only reach 0.2 percent of the literate population. So what we need is some television writer or movie producer to read this book and then produce a popular heartfelt emotional story that pushes us to that change.

What should that story look like? I have no idea. If I did, I'd try to write it myself. A ghost story revived Christmas. Maybe a story about aliens will change it? Stranger things have happened. When seen from the outside of the culture in which it is celebrated, as aliens would, Christmas really is a strange collection of traditions. I wonder what they would conclude about it. Certainly not that it was a religious holiday, given the secular way in which we celebrate it. Then again—they might conclude that consumerism is our religion, and that Christmas is our holiest day of the year. And they might be right. In any event, I'd love for such a story to be written.

But what kind of changes about the way we celebrate Christmas should this story call for?

Don't let anyone decide for you how to celebrate Christmas. I know this sounds strange, given that I am making suggestions about how Christmas should change, but ultimately the main lesson of this book is that we need to make Christmas work for us again. Christmas used to serve a useful purpose; it was a social safety valve that provided for the needs of the poor and that allowed us to relax after the harvest and fatten up for a harsh winter. Now it has simply become something that divides us socially, that indebts us and makes us poorer and fatter, and that makes our children greedy and stupid. We need to make Christmas work for us again, and the best way to do that is for each of us to make Christmas what it needs to be for us.

So, first and foremost, don't tell others how to celebrate Christmas. Choose the traditions that work for you, or even make your own. But also realize that they won't work for everyone. So if you have one of those "Keep Christ in Christmas" stickers on your car, please take it off. If you have made a big stink in the past about people saying "Happy Holidays" or "Merry Christmas," please don't. And don't expect the government to endorse your way of celebrating. As we've learned, although it is fine to celebrate Christmas in a religious way, that is not the original or the only way to celebrate, and it doesn't work for everyone.[+]

GLADE JUL BY VIGGO JOHANSEN (1891), © PD

And please, whoever you are, don't pressure others into celebrating Christmas in the first place. I hope one lesson of this book is that Christmas is for anyone who wants it. Whether you are Christian or not, religious or not, everyone should feel free to celebrate Christmas. But everyone should also feel free to not celebrate at all. Christmas is not for everyone, and no one should be made to feel guilty for not keeping Christmas.

No one should be scared to change the way they celebrate because of tradition. Take any given beloved tradition that you think is ancient and immutable, and chances are it was invented fairly recently and sold to you in order to get your money. Putting lit candles in a dead tree that you just set in your parlor is dangerous. So too are many of our current Christmas traditions. Don't burn down your house in the name of tradition. If you recognize the damage that one of your current Christmas traditions is doing, then change it.

When it comes to gifts, it's better to buy fewer, and it's best to be charitable to the poor. Remember, redistributing wealth down the economic ladder is the best way that gifts create economic value. When you do buy, don't put Christmas gifts on credit cards. If you can't afford it, don't buy it. And if you can afford it, spend wisely. Don't create deadweight loss by "getting things that nobody wants, and nobody cares for after they are got." Remember, gift cards and cash are a wonderful substitute.

Don't blame retailers and corporations for your Christmas spending habits. Yes it's annoying that Christmas ads start in October, that stores play Christmas music in November, and that retailers have begun starting their door-buster sales on Thanksgiving. But realize that they wouldn't do all of that if we didn't spend more money as a result. The entire purpose of businesses and retailers is to make money, and doing those things makes money because, like Pavlovian dogs, when we see "Christmas" we spend, spend, spend. You may think that you can't afford those Christmas presents that you have to buy unless you camp out in front of Best Buy on Thanksgiving. But ask yourself, why do you think you "have to buy" them in the first place? Don't let anyone or anything else dictate what you think you should spend your money on. If we changed our Christmas spending habits, all those annoying things would go away.

Lastly, think long and hard about promoting the Santa Claus lie. It is a lie after all, one that threatens your parental trustworthiness, and risks making your child greedy and credulous. At the least, keep those dangers in mind and try to use the Santa Claus tradition to teach lessons that guard against credulity and promote generosity. And if you still insist on being an ASL (Advocate of the Santa Lie), don't berate your friends who aren't. If they are not telling their children that Santa Claus exists, they probably have really good reasons.

But if there is only one thing you take away from this book, let it be this: Christmas shouldn't own us, we should own Christmas. Although the seven myths I have debunked have stolen Christmas away from us, we can take it back.

ABOUT THE AUTHOR

DAVID KYLE JOHNSON is an associate professor of philosophy at King's College in Wilkes-Barre, PA and is also a professor for *The Great Courses*. At King's he teaches many courses, including a course entitled "Myth Busters: Christmas, Santa, and Other Weird Things." He also lectures and speaks publicly on topics surrounding the Christmas holiday (including on Huffington Post Live and for the American Humanist Association) and has published extensively on Christmas—including for the London School of Economics, the book *The Ultimate Daily Show and Philosophy*, the journal *Think*, and his blogs for *Psychology Today* (Plato on Pop and A Logical Take). His other books include *Introducing Philosophy through Pop Culture (with William Irwin)*, *Inception and Philosophy: Because It's Never Just a Dream* and *Heroes and Philosophy: Buy the Book, Save the World*. He has also written extensively for  Wiley-Blackwell's series *Philosophy and Pop Culture* (20 articles at last court); the topics of his articles range wildly—from *The Hobbit*, *Star Trek* and *Doctor Who* to Quentin Tarantino, Stephen Colbert and Johnny Cash. His academic work includes articles in *Religious Studies, Sophia, Philo, Think*, and *Science, Religion and Culture* and is all available on academica.edu. His courses for *The Great Courses* include *The Big Questions of Philosophy* (available January 2016) and *Exploring Metaphysics* (available now).

Above: The author with Belsnickle at the "Christmas on the Farm" festival in Kutztown, PA in 2011. "It took some doing, but I finally convinced him that doubting his existence didn't count a 'being naughty.'"

ENDNOTES

INTRODUCTION

1   While 90 percent of Americans celebrate Christmas, only about half of them celebrate it religiously; 26 percent of Americans are non-devout Christians and another 16 percent of profess no religious ties at all. See Harper, Jennifer. "Ever Popular: 90 Percent of All Americans Celebrate Christmas." *The Washington Times.* 23 December 2013. www.washingtontimes.com/blog/watercooler/2013/dec/23/what-christmas-wars-90-percent-all-americans-celeb/; Jones, Jeffrey M. "Christmas Strongly Religious for Half in U.S. Who Celebrate It." *Gallup.com.* 24 December 2010. www.gallup.com/poll/145367/christmas-strongly-religious-half-celebrate.aspx; "Religion." *Gallup.com.* 2014. www.gallup.com/poll/1690/religion.aspx; "U.S. Religious Landscape Survey." The Pew Forum on Religion & Public Life. 2013. religions.pewforum.org/reports.

2   Stowe, Harriet Beecher. *Christmas; Or, The Good Fairy. The Writings of Harriet Beecher Stowe.* New York: AMS, 1967.

3   Lewis, C. S. "What Christmas Means to Me," from *God in the Dock—Essays on Theology and Ethics.* Grand Rapids, MI: Wm. B. Eerdmans, 1972, pp. 8-9; pp. 304–305.

4   Forrester, Brent. "[2F14] Homer vs. Patty and Selma." *The Simpsons.* 21 July 1996. www.snpp.com/episodes/2F14.html.

5   Some of this information was relayed to me at the Kutztown, PA "Christmas on the Farm" festival in 2010. The local house was decorated in the German fashion with candles in the tree. They were not lit; I was informed by the Pennsylvania German "head of the house" that such lighting was illegal in Pennsylvania. It was here that I also learned that, since German houses were more often made of stone, this was not as much of a worry back in the homeland.

6   "Holiday and Christmas Tree Fire Safety Outreach Materials." *U.S. Fire Administration.* www.usfa.fema.gov/citizens/home_fire_prev/holiday-seasonal/holiday.shtm.

7   *Centers for Disease Control and Prevention.* 21 November 2013. www.cdc.gov/nchs/fastats/obesity-overweight.htm.

8   Parker-Pope, Tara. "The Skinny on Holiday Weight Gain." *The New York Times.* 22 November 2007. well.blogs.nytimes.com/2007/11/22/the-skinny-on-holiday-weight-gain/.

CHAPTER 1 • MYTH 1: JESUS IS THE REASON FOR THE SEASON

1   For those interested, the name of this fallacy is *post hoc ergo propter hoc* ("after this, therefore, because of this"). Mere correlation does not entail causation.

2   You can see a nice description of Zagmuck and Sacaea in Earl and Alice Count's book *4000 Years of Christmas.* Count, Earl, and Alice Count. *4000 Years of Christmas: A Gift from the Ages.* Berkeley: Ulysses Press, 1997.

3   Here I am quoting David Forbes, who is quoting Lucian, who is (supposedly) quoting Saturn. Forbes, Bruce David. *Christmas: A Candid History.* Berkeley: University of California Press, 2008.

4   See, for example, Doherty, Earl. *The Jesus Puzzle: Did Christianity Begin with a Mythical Christ? Challenging the Existence of an Historical Jesus.* Canada: Age of Reason Publications, 2005.

5   See Ehrman, Bart. *Misquoting Jesus: The Story Behind Who Changed the Bible and Why.* San Francisco: HarperOne, 2005.

6   Besides, even if the Gospel of Luke was written by the historical Luke, its veracity would still be questionable because the historical Luke wasn't one of the 12 apostles; he was a companion of Paul (who also wasn't an apostle).

7   In fact, I've always been a bit puzzled by the phrase "oral tradition." I've only heard this phrase in a religious historical context, and in any other context, we call stories that float around groups and communities—where I heard it from someone, who heard it from someone, who heard it from someone—"rumors." "Oral tradition" seems to be a phrase invented by Christian scholars to distract from the fact that information on which the gospels are based is just not that reliable.

8   I won't bore you with a bunch of ancient biblical names, but if you are curious, see Ehrman, Bart. *Jesus, Interrupted: Revealing the Hidden Contradictions in the Bible (and Why We Don't Know About Them).* San Francisco: HarperOne, 2009.

9   Efforts by apologists to resolve these issues are almost comical. You have to make the Holy Family live in Nazareth, travel to Bethlehem for the census and birth, return immediately home to Nazareth, and then for no apparent reason, two years later, have them leave Nazareth again to return to Bethlehem, then buy a house, and sit around waiting for the Wise Men to visit them there. Then they flee to Egypt to avoid Herod and move back to Nazareth after he is dead. Not only is this explanation completely irrational—it interjects *ad hoc* (non-testable) explanations to save the theory of scriptural inerrancy—but it makes Matthew the worst storyteller ever. The fact that Jesus is born in Bethlehem in Verse 1 would have nothing to do with why he is there in Verse 11 for the Wise Men to find—and all this, despite the fact that Herod sends them to Bethlehem because that is where the King of the Jews is supposed to be born, not because that's where he just happens to be at the time. Matthew just neglects to mention the two treacherous journeys that Mary and Joseph took and that this was all just a giant coincidence? Fortunately, not all Christians are wedded to the (relatively new) idea of complete scriptural inerrancy and can admit the discrepancy.

10 Apologists often claim that Luke also places the birth of Jesus during the reign of Herod. He does not. In Chapter 1, Verse 5, he does place the events of Zacharia's epiphany about the conception of John the Baptist in "the days of Herod," but in Verse 24, he specifically places the conception of John (and thus all subsequent events) after the reign of Herod. It took place "after those days," he says, referring to the days of Herod in which the epiphany took place. Even if we ignore Verse 24 or claim that "days" just refers to the days of Zacharia's ministration (mentioned in Verse 23), there's still a problem. Luke's account would be inconsistent with itself. It can't place the events of Jesus's birth both during the days of Herod and during the reign of Quirinius as governor of Syria. The only way to make Luke internally consistent is to suggest that Zacharia's epiphany occurred during the reign of Herod but that John's and Jesus's conceptions and births happened years later. But, again, that makes it inconsistent with Matthew.

11 Why not 14 years? Because there is no year zero.

12 Scholars agree that both Matthew and Luke had access to Mark. They even copied parts of their gospels directly from it.

13 Mark 6:3.

14 Mark 1:9, 1:24, 10:47, 16:6.

15 Matthew even tells us, in Verse 2:6, about the Old Testament passage that promises this.

16 Then again, he could have been copying one of the many other stories about god-men that were born of virgins that predated Jesus. We'll talk more about that in a moment.

17 See Flynn, Tom. *The Trouble with Christmas.* Amherst: Prometheus Books, 1992.

18 Novella, Steven. "Mithras and Jesus." The New England Skeptical Society. 17 January 2014. theness.com/neurologicablog/index.php/mithras-and-jesus/.

19 Das, Subhamoy. "The Story of the Birth of Lord Krishna." *About.com.* hinduism.about.com/od/lordkrishna/p/krishna_birth.htm.

20 As Bart Ehrman explains it to his students, go outside and try to figure out which star is over the house at the end of the block.

21 Some will argue that *almah* can be translated as "virgin," but nowhere that it appears in the Old Testament demands that translation. I suspect people say this only because it was translated this way in the translation Matthew used.

22 Genesis 40:20–22.

23 Matthew 14:6–11. Origen was particularly fond of pointing this out. Origen, *in Levit., Hom. VIII,* in Migne, Jacques-Paul. *Patrologiae Graecae,* Vol. XII, p. 495.

24 Interestingly, Mark says that Jesus died on Friday, after eating the Passover meal on Thursday night. John, however, says Jesus died on Thursday, the day of preparation for the Passover, at the same time at which the lambs were being slaughtered before the Passover meal. John's theology, which depicted Jesus as the sacrificial lamb, is likely the reason he chose to deviate from Mark's account. See Ehrman (2009), pp. 23–29.

25 Supposedly he converted after having a dream, putting the Chi-Rho [⳩] on his soldiers' shields, and winning a major battle.

26 It comes from the Chronograph of 354. (I know the dates don't match.) For more details see Kelly, Joseph. *The Origins of Christmas.* Collegeville: Liturgical Press, 2004. pp. 68-69.

27 Sechrist, E. H. "Christmas." *World Book Encyclopedia.* Chicago: Field Enterprises Educational Corporation, 1966, Vol. 3, pp. 408–417.

28 Lewis, Judith. "Christmas—Ancient Pagan Holiday Which Was Criminally Illegal until 1907." *The Huffington Post.* www.huffingtonpost.co.uk/judith-lewis/christmas---ancient-pagan-holiday-which-was-criminally-illegal-until-1907_b_2350974.html.

29 This was later reinforced by Constantine in 321 C.E., when he declared that the day of the sun should be a day of rest, and by the Church Council of Laodicea around 364 C.E., who ordered Christian religious services to be held on Sunday.

30 See Kelly (2004), p. 67.

31 Compare, for example, the images seen here www.elistas.net/cgi-bin/eGruposDMime.cgi?K9D9K9Q8L8xumopxCuyfiqdnyuyjjudCUURRWCwuhrCuwymqCRYPTjfb7 and here albumpoles4israel.blox.pl/resource/jesus_thirteenth_century.JPG.

32 McGowan, Andrew. "How December 25th Became Christmas." *Bible History Daily.* 7 December 2012. www.biblicalarchaeology.org/daily/biblical-topics/new-testament/how-december-25-became-christmas/.

33 They also saw the similar date as somehow a sign that Jesus was superior to other gods with the same birthday.

34 Nissenbaum, Stephen. *The Battle for Christmas.* New York: Alfred A. Knopf, 1996, p. 8.

35 Palin, Sarah. *Good Tidings and Great Joy: Protecting the Heart of Christmas.* New York: Broadside, 2013, pp. 68–69.

36 We will learn more about this when we discuss Myth #5.

37 Palin (2013), p. 209.

38 This may be the first example of what we might call "a brand-new old-fashioned tradition." A new practice starts, and within a generation, everyone thinks that the practice is an ancient tradition—that things have always been done that way. We will see many such traditions emerge throughout the book.

39 Anderson, Kevin J., ed. *Tales from the Mos Eisley Cantina.* London: Bantam Spectra, 1995.

40 For more on the origins of beliefs about the Wise Men, see Chapter 4 of Kelly (2004).

41 For more on why and when such things were added to Christmas, see Chapter 3 of Kelly (2004).

42 Although it should be pointed out that the church's plays weren't "Christmas plays" specifically. Performing plays was a major avenue for teaching the illiterate masses about church stories and doctrines, and the church covered much more non-Christmas material in their plays than Christmas material. In addition, because they were performed outside, they took place in the spring, not during the Christmas season. See Kelly (2004), Chapter 4.

43 See Kelly, Joseph. *The Feast of Christmas*. Collegeville: Liturgical Press, 2010, pp. 64–65.

44 Kelly (2004), p. 48.

45 As we will see shortly, in some places "Christ's mass" may have even been bookended by jovial orgies.

46 Boniface. *The Letters of Saint Boniface*. Translated by Ephraim Emerton. New York: Octagon Books, 1973, pp. 81–82, quoted in Kelly (2010), p. 47.

47 Kelly (2004), p. 48.

48 Ibid., p. 65.

49 Nissenbaum (1996), p. 305.

50 Mazza, Ed. "Kirk Cameron Says Pagans Stole Christmas from Christians." *The Huffington Post*. 13 November 2014. www.huffingtonpost.com/2014/11/12/kirk-cameron-christmas_n_6149592.html.

51 Johnson, David Kyle. "Saving Christmas from Kirk Cameron." *Psychology Today.com*. 2014. www.psychologytoday.com/blog/logical-take/201411/saving-christmas-kirk-cameron.

52 I would like to mention, however, that restrictions on Christmas celebrations can go too far. Through email, a reader of my blog shared a story with me about a childhood friend of hers who was a Jehovah's Witness. Jehovah's Witnesses don't celebrate Christmas because (as we have learned) it is not biblical and is rooted in pagan traditions; that I can respect. However, during the class's Christmas party, the friend's parents made him sit out in the hall—where he would just put his head down and sob. The image still made the reader sad 50 years later. I'm not suggesting that Jehovah's Witnesses are obligated to celebrate Christmas at home; but it does seem that isolating a child from their friends, while they drink punch and cookies on the last day before break, because "that's what the pagans used to do" is a bit much.

53 I wouldn't say, however, that all advice on how to celebrate Christmas is bad. I will be arguing a bit later that certain traditions are bad for us and should be abandoned or changed.

....

CHAPTER 2 • MYTH 2: THERE IS A WAR ON CHRISTMAS

1   Blanton, Dana. "Majority OK with Public Nativity Scenes." *Fox News*. 18 Jun. 2004. www.foxnews.com/story/2004/06/18/majority-ok-with-public-nativity-scenes/.

2   "Christmas in Vietnam." Culture-4-Travel. 2013. www.culture-4-travel.com/christmas-in-vietnam.html.

3   Lu, Huaiyuan, and James Melik. "China Succumbs to the Glitz of Christmas." *BBC News*. 23 December 2010. www.bbc.co.uk/news/mobile/business-11991079.

4   "Christmas." Japan-Guide.com. www.japan-guide.com/e/e2299.html.

5   In 2014 one of my students, Jennifer, saw Christmas trees for sale at the local Sam's Club (Wilkes-Barre, PA)...in August.

6   Stewart, John. *The Daily Show*. 3 December 2012.

7   Palin, Sarah. *Good Tidings and Great Joy: Protecting the Heart of Christmas*. New York: Broadside, 2013, p. 7.

8   Ibid., p. 7.

9   Altman, Alex. "The War on Christmas." *Time*. 24 December 2008.

10 Ford, Henry. *The International Jew*. Detroit, MI: Don Lohbeck, 1947.

11 Gibson, Megan. "Rick Perry's 'Strong' Campaign Ad Gets the Web Angry—and Laughing." *Time* NewsFeed. 9 December 2011. newsfeed.time.com/2011/12/09/rick-perrys-strong-campaign-ad-gets-the-web-angry-and-laughing/.

12 Thorp, Brandon. "Mitt Romney and the War on Christmas." *Towleroad.* 18 December 2011. www.towleroad.com/2011/12/mitt-romney-and-the-war-on-christmas.html.

13 "Newt Gingrich Says No Federal Official Is Allowed to Say 'Merry Christmas'" *Tampa Bay Times* PolitiFact. 21 December 2011. www.politifact.com/truth-o-meter/statements/2011/dec/21/newt-gingrich/newt-gingrich-says-no-federal-official-allowed-say/.

14 "O'Reilly: 'War' on Christmas part of 'secular progressive agenda' that includes 'legalization of narcotics, euthanasia, abortion at will, gay marriage'" *Media Matters,* November 21, 2005. mediamatters.org/video/2005/11/21/oreilly-war-on-christmas-part-of-secular-progre/134262

15 Gibson, John. *The War on Christmas: How the Liberal Plot to Ban the Sacred Christian Holiday Is Worse Than You Thought.* New York: Sentinel, 2005.

16 Gill, Sam. "O'Reilly Admits He Falsely Accused Plano of Banning Red and Green Clothing." *Media Matters For America.* 21 December 2005. mediamatters.org/print/research/2005/12/21/oreilly-admits-he-falsely-accused-plano-of-bann/134500.

17 "'Silent Night' Secularized." *WND.* 7 December 2005. www.wnd.com/2005/12/33785/.

18 "Christmas Tree Controversy Takes Root in RI." *Fox News.* 6 December 2011. www.foxnews.com/us/2011/12/06/christmas-tree-controversy-takes-root-in-ri

19 Kovacs, Joe. "Season's Greetings: Christians Banned." *WND.* 2 December 2004. www.wnd.com/2004/12/27819/.

20 Witt, Ryan. "Conservatives Already Decrying a 'War on Christmas' That Liberals Say Does Not Exist." *Examiner.com.* 18 November 2009. www.examiner.com/article/video-conservatives-already-decrying-a-war-on-christmas-that-liberals-say-does-not-exist.

21 Weber, Dave. "TV Reports Wrong: Red, Green OK at Heathrow School." *Orlando Sentinel.* 29 November 2010; "O'Reilly Falsely Claimed a Texas School District Banned Red and Green Clothing, Called Move "Fascism." *Media Matters for America.* 13 December 2005. mediamatters.org/research/2005/12/13/oreilly-falsely-claimed-a-texas-school-district/134426.

22 "Fight the War on Christmas." *Faith & Freedom Coalition.* 9 December 2013. ffcoalition.com/blog/2013-12-09/fight-war-christmas.

23 Ross, Michael. "Todd Starnes Caught Lying about War on Christmas Again." *Examiner.com.* 10 December 2013. www.examiner.com/article/todd-starnes-caught-lying-about-war-on-christmas-again.

24 Boston, Rob. "Is There a 'War on Christmas'?" *Church & State Magazine.* Americans United for Separation of Church and State. December 2007.

25 Something similar could be said of the Chairman of Tulsa's (Oklahoma) parade of lights who replaced the word "Christmas" with "Holiday" in the name of its seasonal parade—something *Fox News* made a big deal about, a year after it first happened.

26 "Rhode Island Gov. Lincoln Chafee's 'Holiday' Tree Remark Angers Thousands—and the Roman Catholic Church." *NY Daily News.* 6 December 2011.

27 Johnson, Luke. "Lincoln Chafee, Rhode Island Governor, Stirs Controversy by Erecting 'Holiday' Tree in Statehouse." *The Huffington Post.* 6 December 2011. www.huffingtonpost.com/2011/12/06/lincoln-chafee-rhode-island-holiday-tree-christmas_n_1132227.html?utm_hp_ref=religion&ir=Religion.

28 Hallowell, Billy. "Battle Brews after RI Governor Calls the State's 'Christmas Tree' a 'Holiday Tree.'" *The Blaze.* 29 November 2011. www.theblaze.com/stories/2011/11/29/battle-brews-after-ri-governor-calls-the-states-christmas-tree-a-holiday-tree/.

29 Wildau, Gabe. "FOX Hypes Stories to Claim 'Christmas Under Siege.'" *Media Matters for America.* 10 December 2004. mediamatters.org/research/2004/12/10/fox-hypes-stories-to-claim-christmas-under-sieg/132428.

30 Dunn, Julie. "Float of Christ's Birth to Join Holiday Parade." *The Denver Post.* 11 October 2005.

31 Ryan (2009). "Video: Conservatives Already Decrying a 'War on Christmas' That Liberals Say Does Not Exist." *Examiner.com*. 18 November 2009. www.examiner.com/article/video-conservatives-already-decrying-a-war-on-christmas-that-liberals-say-does-not-exist.

32 Mikkelson, Barbara. "Wal-Mart Merry Christmas Ban." *Snopes.com*. 12 November 2005. www.snopes.com/politics/christmas/walmart.asp.

33 "O'Reilly: The War On Christmas Is 'Real and We Just Won.'" *NewsHounds*. 17 December 2013. www.newshounds.us/o_reilly_the_war_on_christmas_is_real_and_we_just_won_12172013.

34 It's only a preservative and does not affect the basic function of the vaccine.

35 In fact, O'Reilly's claim is even more irrational than the anti-vaxers. At least autism is a real disease. There is a real problem to solve.

36 Gill, Sam. "Fox Betrays Christmas Crusade, Sells 'Holiday' Ornaments for Your 'Holiday Tree.'" *Media Matters For America*. 30 November 2005. mediamatters.org research/2005/11/30/fox-betrays-christmas-crusade-sells-holiday-orn/134315.

37 Aldrich, Jeremy. "History of 'Happy Holidays.'" *Bloglovin*. 23 December 2011. https://www.bloglovin.com/blog/post/7826487/1078388645.

38 *Christmas with a Capital C*. Dir. Helmut Schleppi. Perf. Ted McGinley, Daniel Baldwin, Nancy Stafford. Ranch Studios, 2011. www.imdb.com/title/tt1640116/.

39 These billboards were erected by a group of women who decided that, if Jesus were alive today, this is what he would say. Kerby, Rob. "Over Morning Coffee, Five Friends Inspire 'Merry Christmas' Billboards." *Beliefnet*. www.beliefnet.com/columnists/news/2011/12/nationwide-merry-christmas-billboards-brewed-up-by-five-women-over-morning-coffee.php.

40 Baum, Geraldine. "Protesting Carolers Disrupt Rhode Island Tree-lighting Ceremony." *Los Angeles Times*. 8 December 2011.

41 Grewal, Daisy. "In Atheists We Distrust." *Scientific American*. 17 January 2012.

42 Palin (2013), p. 150.

43 Palin (2013), p. 155. Sarah did not come up with this idea; she is articulating John Calvin's doctrine of total depravity.

44 Paul, Gregory. "Cross-National Correlations of Quantifiable Societal Health with Popular Religiosity and Secularism in the Prosperous Democracies." *Journal of Religion & Society* 7 (2005): 1–17.

45 Severns Guntzel, Jeff. "Mind and Body." *Utne*. 20 August 2010. See also Zuckerman, Phil. *Society without God: What the Least Religious Nations Can Tell Us about Contentment*. New York: New York University Press, 2008.

46 Santorum recently produced the Christian Christmas movie *The Christmas Candle*. Dir. John Stephenson. Perf. Hans Matheson and Samantha Barks. Echolight Studios, 2014.

47 If Christmas really was like Ramadan—as Sarah Palin suggests—a wholly and only religious holiday invented by the religion that celebrates it, then it would be easier to see how any objection to Christmas would be an attack on the holiday as a whole and on Christianity itself. But, in both history and practice, Ramadan and Christmas are entirely different. See Palin (2013), p. 79.

48 Ibid., Chapter 1.

49 Interestingly "In God We Trust" was first added to some coin money in 1864 in response to a petition by Reverend M. R. Watkinson. This seemed to have been an attempt to declare that God was on the side of the Union army in the Civil War. It didn't appear on all coin money until 1938. For more on the history of the phrase, see: "In God We Trust." *Wikipedia*. en.wikipedia.org/wiki/In_God_we_trust.

50 So do I. How I have always interpreted it is that "establishment" is not a verb, but a noun. The amendment says that congress shouldn't make a law that does a certain kind of thing—respecting. That is the verb, not "establishment." It doesn't say "no law should establish," it's saying "no law should respect." Respect what? An establishment.

What kind of establishment? An establishment of religion—like the Catholic Church, the Methodist Church, etc. In short, I think the first amendment simply says that no law passed by Congress should favor any particular religious organization. But no one, besides me, actually reads it like this, so I relegated this theory of mine to an endnote.

51 "Letter of 7 October 1801, from Danbury (CT) Baptist Association to Thomas Jefferson." Thomas Jefferson Papers, Manuscript Division, Library of Congress, Washington, D.C.

52 Jefferson, Thomas. *The Writings of Thomas Jefferson.* Albert E. Bergh, ed. Washington, D.C.: The Thomas Jefferson Memorial Association of the United States, 1904, Vol. XVI, pp. 281–282.

53 Deists believe that God exists, but does not interfere in the world at all. Basically, God winds up the universe like a watch, and then lets it go, perhaps forgetting about it altogether.

54 Thomas Jefferson, "letter to John Adams, 24 January 1814," found here: www.nobeliefs.com/jefferson.htm.

55 Thomas Jefferson, "letter to William Short," 13 April 1820, found here: www.nobeliefs.com/jefferson.htm.

56 He distributed this as moral teachings to Native Americans.

57 Palin (2013), p. 47. The death toll of these regimes was higher than the Inquisition, but likely because there were more people to kill and more efficient means for killing them en masse. Think about how much worse the crusades would have been if they were fought with today's military technology with today's population density.

58 "Juche Religion." www.billionbibles.org/north-korea/juche-religion.html.

59 While Adams did acknowledge the power religion has to keep some people in line, it's not clear that he thought religion was necessary for morality. Palin ignores the word "moral" in this quote and concludes that Adams was suggesting that, without religion, everyone would misbehave.

60 "The Religion of John Adams, Second U.S. President." *Adherents.com.* www.adherents.com/people/pa/John_Adams.html.

61 "Thomas Jefferson, letter to Dr. Thomas Cooper, February 10, 1814." The entire letter can be found here: www.let.rug.nl/usa/presidents/thomas-jefferson/letters-of-thomas-jefferson/jefl227.php.

62 "Thomas Jefferson, letter to Horatio G. Spafford, March 17, 1814." The entire letter can be read here: founders.archives.gov/documents/Jefferson/03-07-02-0167.

63 "Thomas Jefferson to Alexander von Humboldt, December 6, 1813." The entire letter can be read here: www.let.rug.nl/usa/presidents/thomas-jefferson/letters-of-thomas-jefferson/jefl224.php.

64 Locke argued that we have a natural right to life, liberty, and *property*.

65 Uzgalis, William. "John Locke." *Stanford Encyclopedia of Philosophy.* 2 September 2001. plato.stanford.edu/entries/locke/.

66 Barton, David. *The Jefferson Lies.* Nashville: Thomas Nelson, 2012, p. 35.

67 "Thomas Jefferson to Jon Tyler, May 26, 1810," in Lipscomb, Andrew A., and Albert Ellery Bergh, eds. *The Writings of Thomas Jefferson,* Vol. 12. Washington, D.C.: Thomas Jefferson Memorial Association, 1907, pp. 392–393.

68 "Thomas Jefferson to Horatio G. Spafford, 17 March 1814," in Lipscomb, Andrew A., and Albert Ellery Bergh, eds. *The Writings of Thomas Jefferson,* Vol. 14. Washington, D.C.: Thomas Jefferson Memorial Association, 1907, pp. 119–120.

69 Webster, Stephen C. "'Historian' David Barton's book on Thomas Jefferson pulled from Stores." *Raw story.com.* 10 August 2012. www.rawstory.com/rs/2012/08/10/historian-david-bartons-book-on-thomas-jefferson-pulled-from-stores/.

70 Story, Joseph. *A Familiar Exposition of the Constitution of the United States.* Lake Bluff, IL: Regnery Gateway, 1986, Section 444.

71 You can find all three here: blogs.lse.ac.uk/usappblog/category/authors/david-kyle-johnson/.

72 "Lynch v. Donnelly." *Wikipedia*. en.wikipedia.org/wiki/Lynch_v._Donnelly.

73 "County of Allegheny v. American Civil Liberties Union." *Wikipedia*. en.wikipedia.org/wiki/County_of_Allegheny_v._American_Civil_Liberties_Union.

74 "Nativity Scene, Menorah Removed From Pennsylvania Courthouse Lawn." *Fox News*. 17 December 2009.

75 Gentilviso, Chris. "Festivus for the Rest of Us! Florida Atheist Successfully Puts up Beer Can Pole Display." *The Huffington Post*. 11 December 2013. www.huffingtonpost.com/2013/12/11/festivus-florida-pole_n_4427828.html.

76 Sarah Palin is right about one thing. Such displays are motivated by the desire to eliminate courthouse nativities all together. Those who erect them think that the Reindeer Rule does not go far enough in preventing government-endorsed religion.

77 Hallowell, Billy. "Anti-Nativity Atheist Cancels TX Lawsuit, Citing 'Evil' Death Threats from 'Peace-Loving Christians.'" *The Blaze*. 26 November 2012. www.theblaze.com/stories/2012/11/26/anti-nativity-scene-atheist-cancels-tx-lawsuit-citing-evil-death-threats-from-peace-loving-christians/.

78 Bruinius, Harry. "Culture Wars: Holiday Struggle over Public Spaces Still Very Much Alive (+video)." *The Christian Science Monitor*. 8 December 2013. www.csmonitor.com/USA/Society/2013/1208/Culture-wars-Holiday-struggle-over-public-spaces-still-very-much-alive-video.

79 Dougherty, Justin. "Oklahoma State Representatives File 'Merry Christmas Bill.'" *9 Mobile*. 9 December 2013. m.newson6.com/story/24176594/oklahoma-state-representatives-file-merry-christmas-bill.

80 Palin (2013), p. 44

81 Bruinius (2013).

82 "School Prayer and the Separation of Church and State: The Conflict That Keeps on Giving." *HubPages*. bibowen.hubpages.com/hub/school-prayer#img_url_3780225.

83 Mantyla, Kyle. "David Barton, Jon Stewart, and the Myth of Raymond Raines." *Right Wing Watch*. 2 May 2012. www.rightwingwatch.org/content/david-barton-jon-stewart-and-myth-raymond-raines.

84 Cline, Austin. "School Prayers—Are Prayers Allowed in School?" *About.com*. atheism.about.com/od/churchstatemyths/a/SchoolPrayerBanned.htm.

85 "Operation Christmas Child." Samaritans Purse. www.samaritans-purse.org.uk/what-we-do/operation-christmas-child/.

86 Of course, if one expresses their ultra-right wing views in a public forum, one can reasonably expect others to object, argue against, and even make fun of you. But this does not constitute persecution, nor does it violate freedom of speech. Our freedom of speech protects one's right to express their views without fear of being arrested or fined; it does not protect one from counter argument; it is not against the law for others to exercise their freedom of speech to contradict you.

87 You can check such figures here: tvbythenumbers.zap2it.com/category/cable-news/.

88 *The Daily Show*. Prod. Jon Stewart. "White Santa and Megyn Kelly's Apology." You can view the segment here: thedailyshow.cc.com/videos/tbbd03/white-santa---megyn-kelly-s-apology.

89 French, David. "Christmas skirmishes and the war for American history" *FaithStreet*, December 10, 2012. www.faithstreet.com/onfaith/2010/12/14/christmas-skirmishes-and-the-war-for-american-history/7446

90 Dougherty (2013).

91 Palin (2013), p. 7.

92 Ibid., p. 179.

93 Ibid., Chapter 6.

94 Ibid., p. 48.

95 Ibid., pp. 133–134.

96 Mill, John Stuart, and David Spitz, (ed.). *On Liberty.* New York: Norton, 1975, Chapter 1.

97 Ibid.

98 Fallon, Amy, and Bowcott, Owen. "Uganda Politicians Celebrate Passing of Anti-Gay Laws." *The Guardian.* 24 February 2014. www.theguardian.com/world/2014/feb/24/uganda-president-signs-anti-gay-laws.

CHAPTER 3 • MYTH 3: OUR CHRISTMAS TRADITIONS ARE OLD-FASHIONED

1   Nissenbaum, Stephen. *The Battle for Christmas.* New York: Alfred A. Knopf, 1996, p. 7.

2   Ibid., pp. 6–7.

3   Ibid., p. 7.

4   Ibid. You can find a great article on the Puritan opposition to Christmas here: Ward, Doug. "Cotton Mather's Dilemma." www.unityinchrist.com/history/print/cotton.htm.

5   Crippen, T. G. *Christmas and Christmas Lore.* Detroit: Gale Research Company, 1971, p. 90.

6   Rosenburg, Jennifer. "How FDR Changed Thanksgiving." *About.com.* history1900s. about.com/od/1930s/a/thanksgiving.htm.

7   And that's why we have two giant feast days nearly right next to each other on the calendar. We don't need to celebrate both, and in fact we haven't always done so. Celebrations of Thanksgiving remained sporadic until President Lincoln made Thanksgiving a national holiday in 1863, during the Civil War.

8   Some people have exaggerated this unpopularity, saying that Congress met on Christmas Day for the first 60 years of American history. This is incorrect. (Jon Stewart had to admit that he got this wrong on *The Daily Show* (6 December 2011); that's what he gets for listening to the History Chanel, which also suggests that Nazis had alien technology.) In fact, they didn't meet on Christmas Day—but not because it was Christmas. They usually let out in mid fall, and didn't return until mid January, mainly for travel purposes (they didn't have planes after all), and the fact that "congressman" wasn't their only responsibility.

9   Nissenbaum (1996), p. 25.

10 Franklin also pointed out that papists did attend church on Christmas Day, and in 1789 the Universalists of Boston were holding their first major Christmas church service.

11 Nissenbaum (1996), p. 10.

12 Indeed, one of my first experiences after moving to Pennsylvania was answering the door on Halloween only to have the local children barge their way into my house and sing a song and tell a joke before they accepted the candy that we offered. I later discovered that this tradition is fairly local, only existing in specific parts of the Wyoming Valley, but given that wassailing was popular in parts of Pennsylvania, and Pennsylvania's prominent role in Christmas history, I suspect that this tradition finds its origin in the old wassailing traditions. In fact, trick-or-treating itself, without the song and jokes, likely does as well.

13 Nissenbaum (1996), pp. 10–11. I suspect that this was sung to the tune of "Rock-a-bye-baby."

14 Ibid., p. 10.

15 Howard, Mark. "Ten Conservatives Who Have Praised Slavery." *Salon.* 12 October 2012. www.salon.com/2012/10/12/ten_conservatives_who_have_praised_slavery/.

16 I hope it goes without saying that Christmastime generosity can't make up for the enslavement of other human beings.

17 Nissenbaum (1996), p. 268

18 Ibid., p. 55.

19 Ibid., pp. 56–57.

20 Ibid., p. 58.

21 Pelican Publishing; 2nd ed., 2 November 2009; first published in 1809.

22 Nissenbaum (1996), p. 64.

23 Ibid., p. 65.

24 The true authorship of the poem is disputed, and we will address that when we discuss Myth #5.

25 Nissenbaum (1996), p. 109.

26 Ibid.

27 Ibid., p. 110.

28 Ibid., p. 112.

29 Ibid.

30 Ibid., p. 62.

31 Christmas trees were still not that popular.

32 Standiford, Les. *The Man Who Invented Christmas: How Charles Dickens "A Christmas Carol" Rescued His Career and Revived Our Holiday Spirits.* New York: Crown Publishers, 2008, p. 29.

33 Langager, Chad. "How Many People Watch the Super Bowl Each Year?" *SportingCharts. com.* 30 January 2014. www.sportingcharts.com/articles/nfl/how-many-people-watch-the-super-bowl-each-year.aspx.

34 Nissenbaum (1996), pp. 103–104.

35 Standiford (2008), p. 225.

36 Ibid.

37 Charles Dickens was not a religious person—in fact, he was a bit anti-religious. But he was highly concerned about the plight of the poor in the face of unchecked capitalism. Ghosts, of course, are not Christian either. The only mention of religion in *A Christmas Carol* is when Bob Cratchit mentions that he and Tiny Tim had been to church.

38 "ASCAP [American Society of Composers, Authors and Publishers] Announces Top 25 Holiday Songs." *ASCAP.* 27 November 2006. www.ascap.com/press/2006/112706_xmassongs.html.

39 Forbes, Bruce David. *Christmas: A Candid History.* Berkeley: University of California, 2007, p. 119.

40 Interestingly, Christmas cards predated doodads, and predating Christmas cards were hand-written letters. "Family update letters" are still a common Christmas tradition among many families.

41 This reflects a kind of confirmation bias—a mistake in reasoning—that makes people think the times in which they live are worse than they are; usually they seem like the worst in history. For example, many people believe they live in the end times because, like with Christmas, they think "things have never been as bad as this." In reality, however, we only think this because we are directly aware of the atrocities of our own times, but are not directly aware of the atrocities of times gone by. If you actually look at the statistics, we live in one of the most peaceful times in human history. Even with our increased ability to kill in war on a mass scale, as a percentage, fewer people die as a result of war today than any other time in history. See Singh, Vikas, and Srijana Mitra Das. "Ours Is the Most Peaceful Time in History: Steven Pinker." *The Times of India.* 22 January 2012. timesofindia.indiatimes.com/india/Ours-is-the-most-peaceful-time-in-history-Steven-Pinker/articleshow/11583435.cms?referral=PM.

42 Nissenbaum (1996), pp. 165–167.

43 Ibid., p. 140.

44 Vesilind, Emili. "A Brief History of American Jewelry." *JCK Magazine.* June 2013.

45 "Rudolph the Red-Nosed Reindeer." *Wikipedia.* en.wikipedia.org/wiki/Rudolph_the_Red-Nosed_Reindeer.

46 "The True History of the Modern Day Santa Claus." *The Coca-Cola Company.* 1 January 2012. www.coca-colacompany.com/holidays/the-true-history-of-the-modern-day-santa-claus.

47 "Why Santa Claus Loves Red and White Suit?" *Kvisoft Blog.* www.kvisoft.com/blog/santa-claus-loves-red-white-suit/.

48 Rosenberg, Jennifer. "How FDR Changed Thanksgiving." *About.com.* history1900s.

about.com/od/1930s/a/thanksgiving.htm.

49 The History Channel has a fairly inaccurate history of Christmas trees here: www.history.com/topics/christmas/history-of-christmas-trees.

50 Graves, Dan. "Christmas Eve." *Christianity.com.* July 2007. www.christianity.com/church/church-history/timeline/1501-1600/christmas-eve-11629927.html.

51 Perry, Joe. *Christmas in Germany: A Cultural History.* Chapel Hill: University of North Carolina, 2010.

52 Nissenbaum (1996), p. 195.

53 Ibid., p. 177.

54 Ibid., pp. 196–197.

55 Ibid., p. 212.

56 Interestingly, a generation earlier, spoiled kids like Mary—who wanted or went for their gifts too quickly—would have been put in their place by Belsnickel or Hanstrapp (more on them in the discussion of Myth #5). But our Christmas tree gift-exchange tradition has none of these checks in place—nothing to *actually* punish selfish, spoiled children. I'll argue regarding Myth #6 that this is a good reason to change our Christmas gift-giving traditions.

57 Nissenbaum (1996), p. 245.

58 Ibid., p. 197.

59 "Christmas Tree Production in the United States." *Wikipedia.* en.wikipedia.org/wiki/Christmas_tree_production_in_the_United_States.

60 "White House Christmas Tree." *Wikipedia.* en.wikipedia.org/wiki/White_House_Christmas_tree.

61 Forbes (2007), p. 65.

62 "Rockefeller Center Christmas Tree." *Wikipedia.* en.wikipedia.org/wiki/Rockefeller_Center_Christmas_Tree.

63 Nissenbaum (1996), p. 91.

64 Ibid., p. 93.

65 Ibid., p. 96.

66 Ibid., p. 104.

67 Ibid., p. 228.

68 Ibid., p. 229.

69 Unionization solidified the sentiment as such organizations would not supply assistance to workers on strike.

70 Nissenbaum (1996), p. 230.

71 Ibid., p. 233.

72 Ibid., p. 235.

73 Brace was perhaps too busy writing *Gesta Christi*, a theology book in which he argued that the tone of the New Testament was communistic, favored the distribution of wealth (although not by governmental force) and that Jesus today would likely be considered a socialist—although Brace considered himself a "man of self-reliance." Nissenbaum (1996), p. 236.

74 Ibid., p. 241.

75 "...[T]he American bourgeoisie were facing a real Christmas dilemma. Their own children had become jaded with presents. On the other hand, the actual poor—who were unlikely to be surfeited with gifts—were a sea of anonymous proletarian faces, and in any event they were as likely to respond to acts of token generosity with embarrassment or hostility as with the requisite display of hearty gratitude. Giving to the *children* of the needy would solve the dilemma neatly." Nissenbaum (1996), p. 246.

76 "In any case, from mid-century on—and with what appears to have been increasing frequency in the 1890s—some well-to-do Americans devoted part of their Christmas days to visiting the children of the poor." Nissenbaum (1996), p. 247.

77 Ibid., p. 248.

78 Ibid., p. 253.

79 Ibid.

CHAPTER 4 • MYTH 4: CHRISTMAS SPENDING IS GOOD FOR THE ECONOMY

1   Palin, Sarah. *Good Tidings and Great Joy: Protecting the Heart of Christmas*. New York: Broadside, 2013, p. 86.

2   In fact, the economy's health is often used to predict how heavy Christmas spending will be. Versace, Christopher. *2013—"A Not So Merry Christmas for the Consumer and Retailers?}* Forbes. 26 September 2013.

3   Actually, Christmas spending gives people less to spend.

4   Associated Press, "Pope Decries 'Material Slavery' as Holidays Start." ABC *News*, December 8 2014. abcnews.go.com/Health/wireStory/pope-decries-material-slavery-holidays-start-27445351

5   Waldfogel, Joel. *Scroogenomics: Why You Shouldn't Buy Presents for the Holidays*. Princeton, NJ: Princeton University Press, 2009.

6   If you think you "freely choose" to buy what you buy, try freely choosing to not buy gifts one season and see what happens.

7   Hull, Jason. "What Would Happen if We All Paid off Our Debt?" *U.S. News & World Report*. 12 October 2012. money.usnews.com/money/blogs/the-smarter-mutual-fund-investor/2012/10/12/what-would-happen-if-we-all-paid-off-our-debt.

8   Hull says that prior to the great depression, "it was common practice in the U.S. to have a 50 percent down [payment on a house with a] 5-year interest-only loan."

9   Nissenbaum, Stephen. *The Battle for Christmas*. New York: Random House, 1996.

10 "Chart Book: The Legacy of the Great Recession." *Center on Budget and Policy Priorities*. 11 March 2014. www.cbpp.org/cms/index.cfm?fa=view&id=3252.

11 Waldfogel (2009), Chapter 9.

12 This is the figure reached by Waldfogel in Chapter 3 regarding the 2007 Christmas season. Some make the mistake of thinking that all December sales are Christmas sales, forgetting that a lot of regular spending happens in December as well. This results in exaggerations in the amounts we spend and what we could do with that money instead. See "$469 Billion: How Much Americans Will Spend Shopping During this Holiday Season (and what else you could buy with that much money)." *Last Throes*. 22 December 2011. www.lastthroes.com/2011/12/469-billion-how-much-americans-will.html.

13 "America's Aging Infrastructure: What to Fix, and Who Will Pay?" *University of Pennsylvania*. 10 November 2010. knowledge.wharton.upenn.edu/article/americas-aging-infrastructure-what-to-fix-and-who-will-pay/.

14 Ritholtz, Barry. "Repairing Infrastructure Can Help Repair Economy." *The Big Picture*. 4 July 2013. www.ritholtz.com/blog/2013/07/repairing-infrastructure-can-help-repair-economy/.

15 Wright, Paul. "Looming Crisis: America's Credit Card Debt Bubble-Burst." *Global Research*. 3 March 2010. www.globalresearch.ca/looming-crisis-america-s-credit-card-debt-bubble-burst/17903.

16 Wadfogel (2009), Chapter 8.

17 *Fight Club*. Dir. David Fincher. Perf. Brad Pitt, Edward Norton, and Helena Bonham Carter. Twentieth Century Fox. 1999.

18 Shen, Andrew. "INFOGRAPHIC: Americans Are Spending a Whopping $704.18 On Gifts This Year." *Business Insider*. 20 December 2011. www.businessinsider.com/what-americans-spend-on-christmas-2011-12?IR=T.

19 Paster, Pablo. "Ask Pablo: Holiday Wrapping Paper." *TreeHugger*. 21 December 2010. www.treehugger.com/culture/ask-pablo-holiday-wrapping-paper.html.

20 Waldfogel (2009), Chapter 4.

21 It's not just Christmas gifts that can create deadweight loss. Wedding gifts are good

examples, too. If everyone just "buys on their own," the couple ends up getting things they will never use or multiples of the same item. As a result, the couple has to buy many items that would have made great gifts for them on their own. This is why registering for gifts has become so popular; it guards against wasteful spending. I do not, however, see gift registries as a feasible means to eliminate Christmas waste.

22 Interestingly, websites where you can sell your unused gift cards for cash (but for less than their value) are becoming more common. See www.plasticjungle.com, www.gift-cardrescue.com, or www.cardpool.com.

23 "The Breakers." *Wikipedia.* en.wikipedia.org/wiki/The_Breakers.

24 Sullivan, Missy, "Lost Inheritance." *The Wall Street Journal.* 8 March 2013. online.wsj.com/news/articles/SB10001424127887324662404578334663271139552.

25 Puzzanghera, Jim. "Oxfam Report Highlights Widening Income Gap between Rich, Poor." *LA Times.* 20 January 2014. www.latimes.com/business/la-fi-income-inequality-20140121-story.html. See also, Thompson, Derek. "The World's 85 Richest People Are as Wealthy as the Poorest 3 Billion." *The Atlantic.* 21 January 2014.

26 www.gatesfoundation.org/.

27 Kroll, Luisa. "Inside the 2013 Billionaires List: Facts and Figures." *Forbes.* 25 March 2013.

28 Garcia, Arturo. "Bill Maher's Grinch-like advice for salvaging Christmas: No more gift-giving." *Raw Story.* 22 November 2014. www.rawstory.com/rs/2014/11/bill-mahers-grinch-like-advice-for-salvaging-christmas-no-more-gift-giving/

29 Geisel, Theodor. *How the Grinch Stole Christmas.* New York: Random House, 1957.

30 Dickens, Charles. *A Christmas Carol and Other Stories.* Pleasantville, N.Y./Montreal: The Reader's Digest Association, Inc. 1988, p. 24.

31 Nissenbaum (1996), p. 223.

32 "…Dickens addressed not the great social divisions among classes estranged from one another by wealth, distance, and occupation but the daily, intimate class differences among people who were much closer to one another on the social scale". (Nissenbaum 1996, p. 224) "In other words, *A Christmas Carol* addressed the relationship of the well-to-do not with the faceless poor but with the poor who were personally known and whose predicament might provoke pangs of conscience. It offered a perspective on how to deal with people who neither belonged to one's own family or social circle nor were members of the anonymous proletariat…[T]he creation, in England and America, of vast armies of middle class people and wage earners produced a new type of society in which the old rules of inversion and misrule no longer made much sense". (Nissenbaum 1996, p. 225)

33 Dickens, p. 20.

34 Ibid., p. 21.

35 Ibid.

36 Ibid., p. 69.

37 Ibid., p. 80.

38 Ibid., p. 33.

39 Ibid., p. 101.

40 For more on organizations that support a similar philosophy, see www.adventconspiracy.org and www.buynothingchristmas.org.

· ·

CHAPTER 5 • MYTH 5: SANTA CLAUS IS ST. NICHOLAS

1 Harris, Alisha. "Santa Claus Should Not Be a White Man Anymore." *Slate.com.* 10 December 2013. www.slate.com/articles/life/holidays/2013/12/santa_claus_an_old_white_man_not_anymore_meet_santa_the_penguin_a_new_christmas.html.

2 This sounds rather odd, until you remember that Easter's Mascott is, after all, a rabbit.

3   Harris (2013).

4   For a more detailed response to Megyn, including a highlight of the irony of that statement, see blogs.lse.ac.uk/usappblog/2013/12/22/fox-news-christmas/.

5   Feldman, Josh. "O'Reilly Defends Megyn Kelly: She's 'Correct, Santa Is a White Person.'" *Mediaite.com*. 16 December 2013. www.mediaite.com/tv/oreilly-defends-megyn-kelly-shes-correct-santa-is-a-white-person/.

6   Dolan, Eric. "Bill O'Reilly Uses Image of Dark-Skinned Saint Nicholas to Prove Santa Is White." *Rawstory.com*. 17 December 2013. www.rawstory.com/rs/2013/12/17/bill-oreilly-uses-image-of-dark-skinned-saint-nicholas-to-prove-santa-is-white/.

7   For more on this debacle, see Johnson, David Kyle. "Sorry Megyn, Santa Claus is not White." Psychology Today Blog: Plato on Pop. Dec 10, 2013. www.psychologytoday.com/blog/plato-pop/201312/sorry-megyn-santa-claus-is-not-white

8   Siefker, Phyllis. *Santa Claus, Last of the Wild Men*. Jefferson, NC, and London: McFarland and Company, 1997, p. 5.

9   For example, according to www.catholic.org "[Nicholas's] episcopate at Myra during the fourth century is really all that seems indubitable [sic] authentic." www.catholic.org/saints/saint.php?saint_id=371. *The Catholic Encyclopedia* agrees. Ott, Michael. "St. Nicholas of Myra." *The Catholic Encyclopedia*. New York: Robert Appleton Company, 1911, Vol. 11. www.newadvent.org/cathen/11063b.htm.

10 Lendering, Jona. "Saint Nicholas, Sinterklass, Santa Claus." *Livius.org*. 2006. www.livius.org/ne-nn/nicholas/nicholas_of_myra1.html.

11 Bennett, William. *The True Saint Nicholas*. Brentwood, TN: Howard Books, 2009.

12 Those who want to believe that St. Nicholas exists have very low standards for "convincing evidence." Jeremy Seal, for example, is convinced that there was a real St. Nicholas because the biography of another Nicholas (Nicholas of Sion) includes a mention of him visiting a martyrium named after the original St. Nicholas. But this visit would have been about 200 years after his death (around 550), and a hundred years after the first historical mention of the "original" Nicholas (in 440). There were a host of churches, martyrium, and other buildings named after non-existent saints, and it's no surprise that there were buildings named after Nicholas 100 years after he was first mentioned.

13 See Lendering (2006).

14 Forbes, Bruce David. *Christmas: A Candid History*. Los Angeles: University of Californian Press, 2007, pp. 74–76.

15 Again, apologists reach for explanations. Nicholas's bones were supposedly stolen at one point, but then later those from whom they were stolen claimed to have tricked the robbers, causing them to steal the wrong bones. Of course, all such stories should be taken with a grain of salt.

16 It wasn't so much of a roll, but a list of bishops that voted to support what became the orthodox view of Jesus's divinity. As we shall see, tradition holds that Nicholas supported that view. See Lendering (2006).

17 Scholars universally agree that portions of the relevant passage were embellished. Some argue that the whole thing was confabulated. See Bart Ehrman's *Did Jesus Exist: The Historical Argument for Jesus of Nazareth*. New York: Harper Collins, 2012, pp. 57–59.

18 Lendering brushes past this, only mentioning that it is from a "late source."

19 Lendering cites the fact that the story is embarrassing as evidence for its authenticity. It is assumed the ancients wouldn't make up embarrassing stories about those they admired, and sometimes this reasoning is valid. But if the story is fiction, it would have been made up as an explanation for why he got kicked out—thus wouldn't it have had to been embarrassing? Wouldn't he have had to do something wrong? On top of that, the story seems to be the most honorable way to explain his absence. He was so passionate about the Orthodox view that he punched Arius, the author of the biggest heresy in church history, at the very meeting that heresy became heretical. How is that

even embarrassing? It probably makes people like him more! If the story was that he got taken off the roll because he molested children—then yeah, they probably wouldn't make that up. But as it stands, it is highly unlikely that it is authentic.

20 "Belgian Group Checks Facts." Found in "Saint Makers (Cover story)." *U.S. News & World Report* 126.1 (1999): 52.

21 See Catholic Online's list of saints. www.catholic.org/saints/. Comparing the old calendar with the new would show you who was removed. To see if your favorite saint made the cut, see "Saints of the Roman Calendar." www.ewtn.com/library/MARY/ SAINTROM.htm. But it's probably impossible to find a list of who was cut because most of those interested in saints are Catholic, and Catholics aren't too fond of compiling lists of things they were wrong about. For Pete's sake, it took them 350 years to apologize to Galileo for locking him up after he said the earth revolved around the sun. My guess is that the recommendations of the Bollandists, which led to the "mass defrocking," are locked up in the Vatican somewhere.

22 See Catholic Online's "Saints FAQ's: Whatever Happened to St. Christopher? Is He Still a Saint?" www.catholic.org/saints/faq.php#St.%20Christopher.

23 "Is St. Nicholas a Real Saint?" www.stnicholascenter.org/Brix?pageID=234.

24 Vitti, Jon, "So It's Come to This: A Simpsons Clip Show." *The Simpsons.* 1 April 1993. (The line is Homer's.)

25 *Forbes* (2007), p. 72.

26 Ibid., p. 12.

27 Flynn, Tom. *The Trouble With Christmas.* New York: Prometheus Books, 1993, p. 48.

28 Bowler, Gerry. *Santa Claus: A Biography.* Toronto: McClelland & Stewart, 2005, p. 18.

29 See Lendering (2006).

30 Details about Hold Nickar are hard to come by, but apparently one of the main gifts that he was (or those representing him were) thought to bring was (no joke) psychedelic mushrooms. For more on this see: Larsen, Dana. "The Psychedelic Secrets of Santa Claus." *Cannabis Culture Magazine.* 13 December 2003. www.cannabisculture. com/articles/3136.html; and "Santa Claus Is Coming to Town." PaganParenting.org. www.paganparenting.org/spirituality/wheel/yule/santa.html.

31 Grossman, John. *Christmas Curiosities: Odd, Dark, and Forgotten Christmas.* New York: Stewart, Tabori, and Chang, 2008.

32 Siefker (1997), Chapter 2.

33 Although Moses's horns may be the result of a mistranslation of Exodus 34:29, where Moses's face "shone" after talking with God. The Vulgate used the word "cornuta" for shone, and "cornu" means "horn" in Latin.

34 Siefker (1997), p. 49.

35 Flynn (1993), p. 48.

36 Siefker (1997), Chapter 4.

37 Forbes (2007), p. 94.

38 Siefker (1997), p. 155.

39 Siefker (1997), p. 157.

40 Although he has a similar origin, Black Peter has a noticeably different appearance than the others. Developed by the Dutch while they were under Spanish rule, he looks like a miniature conquistador in black face. It was perhaps inevitable that the Black Peter tradition would come under fire as racist, as it did in 2014. See Iyengar, Rishi "Dutch Blackface Tradition Sparks Festive Fury and 90 Arrests." *Time.com*, November 17 2014. time.com/3588433/netherlands-belgium-christmas-black-pete/

41 Forbes (2007), pp. 78–79.

42 Although it was clearly a combination of the European Nicholas and Wild Man traditions, it seems that Belsnickel was unique to German Pennsylvania—at least, I have yet to find an example of any tradition in Germany that is similar enough to Belsnickel (and enough unlike Nicholas or the Wild Man) to be thought of as another version of Belsnickel.

43 Interestingly, this aspect of the Belsnickle tradition initially carried over into the Santa Claus tradition. My own grandfather, Johney Bryan, used to dress up as Santa and go

house to house on Christmas Eve. Unfortunately, mall Santas seem to have replaced this tradition.

44 Siefker (1997), pp. 19–20. You can see artist Ralph Dunkerlberger's depiction of Pelznickel on page 21 of Siefker's book. You can also see it here: www.volgagermans.net/norka/images/Pelznickel.jpg.

45 Belsnickeling was also a form of begging as those dressed up as Belsnickel would often expect a tip from the home's family in return for their appearance.

46 Nickell, Joe. "The Case of the Christmas Poem." *Manuscripts* 54(4): 293–308; Nickell, Joe. "The Case of the Christmas Poem: Part 2." *Manuscripts* 55(1): 5–15.

47 Kaller, Seth. "The Authorship of 'The Night Before Christmas.'" *Seth Kaller, Inc. Historical Documents, Legacy Collections.* www.sethkaller.com/about/educational/tnbc/.

48 My research made me change my mind on this issue; the authorship of the poem was originally another "Christmas Myth" I was going to address.

49 Nissenbaum, Stephen. *The Battle for Christmas.* New York: Random House, 1996, p. 85.

50 Here I am quoting Kaller who is quoting the *New-York Historical Society Quarterly Bulletin,* January 1919, See pp. 111 and 114.

51 If you dig into this a bit further, you may find that the Belsnickel tradition was celebrated by the "Pennsylvania Dutch" and thus think that Livingston's Dutch origins would make him familiar with the Belsnickel tradition. But, ironically, the Pennsylvania Dutch are not Dutch at all—but are one and the same with the Pennsylvania Germans. The confusion began right after their immigration to the Americas. When asked where they were from, they would refer to their homeland of Germany in their native tongue—calling it "Deutschland." Uneducated Americans thought they were saying that they were Dutch, and thus began calling them "Pennsylvania Dutch." The name stuck, and is still preferred by the "less educated" Pennsylvania Germans.

52 Interestingly, the common Dutch phrase "Dunder and Blixem" (thunder and lightning, which was often used as a Dutch curse) is in the original 1823 "anonymous" version of the poem, but was changed to the German "Donder and Blitzen" by Moore in the 1844 official publication. Some claim this is evidence that the poem was originally written by the Dutch Livingston, but later changed by Moore when he stole it. What is more likely is that Moore first used "Dunder and Blixem"—a phrase he didn't fully understand but knew was Dutch—to make it seem more authentically Dutch. He likely changed it when he published it in 1844 simply because it rhymed better (Vixen/Blitzen).

53 You can see a depiction of Thor, with his goats Gnasher and Cracker, pulling his chariot here: saxons.etrusia.co.uk/images/thor.jpg.

54 Yzermans, Vincent A., *Wonderworker: The True Story of How St. Nicholas Became Santa Claus.* Chicago: ACTA Publications, 1994.

55 Siefker (1997), p. 161.

56 Here are a few suggestions I found. William Hooper (in his self-published *The Heathen's Guide to Christmas*) suggested that in the Middle Ages the church used St. Nicholas as a threat, to make sure that all people—not just kids—obeyed. "Pay your tithe, or Nicholas will get you on December 6th." People, in turn, threatened to lock their doors and windows to prevent his entry. The church retorted, "he is so resolute, he'll come in the one place you can't lock up in the winter: your chimney!" On the other hand, Yzermans suggested that Laplandish Christmas visitors would come in through the holes in their teepees, where the fire escaped. I doubt both explanations.

57 Siefker (1997), p. 103.

58 Nissenbaum (1996), pp. 72–73; Bowler (2005), p. 28."

59 This is another possible origin for the idea that Santa lives at the North Pole; the 1857 drawing depicts him in an icy and snowy place. See Harper's Weekly, December 26, 1857 (pp.820-1) which can be found here www.hymnsandcarolsofchristmas.com/santa/Wonders/wonders_of_santa_claus.htm. For more on the history of Nast's Santa images, see Kennedy, Robert. "Santa Claus and His Works" New York Times: On This Day. December 25, 2001. www.nytimes.com/learning/general/onthisday/harp/1225.html

60   You can see the first Coca-Cola Santa, as depicted by artist Haddon Sundblom in the *Saturday Evening Post*, in 1931 (and a number of other Coca-Cola Santas) here: www.thecoca-colacompany.com/heritage/cokelore_santa.html.

61   Brown, R. J. "Thomas Nast: The Power of One Person's Wood Engravings." *HistoryBuff.com.* www.historybuff.com/library/refnast.html.

62   Three of my personal favorite modern renditions of Krampus can be seen here: www2.bgsu.edu/departments/greal/NewAYA/salzburg_info/subpages/images/krampus.jpg; f742a291acf7f6ce2375-d87d8e7b51bb281f7a964c4a606459da.r10.cf1.rackcdn.com/krampus_21.jpg; upload.wikimedia.org/wikipedia/commons/6/6a/Krampus_Morzger_Pass_Salzburg_2008_10.jpg.

63   You can see his appearance here: www.colbertnation.com/the-colbert-report-videos/258162/december-09-2009/the-blitzkrieg-on-grinchitude---hallmark---krampus.

64   You can see it here: www.youtube.com/watch?v=9p1JYvV178E&feature=youtu.be.

65   Brom. *Krampus: The Yule Lord.* New York: Harper Voyager, 2012.

66   "Dwight Christmas." Wikipedia. en.wikipedia.org/wiki/Dwight_Christmas.

67   Basu, Tanya. "Who Is Krampus? Explaining the Horrific Christmas Devil." *National Geographic.* 17 December 2013.

68   "Twelve Days of Krampus." 13 December 2013.

69   "Minstrel Krampus." 15 December 2013. This episode was originally scheduled for 2012, but pushed back a year because it has a shootout at the end that was too reminiscent of the Sandy Hook Shootings of that same year. See McFarland, Kevin. "American Dad, 'Minstrel Krampus,' Season 9, Episode 8." *A.V. Club.* 16 December 2013. www.avclub.com/tvclub/minstrel-krampus-106512.

70   The only reference I could find that predates my interest in Krampus is an 11-minute Venture Brothers special from 2004. venturebrothers.wikia.com/wiki/A_Very_Venture_Christmas.

71   Janelle, "Krampus is Coming" *Last Gasp.* November 25, 2014. www.lastgasp.com/story/2014/11/krampus2014

72   Eddy, Melissa. "He Sees You When You're Sleeping, and Gives You Nightmares." *The New York Times,* Europe: Munich Journal. Dec 21, 2014. www.nytimes.com/2014/12/22/world/europe/krampus-he-sees-you-when-youre-sleeping-and-gives-you-nightmares.html

73   Woerner, Meredith. "Joyful Krampus Gifs Tease Next Year's Holiday Horror Movie." Dec 20, 2015. *Io9* io9.com/joyful-krampus-gifs-tease-next-years-holiday-horror-mov-1673336754

···

CHAPTER 6 • MYTH 6: THE SANTA CLAUS LIE IS HARMLESS

1   *Daily Mail* reporter. "Primary School Teacher Who Told Children: 'Santa Does Not Exist' Is Fired." 11 December 2008. www.dailymail.co.uk/news/article-1093535/Primary-school-teacher-told-children-Santa-does-exist-fired.html.

2   Sudo, Chuck. "Fox News Chicago's Robin Robinson Apologizes for Saying There Is No Santa on Air." *Chicagoist.* 2 December 2011. chicagoist.com/tags/robinrobinsonapologizesforsayingsantaisn'treal. To boot: right before the publication of this book, a mother in California was threatened with a lawsuit because her son told other children at his school that Santa wasn't real. The lawsuit even calls for her to pay a Santa to come to one of the kids houses, where all the disillusioned kids will be waiting, to trick the kids into believing again. See Rose, Tammy. "California Mom Threated With Lawsuit After Her Son Tells Friends that Santa Claus Isn't Real" *Inquisitr* (October 2, 2015). www.inquisitr.com/2464571/california-mom-threatened-with-lawsuit-after-her-son-tells-his-friends-that-santa-claus-isnt-real

3   Take, for example, a story accounted to me by Marty Michelson, my undergraduate Old Testament professor. While working as a children's pastor in Colorado Springs to more than 250 kids in the 90's, he had parents adamantly complain about a married couple—extremely faithful, reliable and hardworking volunteers—because they clarified, to their 8 and 9 year old Sunday School students, that while Santa was make-believe, Jesus was not. Parents who had never even bothered to make themselves known to him, made it a point to seek Marty out and complain. "I'm confused," he asked, "the Sunday School teacher taught your child the truth. Is it your hope the teacher will lie to your children?" "Yes," most of them replied, "about this one issue."

4   See Johnson, David Kyle. "Sorry, Virginia..." *Baltimore Sun*. 13 December 2009; Johnson, David Kyle. "Against the Santa Claus Lie: The Truth We Should Tell Our Children." Chapter 12 (pp. 139–150) in Scott Lowe's *Christmas—Philosophy for Everyone*. Oxford: Wiley-Blackwell, 2010; Johnson, David Kyle. "Say Goodbye to the Santa Claus Lie." *Psychology Today*. Blog: Plato on Pop. 17 December 2012. www.psychologytoday.com/blog/plato pop/201212/say-goodbye-the-santa-claus-lie; Johnson, David Kyle. "Let's Bench the Elf on the Shelf." *Psychology Today*. Blog: Plato on Pop. 19 December 2012. www.psychologytoday.com/blog/plato-pop/201212/let-s-bench-the-elf-the-shelf; Johnson, David Kyle. "The Santa Claus Lie Debate: Answering Objections." *Psychology Today*. Blog: Plato on Pop. 9 December 2013. www.psychologytoday.com/blog/plato-pop/201312/the-santa-claus-lie-debateanswering-

5   And as one person reminded me in an email, Santa also helps distract from the fact that many of the toys weren't made in his workshop—but in sweatshop like conditions, by other children, overseas.

6   I first mentioned this story in Lowe (2010), p. 143.

7   Although it is not fun for all children. See the marvelous book *Scared of Santa: Scenes of Terror in Toyland* by Denise Joyce and Nancy Watkins. New York: Harper Publishing, 2008.

8   Statistics on this are hard to find. One 1979 study suggested that although 39% of kids were disappointed by learning the truth, only 6% of them felt betrayed. These numbers were up from an 1896 study, however, and I wonder what they would be now. At any rate, I would not consider this one single study to be authoritative and I was unable to check its methodology. "Why Do We Believe in Santa?" *Universte de Montreal, News Digest*. 8 December 2008. www.nouvelles.umontreal.ca/archives/2007-2008/content/view/2121/248/index.html.

9   Comte-Sponville, Andre. *A Small Treatise on the Great Virtues*. New York: Holt Paperbacks, 2002, Chapter 1.

10 She defends the lie in the name of imagination. I'll deal with this argument shortly.

11 Moyer, Melinda Wenner. "The Santa Lie: Is the Big Christmas Con Hurting Our Kids?" *Slate Magazine*. 6 December 2012. www.slate.com/articles/double_x/the_kids/2012/12/the_santa_lie_is_the_big_christmas_con_hurting_our_kids.html.

12 Hume, David. "Section X: Of Miracles." *An Enquiry Concerning Human Understanding: A Letter from a Gentleman to His Friend in Edinburgh*. Indianapolis: Hackett Publishing, 1977.

13 Clifford, W. K. *The Ethics of Belief and Other Essays*. Amherst: Prometheus Books, 1999, p. 138.

14 Schick, Theodore, and Vaughn, Lewis. *How to Think about Weird Things: Critical Thinking for a New Age*, 7th ed. New York: McGraw Hill, 2014, p. 2.

15 Sometimes they use such treatments in place of working medical treatments and die of curable conditions.

16 Schick and Vaughn (2014), p. 6.

17 Williams, Rob. "One in Four Americans 'Don't Know the Earth Orbits the Sun' and Only Half Believe in Evolution." *The Independent*. 16 February 2014. www.independent.co.uk/news/science/one-in-four-americans-dont-know-the-earth-orbits-the-sun-and-only-half-believe-in-evolution-9131721.html.

18 For more on this, see Schick and Vaughn (2014), Chapter 5.

19 "The Innocence Project—Reevaluating Lineups: Why Witnesses Make Mistakes and How to Reduce the Chance of a Misidentification." *The Innocence Project*. www.innocenceproject.org/Content/Reevaluating_Lineups_Why_Witnesses_Make_Mistakes_and_How_to_Reduce_the_Chance_of_a_Misidentification.php.

20 Preidt, Robert. "Memories Can Be Unreliable, Manipulated—Neurology (Brain and Nerve) Conditions, Diseases, Medications, Procedures, Tests, Treatment, Prevention, and Prognosis Information on MedicineNet.com." *MedicineNet*. 3 August 2011. www.medicinenet.com/script/main/art.asp?articlekey=147786.

21 "Cognitive Science: An Introduction/Biases and Reasoning Heuristics." Wikibooks. en.wikibooks.org/wiki/Cognitive_Science:_An_Introduction/Biases_and_Reasoning_Heuristics.

22 *Search for Santa*. Dir. Douglas Cheney. CustomFlix, 2006.

23 In an homage to the Zapruder film, that captured JFK's assassination, they call it the "Swoboda film."

24 Lowry, Lauren. "Fact or Fiction? The Top 10 Assumptions about Early Speech and Language Development." *The Hanen Centre*. 2011. www.hanen.org/Helpful-Info/Articles/Fact-or-Fiction--The-Top-10-Assumptions-about-Earl.aspx.

25 "The Truth about Kids and the Santa Claus Lie." *The Huffington Post*. 16 December 2013. live.huffingtonpost.com/r/segment/the-truth-about-kids-and-santa-claus/52a89400fe344438aa00025c.

26 Stuever, Hank. *Tinsel: A Search for America's Christmas Present*. Boston: Houghton Mifflin Harcourt, 2009, p. 181.

27 Beckford, Martin. "Harry Potter Fails to Cast Spell over Professor Richard Dawkins." *Telegraph.com*. Updated 5 July 2009. www.telegraph.co.uk/news/3255972/Harry-Potter-fails-to-cast-spell-over-Professor-Richard-Dawkins.html.

28 "Is There a Santa Claus?" *New York Sun*. 21 September 1897, p. 6.

29 If you have not read it in a while, I suggest you do before reading the rest of this section. You can find it here: www.newseum.org/yesvirginia/.

30 "Is There a Santa Claus?" *New York Sun*. 21 September 1897, p. 6.

31 Another classic sample of something we believe in that we can't see is the wind. But the same holds true with it. We believe the wind exists because we see its effects. If the trees are not swaying and you feel no air on your face, you are not justified in believing that there is wind that day.

32 Church does something similar in the first paragraph when he says that our inability to detect Santa is merely a result of the smallness of our minds.

33 McCormick, Rich. "Map of Preventable Disease Outbreaks Shows the Influence of Anti-vaccination Movements." *The Verge*. 21 January 2014. www.theverge.com/2014/1/21/5329478/vaccine-preventable-disease-outbreaks-show-anti-vaccine-movement-influence.

34 What's the Harm? whatstheharm.net/.

35 University of Michigan. "US Public's Knowledge of Science: Getting Better but a Long Way to Go, Study Finds." *ScienceDaily*. 17 February 2011. www.sciencedaily.com/releases/2011/02/110216110857.htm.

36 "Ganges River." www.sacredland.org/ganges/.

37 If someone does think that there is proof that God doesn't exist, but that it's acceptable—even rational—to just believe it anyway, I suggest this person reevaluate their priorities. They may have believed in Santa despite the evidence a little too long.

38 *Psychiatric Bulletin* (2004) 28: 455–456. pb.rcpsych.org/content/28/12/455.

39 Moyer (2012).

40 Similar arguments have made on the TrainingZone. See "The Power Of Imagination, Santa Claus, and Telling the Truth." *TrainingZone*. 13 December 2012. www.trainingzone.co.uk/blogs-post/power-imagination-santa-claus-and-telling-truth/182977. See also Wang, Shirley S. "The Power of Magical Thinking." *The Wall Street Journal*. 22

December 2009; Wang, Samantha. "Santa Claus Brings Children Gift of imagination." *University City High School Commander*. 16 December 2011. www.uchscommander.com/ opinions /2011/12/16/santa-claus-brings-children-gift-of-imagination/; and "Child Development Expert Says the Magic of Santa Claus Is No Lie." *Phys.org*. 7 December 2009. phys.org/news179429017.html.

41 Any benefit to scientific reasoning skills would be likely be undone by the credulity the lie promotes.

42 Kaplan, Eric. *Does Santa Exist?: A Philosophical Investigation*. Dutton Publishing. 2014.

43 Kaplan, Eric. "Should We Believe In Santa Claus?" *New York Times: The Stone*. December 20, 2104. opinionator.blogs.nytimes.com//2014/12/20/should-we-believe-in-santa-claus

44 Johnson, David Kyle. "Does Santa Exist? A Review." *Psychology Today* Blog: Plato on Pop. Dec 5, 2014. www.psychologytoday.com/blog/plato-pop/201412/does-santa-exist-review

45 Principe, Gabrielle, and Eric Smith. "The Tooth, the Whole Tooth and Nothing but the Tooth: How Belief in the Tooth Fairy Can Engender False Memories." *Applied Cognitive Psychology* 22(5): 625–642.

46 This includes Tony Woodlief who hesitates to tell his children the truth about Santa when they ask because he wants to encourage their belief in the impossible, which he sees as necessary for belief in God. Tony makes the same mistake that Church makes, failing to recognize that, unlike Santa, belief in God shouldn't require belief despite evidence to the contrary. If he really thinks that God is impossible, then he shouldn't believe; if he thinks that belief in God is equivalent to belief in Santa, he really ought not believe. See Woodlief, Tony. "OK, Virginia, There's No Santa Claus. But There Is God." *The Wall Street Journal* Digital Network. 19 December 2008. online.wsj.com/ article/SB122963990662019887.html.

CHAPTER 7 • MYTH 7: CHRISTMAS CAN'T CHANGE

1 See McGrane, Sally. "The Netherlands Confronts Black Pete." *The New Yorker*, 4 November 2013. www.newyorker.com/culture/culture-desk/the-netherlands-confronts-blackpete. See also Bahceli, Yoruk. "Schools in Dutch city to do away with 'Black Pete' on racism grounds." *Reuters*. 17 September 2015. www.reuters.com/article/ 2015/09/17/us-netherlandsracism-idUSKCN0RH1YT20150917

2 Keohane, Joe. "How Facts Backfire." *Boston.com*. 11 July 2010. www.boston.com/bostonglobe/ideas/articles/2010/07/11/how_facts_backfire/.

3 See "A Christmas Carol." Wikipedia. en.wikipedia.org/wiki/A_Christmas_Carol. See also Petro, Bill. "History of A Christmas Carol: A Ghost Story of Christmas." 19 December 2013. billpetro.com/history-of-a-christmas-carol.

4 And if anyone from Fox News is reading this, please stop perpetuating the idea that there is a war on Christmas. There is not. All you are doing is adding fuel to the culture war, and the culture war is already bad enough. I know it generates viewers, but please—just stop.